LISTEN, YANKEE!

LISTEN, YANKEE!
WHY CUBA MATTERS

TOM HAYDEN

Based in part on conversations with Ricardo Alarcón

SEVEN STORIES PRESS
NEW YORK • OAKLAND

Copyright © 2015 by Tom Hayden

First trade paperback edition January 2017

All rights reserved. No part of this book may be reproduced, stored in a retrieval system, or transmitted in any form or by any means, including mechanical, electronic, photocopying, recording, or otherwise, without the prior written permission of the publisher.

Excerpts from Roque Dalton's poems "Tense Conversation" and "Soldier's Rest," from *Small Hours of the Night: Selected Poems of Roque Dalton*, edited by Hardie St. Martin (Willimantic: Curbstone Press, 1996). Reprinted courtesy of Curbstone Press.

Excerpt from Bertolt Brecht's poem "To Posterity," from *Selected Poems*, translated by H. R. Hays (New York: Grove Press, 1959). Reprinted courtesy of Grove Press.

Seven Stories Press
140 Watts Street
New York, NY 10013
www.sevenstories.com

College professors and high school and middle school teachers may order free examination copies of Seven Stories Press titles. To order, visit http://www.sevenstories.com/contact or send a fax on school letterhead to (212) 226-1411.

Book design by Jon Gilbert

Library of Congress Cataloging-in-Publication Data

Hayden, Tom.
  Listen, yankee! : why Cuba matters / Tom Hayden.
  pages   cm.
  ISBN 978-1-60980-596-8 (hardcover)
  ISBN 978-1-60980-722-1 (paperback)
  1. United States--Foreign relations--Cuba. 2--Foreign relations--United States. I. Title.
  E183.8.C9H39 2015
  327.7307291--DC23
                        2014038293

Printed in the United States

9 8 7 6 5 4 3 2 1

Dedicated to Jean Stein

And to the memory of Saul Landau and Len Weinglass

CONTENTS

PREFACE

The Day They Said Would Never Come

xi

INTRODUCTION

Two Old Guys Talking

I

CHAPTER 1

"A Heroic Creation"

11

CHAPTER 2

The Revolutionary War, 1956–59

23

CHAPTER 3

The Cuban Revolution and the American New Left

31

CHAPTER 4

C. Wright Mills, Cuba, and the New Left

35

CHAPTER 5

From the Cuban Missile Crisis to Counterinsurgency

45

CHAPTER 6

JFK's Assassination

59

CHAPTER 7

Latin American Revolution

73

CHAPTER 8

Enter and Exit Régis Debray

85

CHAPTER 9

The Revolutionary Flame

109

CHAPTER 10

The Cuban Revolution Goes Global

125

CHAPTER 11

The Liberal Democrats' Default: The Carter Era

145

CHAPTER 12

The Clinton Years: Yielding to the Cuban Right

165

CHAPTER 13

Rethinking Marxism, Rethinking the Americas

185

CHAPTER 14

A New Model in Our Americas

199

CHAPTER 15

Rescuing Elián González, Losing Al Gore

213

CHAPTER 16

Listen, Yankee!

223

EPILOGUE

245

ACKNOWLEDGMENTS

247

NOTES

253

INDEX

279

The Day They Said Would Never Come

When I started writing this memoir in 2013, I had two purposes in mind. The first was to claim that an improbable future was rising before our blinded eyes: that normalization between the United States and Cuba would take place in president Barack Obama's second term of office and before the deaths of either president Raúl Castro or his older sibling Fidel. No one believed me at the time. Even I doubted it would happen. Then it did. On December 17, 2014, the change I had foreseen was announced by the presidents of both countries—after fifty-five years of antagonism.

The second purpose was more personal as well as historic: my quest to understand the long history of the sixties generation through the prism of the Cuban Revolution and the American response. The same turbulent times gave birth to social movements in both countries. Third world revolution was disrupting the comfortable status quo of American-backed dictators like Fulgencio Batista in Havana, just as a civil rights revolution was breaking up the segregationist order in Montgomery, Birmingham, Selma, and Harlem. The bearded ones in the Sierra Maestra touched our bearded ones in the Haight-Ashbury. When Fidel visited the United Nations in 1960, he electrified Harlem, Harvard, and Hollywood. As a student at the Uni-

versity of Michigan, I went on a date to a Fair Play for Cuba
meeting before the Students for a Democratic Society was born.
No one could have foreseen then that the triumphs, traumas,
and tribulations between our two nations would continue for
another fifty-five years.

The normalization of relations could not have been more timely.
President Obama and Cuban president Raúl Castro have made it
part of their legacy. It preceded Fidel Castro's passing, about which
rumors circulated constantly, as either having already happened, or
being imminent.¹ It permitted and made much more likely that
the president of the United States would be present at his funeral,
a long-overdue sign of respect and one that is symbolic of this new
and better chapter of US-Cuban history. (Conversely, for President Obama to have been among the only world leaders without
the option of attending such an important world event would have
been, in my view, shameful and embarrassing.)

While the prediction of normalization has come true, the
larger story of the US-Cuban relationship is still in danger of
being lost in time, or frozen in stereotypes. But at least now
we can hope for a very different kind of future, all the while
exploring the lessons of the past that brought us here.

I chose as my partner in developing this book Ricardo
Alarcón, a Cuban who, like myself, was a radical student leader
almost six decades ago, Ricardo at the University of Havana
while I was at the University of Michigan and editor of the
Daily, both of us philosophy graduate students who dropped
our studies to immerse ourselves in causes for which we were
willing to die. He became a top leader of the Cuban Revolution,
foreign minister, United Nations representative, and president of
the National Assembly. My own path led through forty years of
social activism, ten arrests on charges of conspiracy and civil disobedience, eighteen years in the California legislature, and a long
span of writing and teaching. The radical movements to which I
belonged were able to change much about American culture, but
failed to achieve political power because of the assassinations of

national leaders, which destroyed our full potential as a movement and as a country. I stood in an honor guard besides Robert F. Kennedy's casket, wearing an olive green Cuban army cap. It would not have bothered Bobby, who evolved from Fidel Castro's early enemy to a strong supporter of dialogue and coexistence.

Think of this book as an archeological dig into decades of lessons worth studying and debating lest they recur. Only by understanding our common past will we understand why the normalization breakthrough happened, and where the intertwined Cuban-US relationship may go from here. This book, which began as a prediction, can be read as both a history and a prologue.

THE DAY OF LAZARUS IN CUBA

In Cuba, December 17 ends a three-day religious pilgrimage to honor Lazarus, the poor beggar afflicted with leprosy in the Gospel of Luke and in an older Afro-Cuban legend. Jesus restored Lazarus to life after arriving just after Lazarus had died. The *milagro*, or miracle story, is about having the power to transcend death, and is memorialized by several thousand Cubans each year who carry themselves in pain of one kind or another on a walk to Rincón, twenty-five miles from Havana. Pope John Paul II visited them in 1998 to identify with their experience. Fortunately, the Cuban Revolution's health programs mostly wiped out leprosy, which had ravaged the island since the eighteenth century. In 1962, the old Rincón leprosorium was replaced by a dermatology hospital.[2]

On this December 17, 2014, a new "miracle" was proclaimed by thousands of Cubans in their homes and on street corners. Precisely at noon, in simultaneous televised press conferences, Raúl Castro and Barack Obama were announcing the end of another kind of affliction and launching the official healing of relations between the two countries.

In a world accustomed to the usual sorts of modest diplomatic tinkering, the December 17 announcement between the United States and Cuba was stunning:

- Full diplomatic relations would be restored immediately, with the two Interest Sections established during the Carter era turned into full-scale embassies;

- The United States would soon remove Cuba from the sanctions created by its inclusion on the State Department's list of "terrorist states." Also on December 17, at the Cuba-sponsored Colombian peace talks in Havana, the Colombian guerrilla insurgents declared a unilateral ceasefire in their forty-year civil war against the US-supported repressive Bogota regime;

- Constraints on American travel to and from Cuba would be substantially lifted. General travel licenses would be expanded to include public performances, sports, humanitarian activity, "information dissemination," private foundation events, and the licensed export of more products in addition to the telecommunication licenses issued by Obama in 2009;

- Licenses for tourism would continue to be restricted pending US congressional action;

- Banking and trade would be widened to include opening accounts at Cuban financial institutions, the use of credit and debit cards, freeing of US entities in third-party countries to do transactions with Cubans in those countries, the export of building materials and agricultural equipment, telecommunication investments, and allowances permitting the import of up to $400 from Cuba including $100 worth of cigars or alcohol;

- Remitttances from Cuban Americans to their relatives in Cuba would be further increased (nearly one billion in US dollars already flows yearly).

Obama could not lift the rest of the embargo because that power was transferred to Congress in the 1996 Helms-Burton legislation signed by President Clinton, who would come to regret that giveaway of executive authority. Clinton's concession enabled the small bloc of right-wing Cuban Americans in Congress and their vociferous lobby to gain a monopoly over Cuban policy. The Cuban Right's goal, written into federal law, prohibited US recognition of any Cuban government led by a Castro, and required the establishment of a market economy and multiparty political system on the island—among other onerous conditions—before the embargo and diplomatic isolation of Cuba could end. In short, regime change would have to be imposed first, a US demand that had lasted through fifty-five years without achieving its stated goal.

A VICTORY FOR CUBA

Though it wasn't acknowledged as such in the mainstream discourse, the December 17 agreement was a victory for the Cuban Revolution. Obama was recognizing the Castro- and Communist-led government that previous American presidents had refused to accept or had actively tried to overthrow. Obama's easing of travel and economic restrictions would hollow out the embargo from within by allowing more dollars to flow to the island. His lifting of the terrorism designation would permit Cuba to receive loans from the International Monetary Fund. The upgrading of the Interest Section building in Havana to an American embassy would symbolize, and help normalize, the new reality. The scaffolding of the embargo would remain on the books for a time, but the content would be hugely diminished. American demands for free elections and human rights were no longer stumbling blocks to improved diplomatic relations, but could be taken up with a much reduced external threat. Overall, the agreement codified respect for and recognition of the sovereign national rights for which the Cuban revolutionaries had fought.

Of course, the world context had changed. The Cold War was over, the Soviet Union gone. The Russians were sending aid to Cuba but so were many other countries in the world, especially Brazil and Venezuela. The United States was isolated diplomatically on the Cuban question at the United Nations where Cuba enjoyed almost unanimous backing. Many of the Cuban-supported guerrillas of the sixties had become political leaders in the new Latin America. Globalization required that Cuba adjust to the market system and the Internet while still pursuing its socialist model in health care, education, and humanitarian missions abroad, as it has in the battle against Ebola. Whatever political transition is to occur in Cuba, it is likely to be cushioned and facilitated by regional diplomacy, not by American overseers.

American public opinion had changed too, with a significant majority favoring diplomatic relations and lifting of the embargo, even in states that the right-wing Cubans long have considered their strongholds, like Florida and New Jersey. The agreement was denounced by the Cuban American bloc in Congress and most of their Republican backers as a feckless sellout by Barack Obama to communism. The critics much preferred the Bush era when Cuban Americans couldn't travel home or send remittances on the grounds that their spending was subsidizing a totalitarian state. They said Obama was bailing out a dysfunctional state that would have fallen in the near future, a prediction heard since 1960. Otherwise intelligent conservatives like the *Wall Street Journal*'s Peggy Noonan became quite addled, dismissing Cuba as a "defeated foe," a "floating prison," with a dead economy.[3] These diatribes simply ignored the fact that, despite its serious problems, Cuba is regularly ranked in the upper tier of the United Nations Human Development Index for its education, health, and welfare programs, and enjoys strong diplomatic and economic ties with most of Latin America, Europe, and Russia.

Obama answered that the previous US policies had failed, and that greater diplomatic and economic engagement would draw more Cubans into a friendlier attitude toward the United States. Obama could also point to the prospect of vastly improved relations between the United States and Central and Latin America as a direct outcome of December 17. There would never again be humiliating 188-2 votes in the United Nations against America's Cuba policy. With a rising immigrant rights movement changing American domestic politics from within, it is becoming possible to embark on a constructive new foreign policy toward the Americas not seen since the Good Neighbor policies of president Franklin Roosevelt in the thirties. As Ricardo argues in these chapters, the third world is no longer a remote zone of Yankee exploitation but now has "penetrated" the American working class as the result of immigration trends spurred by trade policies that uproot indigenous people and send them on their journeys to the North. The new relationship will be on display at the Summit of the Americas in Panama in March 2015, where Obama and Raúl Castro will both be present.

QUESTIONS FOR THE LEFT

The December 17 agreement also jarred some on the Left, domestically and internationally, who shared the Right's conviction that US policy would never change, it being imperialist at the core. In this cynical view, the United States still wanted regime change, but was trying a new approach. "Now they will suffocate them in their embrace," the *New York Times* quoted one Russian minister.[4] When I first began predicting the coming normalization in 2013, a few Cuba supporters criticized me as being either wrong or opportunistic. I repeatedly heard moaning that Cuba soon would have a Starbucks on every street corner and lose its "charm" under a flood of crass North American tourists. But as

Ricardo says in our interviews, the purpose of the revolution was not to prevent Starbucks or sunbathing Yankees. There is nothing in Marxism-Leninism, he says wryly, requiring that barbershops or restaurants be state owned. And as for the flood of "decadent" tourists, he notes that Cuba received one million visitors from Canada alone last year—without causing any Cubans to bow to the Queen of England. The Western tourists come to relax, buy rum and cigars, and enjoy the beaches in winter, not to demonstrate on behalf of capitalism.

There remain heavily contested issues between the United States, Cuba, and Latin America, of course, but now these will play out along political and economic lines instead of through military confrontation or secret information wars. Chief among these is the Americans' continuing embrace of what is called neoliberalism in Latin America, or the dismantling of New Deal-style government programs in education, health care, pensions, welfare, and environmental protection, in favor of an approach favoring privatization of markets. Starting several years ago, the Cubans began carefully to open their state-controlled economy to private investment and enterprise. But like most governments in Latin America, the Cubans believe in a leading role for the state in economic development and social programs.[5] With the United States suffering from increased economic inequality, it is possible there will be growing convergence between a renewed American populist Left and a new Latin America, including Cuba, that considers itself much more than a sweatshop haven or a storehouse of raw materials for American corporations.

There also will be conflicts over the continued role of the US-supported dissidents on the island, a small faction numerically who are widely supported by the human rights community and the Catholic Church. The December 17 agreement released fifty-three dissidents from Cuban prisons, the number listed by Amnesty International. One reason the dissidents have been maligned in Cuba has been their alignment with the interests of the United

States and funding by US agencies or foundations. Most of them are seen, correctly, as recipients of US support for regime change and the chaos that would follow. Now with relations normalizing, the dissidents' future is in question. They are demanding formal recognition in the forthcoming Summit of the Americas, giving them status as the legitimate Cuban opposition. That institutionalized role is likely to be rejected, but a much larger space is opening up for dissent and debate among mainstream Cubans as US hostility recedes. How the traditionalists in the Communist Party and state bureaucracies respond to that larger thaw will partly determine how the drama is played out.

DECEMBER 17 IN HAVANA: GUARDED JOY

"There's joy in the street here," wrote José Pertierra when I emailed to ask where he was on Lazarus Day. José is a Cuban American human rights lawyer living in Washington and married to a key journalist in Havana. His son Andrés, who attended philosophy graduate school in Cuba, was my main research assistant on this book.

JOSÉ PERTIERRA: *Perfect strangers hug each other with tears in their eyes. Although the* [Helms-Burton] *legislation is still on the books and despite Obama wanting to stick Cuba with Torricelli's Track 2 on Viagra, the blockade is over.*[6] *The executive is legislating travel, commerce, and banking. It's over, Tom, it's over. It's up to Cuba to manage its way through these massive changes.*

I told him how sorry I was that two close friends, Leonard Weinglass and Saul Landau, longtime supporters of Cuba, had both passed away in the two years before this moment. Like many thousands around the world, their support for Cuba extended over many decades. Len was a close friend whom I encouraged to take on the legal challenge of the Cuban Five;

Saul, a writer and filmmaker, made contributions to my research through his long association with Cuba's leaders.

JOSÉ: *When I was listening to the statements by Raúl and Obama with Cubans and Americans side by side who had been fighting for decades to end the blockade, I saw Lenny and Saul in my mind. It was Lenny who first and best brought the story of the Cuban Five to the American public, and it was Saul who introduced the Cuban people to the American people through his films and presentations. All of us there in the conference hall at noon saw their faces and heard their voices as Obama and Raúl spoke.*

Ricardo would express the same sentiments in the following days, a window into the de facto closeness and solidarity developed between many Cubans and Americans over five decades in spite of the embargo and travel bans:

RICARDO ALARCÓN: *How could I forget Lenny when I asked him to take on the main role in defense of the Five and he asked for nothing in exchange, and only responded by thanking me? And his visits to the comrades in the prisons and his speeches and declarations in and beyond the United States? And his tireless, meticulous, and profound work in the appellate process, all of that in spite of his gravely fragile illness?*

How to forget that on his last visit to Cuba, as I was taking him in an emergency to the doctor, he demanded to return because he needed to meet with Adriana? Or when he returned to New York and needed surgery without delay, he refused to be admitted to the hospital until he could speak with Gerardo? And when he finally went, it was to the South Bronx where he felt happy together with the poor, with the immigrants, the persecuted, his "old clients" as he liked to joke when he answered those who scolded him for not being in a more sophisticated medical center.

How can I forget his last photograph, in his last stages, reviewing the Habeas Corpus papers of the Five?

Long before Len Weinglass—my closest friend for years—took up the case of the Cuban Five, many thousands of young Americans journeyed to Cuba in violation of the US travel ban to cut sugarcane and open themselves to the realities of Cuba. Thousands were harassed, searched, had their articles confiscated by customs agents enforcing the ban and blockade. Many were attacked, bombed, or threatened by Cuban exiles in America. Others, like Len and Saul Landau, were subjected to campaigns of ridicule and dismissal for their professional work in law and filmmaking. On December 17, all that pent-up frustration burst in a moment of euphoria. It all seemed worth the wait.

And what of Ricardo Alarcón, the one who played such a leading role in it all?

He was in Havana, recovering from two cataract operations. His wife, Margarita, whom he met in the romantic days of revolution, had passed away in 2008 from a long struggle with Parkinson's. His family now consists of his daughter, Margarita, and her ten-year-old son, Ricardito, or Ricky. He lives alone in an apartment walled with books in many languages. He is retired from his many positions, though he keeps a small office at the presidential palace under the auspices of Raúl. His official entourage is gone. His closest aide, a person privy to all his meetings, is in a Cuban prison after being arrested for espionage just before these interviews began in 2012.[7]

Every few days Ricardo goes out with old friends for drinks and conversation. He had become the face of an old regime, sometimes the subject of snide criticism by the dissidents and American Cuba watchers like Ann Louise Bardach, whose gossipy books are considered authoritative in the American media. When I met Bardach in her Santa Barbara home a few weeks before December 17, she couldn't figure out how Alarcón had survived so many decades and, in her account, so many purges. I told her that perhaps the problem lay in her model of Cuba, which reduced the island's history to internecine family vendettas, bloodletting, and executions. I assume that Ricardo's long experience is of some value. That was also the view of Cuba's current UN representative, Rodolfo Reyes, when I interviewed him earlier in 2014. "Ricardo Alarcón is regarded as one of our few Cuban experts on the United States with a long memory. His insights are unique and valuable."

When I caught up with Ricardo in the hours after December 17 by email, his immediate answer was typically terse and to the point:

RICARDO: *I was at my office and watched the announcements as they came out. I was aware that something was going on but was not personally involved in the last talks that were kept in strict secrecy as they should have been. I was convinced* [this was going to happen] *because I knew that our three Cuban* [prisoners] *had been taken out of their American prisons.*

Now a party has broken out in Cuba and far beyond that hasn't ended yet.

He invited me back to Cuba, saying, *"I think it may be useful in these days when many are involved in the rewriting of history."* About a week later, on December 26, Ricardo's first published observations appeared:

It took courage. Obama is attempting to assure his place in history with immigration reform and now with the start of a different relationship with Cuba. Perhaps he will try other reforms as well. For that he deserves respect and support.[8]

I found his daughter Margarita by phone in New York City where she was intent on taking her ten-year-old ice skating for the first time. She had grown up in New York during the years that Ricardo was stationed at the United Nations, making her a cultural hybrid of sorts. I was very sorry, I told her, that her mother hadn't lived to see this day.

MARGARITA ALARCÓN: *I thought about her a lot yesterday. She would have loved to see this.*

Margarita then spoke lovingly of the three Cuban prisoners released as part of the December 17 deal. Virtually every Cuban knows the Cuban Five as family after so many years' of high-profile detention.

MARGARITA: *In any event, Gerardo* [Hernández] *is out and free. Tony* [Guererro] *is spunky and so much smarter than I ever imagined, and Ramon* [Labañino] *is a darling.*

But she also struck a more cautious note than José Pertierra.

MARGARITA: *Cubans have seen this before. Well, not like this. But there are deep memories of hoping for change and those hopes being dashed. Carter promised normalization but it was stopped for Cold War reasons.*[9] *We got an Interest Section, then came Reagan. Under Clinton there was an effort but then came Helms-Burton. Now it's Obama, and we'll have to see if it lasts or not."*

Over our lifetimes, Ricardo Alarcón and I both have been enthusiasts of the radical American sociologist C. Wright Mills, who visited Cuba and wrote the best-selling polemic *Listen, Yankee* (1960) before his death from heart failure in 1962. I have on my desk a yellowing edition of Mills's book with an inscription by Ricardo from 1968, a time of cresting revolutionary dreams. Mills's thesis was that the US leaders' historic failure to *listen* to the voices of the original Cuban revolutionaries was at the heart of a tragic misunderstanding.

It may be that Barack Obama is the first Yankee president to listen.

HOW DECEMBER 17 HAPPENED. THE IMPORTANCE OF THE "CUBAN FIVE"

The December 17 agreement was long in preparation, but would not have occurred without a prisoner exchange that was orchestrated with extreme secrecy and care. On the one hand, the Obama administration badly wanted the Cubans to release Alan Gross, a US contractor, from the Cuban prison where he had been held for five years. If Obama couldn't get a single American aid worker out of a Cuban jail, his critics argued, it proved his fecklessness as commander in chief. Gross, it turned out, was not your everyday handyman distributing consumer appliances to the Jewish community and Masonic lodges. His funder, the Agency for International Development (USAID), was channeling tens of millions of dollars of US funds into covert "democracy programs," in this case highly sophisticated communications equipment that would allow Cubans to secretly work in undetectable Wi-Fi hotspots without the government's knowledge. The program was a fiasco like many others, infiltrated by Cuban informants and intelligence agents. But Gross persisted, taking five trips in 2009 alone. He knew he was into "risky business," according to notes he supplied his employers. He was arrested by the Cubans on December 3, 2009, not long after the US Supreme Court had refused to take up an appeal in the case of the Cuban Five. There seemed to be a connection.

To achieve the December 17 agreement, Cuba and the United States first had to negotiate a de facto swap of Alan Gross for the Cuban Five, three of whom remained in US prisons, a resolution which the United States government, both political parties, and the mainstream media initially and unanimously denounced as absurd.[10] The Five, whose story will be recounted at length in this book and whose defense was led for years by Ricardo Alarcón, were charged with conspiring to spy on Cuban exile forces who were training in Florida swamps and flying on provocative missions into Cuban airspace on harassment maneuvers. After numerous warnings from Cuba which the Clinton administration failed to act on, the Cuban government ordered a shootdown on February 24, 1996, killing four pilots. That affair ended any possibility of rapprochement and led directly to the draconian Helms-Burton law. In researching this book, I interviewed the lead official in the Clinton administration during those days, Morton Halperin, who told me that the Miami-based Cuban exiles actually wanted to provoke the shooting down of their own planes in order to provoke the crisis that followed. There exists plenty of evidence that Halperin was right.

Three of the Cuban Five, as they came to be known, had served as soldiers in Cuba's seventies' African wars against Portuguese colonialism and South African apartheid, during a time when liberation struggles elsewhere in the world were considered by Havana to be a rebirth of the Cuban Revolution. After their arrest, the Cuban Five were subjected to a hostile Miami courtroom and a mainstream press that was fed false information by the US government, and were put behind bars, often in solitary confinement, in 2001. It would take the miracle of December 17 for them to be released. Two of them had been sent home under "supervised probation" with the consent of Obama's Justice Department while I was writing this book. I met one of those men, René González, with Ricardo in Havana in June 2013 and found him animated by a passion typical of so many Cubans. He was reunited with his wife and dedicated to fighting for the release of the other three. He refused to believe that Obama was interested in their release. That suspicion was pervasive on the island as the secret talks were unfolding.

During the past two years, I talked on condition of anonymity with a central participant in the talks that led to the December 17 agreement. That anonymity ended on December 17, when that contact was revealed to be Tim Rieser, longtime aide to Sen. Patrick Leahy (D-VT). Leahy, a respected senior senator, plunged into the Cuba debate as long ago as the nineties. He took multiple trips to Cuba where he spoke with senior officials, often bringing Rieser with him. Their continuous, many-sided approach to diplomatic conflict resolution was kept top secret for fear of backlash. The continuous dialogues were frustrating and time consuming, but eventually resulted in the White House and Cuban governments embracing the detailed policies announced on December 17.

TIM RIESER: *It was a long saga. Secrecy was the only way by which I could* [obtain] *information from the White House. People like Senator Leahy had been working on Cuba issues since the nineties, twenty-five years. He, like many others, wanted to change the policy that had failed to achieve any of its objectives. We knew early on that it would be impossible to change US policy toward Cuba without getting Gross home and that was impossible without resolving the case of the Cuban Five. The administration did not even want to consider that initially. But either Gross would die in a Cuban prison and the president would lose the chance to change the policy, or we would have to resolve the case of the Cuban prisoners. I told the Cubans that if they didn't release Gross the whole project was over and it would be many years before it could be restarted. I didn't want the Cubans to think that if they just waited us out everything would be fine.*

But the administration was going about it wrong by simply demanding that the Cubans release Gross and refusing to negotiate. That had accomplished nothing and we needed to approach the problem differently.

I talked to Alan every two or three days but I could not tell him everything I knew. I only told him that we were making progress, that he should feel positive, and that if things changed for the worse I would tell him. So instead we talked about a lot of other things, like food, movies, places he or I had been, books, etc.

Rieser's cover was blown shortly after December 17 when the *New York Times* answered the riddle of "How a Cuban Spy and His Wife Came to Be Expectant Parents," in a December 22 exposé. Gerardo Hernández, who was sentenced to a double-life term, was photographed in Havana touching the pregnant stomach of his wife Adriana Pérez. How could this miracle of life have happened? It turned out that Rieser had practiced "sperm diplomacy" as a humanitarian gesture. Gerardo's wife in

Havana asked Leahy in February 2013 to help her become pregnant with her husband. Rieser discovered that while US prisons ban conjugal visits, artificial insemination was permissible. The Cubans obtained sperm samples on two occasions from Gerardo, and finally Adriana became pregnant in early 2014. In exchange, Rieser got the Cubans to improve the humanitarian situation of Alan Gross.

TIM RIESER: *It was a purely humanitarian gesture on the part of Senator and Mrs. Leahy. Adriana Pérez was forty-three and believed that her husband would never be released from prison. Senator Leahy had also asked the Cubans to do several things to improve their treatment of Alan Gross, and to permit American doctors to travel to Cuba to examine him, which had never happened before and the Cubans ultimately agreed. Senator Leahy believed it was in the US interest to try to improve the tone of the relationship between the United States and Cuba, and one way to help do that was to respond positively to humanitarian concerns.*

When I asked him about Rolando Sarraf, the pivotal CIA spy held in a Cuban prison who was exchanged in the deal for Gross, Rieser's answer was discreet:

TIM RIESER: *This is best discussed with the White House.*

I had no luck asking the White House to reveal its hand. When I emailed Ricardo, he replied that he'd never heard of Sarraf, who was in a Cuban prison for twenty years. I heard from René González by email that Sarraf was "just a traitor with some technical knowledge who was able to pass on some good information to the CIA, some related to [our] arrests." Obama might be inflating his importance to justify the swap in his opponents' eyes.

If we take Obama at his word, Sarraf was an informant hidden within Cuban intelligence who played a role in cracking open the secrets of the Cuban Five. Assuming so, the swap could be considered spy-for-spy, leaving Alan Gross defined as an innocent contractor.

The truth may not be known until classified documents are released by both sides. It should be clear, however, that the Cubans were spying on the operations of Cuban American exiles bent on overthrowing the Castro government from a Florida base. They were not "spying" on the US government at all; indeed, their files on the exiles were provided to the FBI at one point, in a secret conference in Havana. Alan Gross, on the other hand, was engaged in trying to subvert the Cuban government by supplying sophisticated communications technology to dissidents on the island. In all probability Gross was taken in when the Cubans realized that there was no hope for appeals in the US courts. Obama was under pressure to obtain Gross's release or be accused of superpower weakness, while the Cubans were unwilling to leave their five behind. The larger desire for a new relationship made the swap an imperative.

TIM RIESER: *There were a number of meetings between Leahy and other members of Congress, including Jim* [McGovern], *and the president, the secretary, the attorney general, and White House staff. But in terms of meetings with Cuban officials in Canada, those secret negotiations had nothing to do with Congress. I was informed months after those talks began. I was not part of the process directly. The White House privately kept me informed of the progress.*

We had meetings with Josefina Vidal,[11] *the Cuban foreign minister, and Raúl Castro—Leahy bought Flake, McGovern, and others to Cuba. In New York City, Leahy met with the Cuban foreign minister and Josefina Vidal, or I met with them alone in Havana. We were confident that Leahy's views expressed in those meetings were being passed on to other Cuban officials.*

We told the Cubans there was a finite window in which to conclude agreement, and that the Cubans needed to reciprocate. I urged them to make it as easy as possible for President Obama to make the right decision.

RICARDO: *I was following Carter's release of the Puerto Rican nationalists in the seventies, reading classified documents by Brzezinski, etc. For the Americans it was important not to appear as swapping. It was better to appear as a humanitarian act facilitating family reunion. Their main consideration was that it was in their best interest not to continue having the nationalists incarcerated, including a woman, Lolita Lebrón, who at the time was serving the longest sentence ever for a woman. There was an international campaign for their freedom and Carter was supposed to be a human rights champion. Finally, a group of Americans* [associated with the] *CIA being held in Cuban prisons were freed and went back to the United States. The Puerto Ricans were released separately.*

TIM: *I told the White House staff, and they shared this same view, that getting Alan Gross home was an essential step, but the larger goal was to transform the policy itself.*

We met with Kerry, conversed with his staff, he was informed, but the negotiations were not conducted through the State Department nor the Cuban Foreign Ministry.

The pope did play an important role. In one of the meetings with the White House staff early on, the issue of the prisoners came up and they dismissed the idea of an exchange for Gross. Senator Durbin said maybe we can get the pope involved. I thought we might as well try anything. So I drafted a letter for Senator Leahy to send to the cardinal[12] *in Havana whom we knew from years before, and asked him to urge the pope to raise the issue of Gross and the Cuban prisoners when he met Obama. The letter suggested that this was the way for the two countries to get to a different relationship, and the Cuban people would benefit. The pope did discuss it with the president, and he then wrote to both Castro and Obama, and we later learned that the Vatican played a key role at the end of the negotiations.*

It was a collective [achievement]. *Senator Leahy helped focus the administration's attention early on the opportunity to change the policy. It was something the president wanted to do. But there was this obstacle, Alan Gross, and they were going about it ineffec-*

tively. The Cuban government insisted they wanted a different relationship, and an end to the embargo. The Cubans had the primary responsibility for the Gross problem. We made it clear the White House needed to negotiate with the Cubans and deal with the Five. At first the idea of clemency was dismissed out of hand, as if we were suggesting the impossible. I told them that then Gross will die in Cuba and that will be the end of any chance for this administration to change the policy. Eventually they did start talking to the Cubans [about Gross and the Five]. *Senator Leahy pushed the Cubans to meet the White House halfway, and we had to keep Gross from losing hope because he had lost confidence in both governments.*

We studied the history of the case of the Cuban Five, the legal and political precedents, and provided a lengthy memorandum to the White House.

Senator Leahy felt that their trial had suffered from serious inadequacies, the sentences were excessive, and the case was not a good example of American justice. Apart from that, they had served a long time and if we wanted to obtain Gross's freedom we needed to talk with them about the Cuban prisoners.

We believe that Gross was arrested in part to be used by the Cubans as a bargaining chip. They also felt that the Five had been subjected to a miscarriage of justice.

We were trying to change the ways we were dealing with each other, from acrimony to a more constructive and respectful manner, despite our strong disagreements, and to act where there were opportunities. We felt, "Why not change the way that we talk to each other?

It was very important for the atmosphere to improve. Both sides expressed appreciation that it became more positive. We still disagreed but made more progress. That was a key reason why Senator Leahy helped Adriana Pérez. If there was something we could do that could improve the relationship, that did not require major costs on our part, then he felt we should do it. Why be unresponsive or vindictive?

I remember one conversation in Cuba with the foreign ministry, planning what to do with some visiting members of Congress. I was the go-between, and asked why can't you and the US Interest Section give each other your cell phone numbers, but realized they couldn't. These were diplomats who believe in communication, I realized, it wasn't their fault, it wasn't their decision, they were diplomats but their hands were tied. Sometimes the State Department would say unhelpful things. I told them sometimes it's best to say nothing."

I asked Rieser whether there was a "winner" in the December 17 agreement.

TIM RIESER: *It's impossible to quantify. This is a process that will unfold over many years. I don't see it as a win or lose situation. The question is whether this is a better approach to help achieve a more open, freer society in Cuba.*

I think it's going to be determined by the next generation. There is a lot about Americans they love.

The agreement does not include the $20 million for democracy programs.[13] The appropriations committee is responsible for 2015. The administration request was for $20 million, but the appropriations act for the first time doesn't specify an amount and instead says, "Funds should be made available for programs in Cuba."

I think if you asked most Americans if they think we should have an embassy in Cuba, they would respond, "There isn't one?" A half million Americans travel to Cuba each year so of course we need an embassy, but for a whole lot of other reasons as well. If Republicans block an ambassador, then there will be a chargé d'affaires. But it is too soon to tell how things will evolve.

I asked about lifting the terrorism designation, an action recommended by the secretary of state, carried out by the president, and reversible by a two-thirds vote of the Senate.

TIM RIESER: *It will not be easy to overrule the president.*

Two Old Guys Talking

wo old guys talking. That was the reason given to me, with a smile and shrug, by thirty-something Margarita Alarcón when I asked her why on earth her father Ricardo wanted to interview me. Cuba's former foreign minister, United Nations representative, and then-president of Cuba's National Assembly, Ricardo Alarcón was a busy man. It was 2006, and he wanted to see me in Havana. I knew him only slightly at the time, but I flew down to the island on wings of curiosity.

Six years later, pushed by my good friend Jean Stein in New York, I went back to begin a round of my own interviews with Ricardo, as I came to know him. He was seventy-six, no longer in power, had lost his wife to a long illness, and wanted to compose some reflections on his fifty years in official positions. He was a man of widely respected intelligence and, by my reckoning, probably had met more revolutionaries, political leaders, diplomats, and heads of state than anyone on the planet. He was a rare treasure of worldly information, but off-limits to direct contact with the United States because of our embargo. Ricardo had been denied permission to travel to the United States even when invited by academicians or members of Congress. Who was really being isolated, I wondered, Ricardo, who could meet those professors and politicians in Cuba at any time, or the United States from vital contact with key representatives of an important neighboring country?

1

In Havana we met, day after day, on the sixth floor of the venerable Hotel Nacional, where one feels all the currents of recent Cuban history. Opened in 1930, it sits on a promontory overlooking Havana harbor, atop an ancient cave and surrounded by a few of the remaining Spanish cannons that have defended Havana from Englishmen and pirates. Its "who's who" roster includes hundreds of the world's most famous celebrities and leaders. The Cosa Nostra—when Meyer Lansky was running things—operated from its floors; according to the delicate wording of the hotel's own history, it was here that Lansky "arranged with Batista the business of the casinos." Charles "Lucky" Luciano, Vito Genovese, and a rival mobster, Santo Trafficante, all hung out here. Frank Sinatra was an entertainment luminary. A cell of Fidel's revolutionary 26th of July movement also came to operate here clandestinely. The lurid contradictions of its history are famously dramatized in Francis Ford Coppola's *The Godfather Part II* in a scene where the mobsters enjoy a sunlit penthouse rooftop while a young Fidelista blows himself up on the streets below rather than be taken alive. Looking down from the same heights where I sat with Ricardo, the fictional Michael Corleone commented to the Lansky character,

"[But] it occurred to me. The soldiers are paid to fight. The rebels aren't."

"What does that tell you?" asks Roth.

"They can win," Corleone replies.

In Coppola's film, the dates were changed so that the mobster meeting occurred on the eve of the 1959 revolution, but the essential theme was true to life.

The conversations between Ricardo and myself are the backbone of the book you are holding in your hands. While most of the writing and all of the opinions are mine, they arise from tens of hours of interviews. In addition to my writing you will see whole paragraphs in italics representing Ricardo's running commentaries on the subject that has always been of passionate interest to us both—the decades-long, intertwined histories of our two nations, an intense relationship some have described as being "the closest of enemies."

Ricardo was a philosophy student at the University of Havana and leader of the Federación Estudiantil Universitaria (FEU). The FEU was founded in 1922 by student leaders who were desirous of radical reforms. It became the breeding ground for many of the most important reformist and revolutionary political figures that would dominate the succeeding decades, including Fidel Castro. Ricardo's generation made a great refusal of the Mafia axiom that everyone has a price. They fought a revolution and won.

Now it was fifty-five years later, and we were "old guys talking." The Nacional had endured. A few sunburned tourists lay outside by the pool. The hotel's special ice cream was being served in bucketfuls. Busy conferees bustled back and forth to their meetings. A seminar was underway on the expansion of airline services. The Chinese ambassador, speaking perfect Spanish and looking Cuban, politely introduced himself. Beautiful models posed for fashion photographers by the old Spanish cannons. Middle-aged lefties gathered in tour groups bearing their maps and cameras. A tiny modern tourist shop was open, selling sunscreen, near the currency exchange counter. At the marble-topped front desk they were selling the writings of Fidel, Che, and Camilo Cienfuegos in paperback editions. The hotel had withstood time's passing, while history without end continued being made here.

The Nacional's hotel workers were brisk and dignified, and efficiently served cup after cup of strong Cuban coffee as I sat on an outdoor couch asking question after question of Ricardo. Occasionally we were interrupted by friends dropping by to shake his hand before going off to Old Havana, the famous Malecón promenade, or the sparkling beach below us. Cuba, now dependent on tourism, was welcoming millions of Canadians and Europeans, and even one hundred thousand Americans this year.

Up on the sixth floor, we two old guys talked on, as the world below rapidly changed. Hour after hour, day after day, Ricardo answered my questions. Since those weeks, he has answered even more of my queries by email.

I understand Ricardo as a voice of Cuba rarely heard in the United States even though he has lived here more years than any other high Cuban official. He is basically embargoed. The Cuban ambassador to the United States who-might-have-been. His range of experience and contacts is vast, from Latin America to Africa, spanning nine US administrations. Yet his life has been officially circumscribed by US executive order: to a twenty-five-mile radius from the United Nations or the metropolitan limits of Washington, D.C. He was denied a visa to attend meetings with academics and congressional officials.

I thought Ricardo might shed light, as a man of several worlds, on the long roads we had traveled in parallel. When he and I were both idealistic revolutionary student leaders, at universities in Havana and Ann Arbor, the Cuban Revolution was an inspiration to the black civil rights movement, the emerging Chicano movement and the American New Left overall. We mutually survived the danger of nuclear incineration in 1962, he on the island and I at a vigil in Washington, D.C. We both felt the suffocating burden of the Cold War, I as a dissenter from thoughtless anti-communism and militarism, he as a socialist with reservations about the Soviet Big Brother. Each of us was deeply influenced by the writings of the radical sociologist C. Wright Mills, who inspired Students for a Democratic Society (SDS) and spent two weeks in Cuba in 1960,[1] including three and a half eighteen-hour days interviewing Fidel, researching his best-selling *Listen, Yankee*. Long after Mills died in 1962, Ricardo wrote a book and I published an essay lamenting his early passing.[2] One of the reasons Ricardo invited me to Cuba in 2006 was to describe the 1962 Port Huron Statement, the founding document of SDS, which I had drafted. Ricardo was president of the National Assembly of People's Power at the time, charged with stimulating greater mass participation in decision making. He felt that Cuba, in its own way, was moving toward participatory democracy, the central tenet of the Port Huron Statement.

Toward the end of the sixties, some young American radicals from SDS joined armed undergrounds, inspired by Che and the writings of a young protégé of Fidel Castro's, Régis Debray, whom Ricardo knew well and with whom he disagreed. Both Ricardo and I became deeply involved in fighting South African apartheid, Ricardo as Cuba's UN ambassador and I as a legislator who brought Desmond Tutu to America when I was banned from entry into South Africa. When corporate globalization became triumphant after the Cold War, I joined the 1999 Seattle protests against the World Trade Organization, while Ricardo was inspired by Latin America's populist surges against neoliberalism and pondered whether what was emerging was "Marxism without Marx." We both believed that forms of participatory democracy were coming alive in the new revolts in Latin America.

NEW PERSPECTIVES ON CUBA

In writing this book, I have gained new information and insights on several chapters of historical interest, information that should help us understand the history of Cuba and the United States in new ways that will stand in stark contrast to the story told in the American media. Most of these insights illustrate plainly the price we have paid for isolating ourselves from Cuba:

- That Cuba countered the US effort at isolation with foreign policies that have had a global impact completely out of proportion with its being a tiny country of eleven million people. Most recently, Cuban medical personnel have made the "most robust" contribution of any country in the world to the fight against the Ebola epidemic.[3]

Similarly in 2011 the Cubans were at the forefront of the battle against cholera in Haiti. Cuba has sent many thousands of doctors, nurses, teachers, and other specialists on humanitarian missions to third world countries. These programs surpass in scale the American Peace Corps, which was designed by the Kennedy administration as a free-world answer to Cuba.

Decades ago, the Cubans made a dramatic decision to send tens of thousands of troops to fight against colonialism in Angola and the apartheid regime in South Africa in the seventies. Cuba gained enormous respect and even a heroic status globally by its efforts. Meanwhile the United States was opposing sanctions and divestment against South Africa and offering only "quiet diplomacy" and "constructive engagement." Ricardo was a signatory to the peace agreement in southern Africa and talks about that experience here. As a result, Cuba became the leader of the Non-Aligned Movement among third world nations during the late sixties, and gained the support of Latin America, Asia, and Africa within the UN General Assembly;

- That the draconian US policies of nonrecognition often led to follies in practical diplomacy. Ricardo enjoyed handshakes and cocktails with top American officials in southern Africa while remaining officially a nonperson in terms of US diplomacy. US talks with Ricardo Alarcón on serious issues like immigration required him to be hidden in the backseats of official cars or spirited to secret meetings in Toronto hotels—without the knowledge of the very US officials technically in charge of Cuba policy;

- That such secret contacts were considered necessary by the White House because the Cuba lobby had infiltrated key offices within the US executive branch;

- That Ricardo was engaged in top-secret talks with top US officials while at the same time being rejected in his visa requests to visit the United States at the invitation of members of Congress;

- That the federal government kept secret its plans to return six-year-old Elián González to Cuba in June 2000 because the Miami FBI, police and media were considered too closely connected to Cuban exile groups; the de facto conspiracy to return Elián González was coordinated between US officials and Ricardo Alarcón, who welcomed the youngster home at Havana's international airport;

- That the federal government and CIA built and granted immunity to a de facto armed settler sanctuary in Miami, a "Mafia state" to Ricardo Alarcón, for training and weapons stockpiling, putting lethal power in the hands of the exiles launching attacks on Cuba. All this was in the name of exporting democracy to Cuba while it left a cancer on democracy in the United States;

- Ironically, members of Ricardo's generation, symbolized by Fidel and Che, have been resurrected as heroic icons in the triumphant democratic revolutions across Latin America over the past twenty-five years;

- That solidarity work and cultural exchanges allowed the Cuban Revolution to build a significant base of support for Cuba in the United States, circumventing the walls of the embargo. The cane-cutting solidarity movement known as the Venceremos Brigades sent at least eight thousand Americans to work and learn in the Cuban countryside over two decades, with 1,300 in 1969–1970, more than the 1,100 volunteers who journeyed to Mississippi in 1964 for the far more visible Freedom Summer project. In both cases the thousands of volunteers were taking risks; the Venceremos volunteers by breaking the travel ban, the Mississippi volunteers suffering three deaths and many arrests. More so-called solidarity movements would grow during the Central American Wars of the 1970s–1980s. Many of those *brigadistas* later became mayors, members of Congress, and influential Americans in many fields. They are an invisible backbone of support for normalized relations today.

In addition, hundreds of thousands of Americans have visited Cuba, legally and illegally, as tourists, most of them bringing back deep sympathy for the island. Those two blocs—solidarity activists and progressive tourists—have given Cuba an important and growing base of sympathetic support within the United States, a potential counter to the Cuba lobby's crusade to demonize the island. Now that the road to normalization has been chosen, those networks of support will be key bridges in bringing our two peoples together. In addition, they should be recognized as an important source of influence on Cuba's evolution in human rights and democracy, a constructive alternative to the failed and contradictory US policy of covert "democracy programs."

In researching why our government embargoed Cuba for so long and in such an exceptional way, while recognizing and doing business with so many undemocratic regimes, I point to several trends that suggested to me the coming change. First, Cuba is being integrated into the new Latin American region as a whole, where it enjoys deep popular support and draws vast economic assistance from countries like Venezuela and Brazil. As China becomes a power in Latin America, it too provides an independent source of financial backing for Havana. The geopolitics are reversing. With the bogeyman of the Soviet Union gone, the United States is becoming isolated diplomatically in the region, unable to find its way back to acceptance except through normalizing relations with the government in Havana. Normalization will go a long way toward opening doors for

Obama and future US presidents, doors that have been closed to US during the years of the embargo.

Meanwhile, the politics of immigration have changed, and the United States is becoming a Latinized nation. Nearly five hundred thousand Cubans from Florida and New Jersey travel to and from the island every year. These are not the bitter exiles of 1960 plotting their revenge. They are not so overwhelmingly white as were the original exiles, but black, brown, and struggling economically. They are traveling for family or economic reasons, and the right-wing Cuban American politicians cannot easily deter them with charges that they are subsidizing a Communist dictatorship with their business, commerce, and family remittances. The Barack Obama Democrats have the vote of these new Cubans, in Florida and elsewhere, however they choose to use it. This Cuban diaspora is bridging the divide, reshaping Cuba on both sides of the Straits. The future is being discussed again around family dinner tables.

Ricardo's daughter Margarita, now in her forties, is a symbolic forerunner in this process, unique only because of her elite lineage. She spent fourteen years growing up in New York in the home of a Cuban revolutionary diplomat:

MARGARITA ALARCÓN: *In the end, I wasn't Cuban or American, I wasn't Latina or black or white, in the end I was a true New Yorker, a person of no predetermined race or religion who adapted and accepted.*

I think it is precisely because of the times that I lived in NYC, and the life I led, that I can empathize with Martí when he said "I have lived inside the monster and I know its entrails," but not because I was seeing it as all bad, it was because of the moment in history and because it was in NYC. Remember, it wasn't until after 9/11 in 2001 that the City was once again accepted back into the Union of the United States, before that, New York was a separate place, almost the Basque nation of the United States.

Margarita's story illustrates that the diplomatic term "normalization" is insufficient to convey the many contradictions and possibilities dividing and joining our two countries. There are at least two levels of coexistence that are evolving: first, coexistence between the Cuban nation-state and the Cuban Americans who consider themselves still related to the Cuban nation as a diaspora; and second, coexistence between the United States, which long has considered itself the dominant power, and the Cuba that emerged with the 1959 revolution. In both cases, there is an important role for American progressives if they engage politically in the new space that comes with normalization. Finally, behind this drama of seeking peaceful coexistence with Cuba lies the larger challenge of transitioning to a new and more equal relationship between the United States and Latin America, not only in the region to our south but with millions of Latinos at the center of the immigration debate here inside the United States. Ricardo Alarcón has been at the forefront of rethinking what these profound changes mean for the future of the Left.

Hopefully, the reflections of "two old guys talking" in these pages will flow into this incredible historical moment in a useful way, lending substance to the vision of Cuba's "National Hero" José Martí, the exile who took sanctuary in America before dying in battle in Cuba in 1895. Martí believed in "our America," an integration of the people of all the Americas, equal to and independent from the United States, their enemy-brother with a common destiny. On the US side, we are finally, hopefully, moving away from the hegemonic doctrine of Manifest Destiny, foreshadowed by Franklin Roosevelt's tentative embrace of a Good Neighbor policy many decades ago. But as the United States becomes more Latino and varied in its national makeup, a new opportunity is here for policies of mutual respect and interdependence between our two countries in a new version of the New World.

CHAPTER 1

"A Heroic Creation"

Bliss was it in that dawn to be alive,
But to be young was very heaven!
—WILLIAM WORDSWORTH, 1805

Knowing his biography, it is hard to believe that Ricardo was predestined to be a Politburo member of the Cuban Communist Party or, more generally, that Cuba's journey into Marxism-Leninism was inevitable. The island's long battle for real independence from the United States, combined with America's Cold War version of Manifest Destiny, produced those outcomes.

Ricardo Alarcón de Quesada was born in 1937, blue eyed and blond haired, into a family he describes as "the Camagüey aristocracy" but which also included a long line of nationalist ancestors.[1] Ricardo was sixteen years old when Fidel and 160 others assaulted Batista's Moncada army barracks on July 26, 1953, leaving at least eighty young revolutionaries dead,[2] and Fidel and Raúl Castro imprisoned with others.[3] Just the year before, Fidel was attempting to confront injustice by political means. Wanting to combat corruption and seeing himself as the heir to the Orthodox Party, whose leader, Eduardo Chibás, had committed suicide in 1951 after a militant radio speech.[4] Fidel ran for Cuba's House of Representatives, driving his American Chevrolet fifty thousand kilometers across the island before the elections were suspended when Batista seized power. Ricardo would become devoted to the 26th of July movement.

These young Cuban revolutionaries were plagued by the divisions that confront many social movements. Their ranks included nationalists, Marxists, Trotskyites, constitutionalists, torch carriers, bomb makers, clandestine couriers, and furious militants seeking revenge, united temporarily in a sea of boiling currents. Though a member of the 26th of July, Ricardo grew up with many friends in the revolutionary Directorate, or Directorio, a student-led movement devoted to overthrowing the dictator.[5]

RICARDO: *I was not a member of the Directorio but was close to many of its members, especially Fructuoso.*

His friend Fructuoso Rodriguez was the student leader who helped lead the audacious but unsuccessful attack on Batista's presidential palace on March 13, 1957. These extraordinary instances of student-led urban uprisings—Moncada in 1953, the palace attack in 1957, and another in Santiago in 1956 meant to accompany Fidel's landing in the leaking *Granma* vessel—all in less than five years—would mark forever the lives of those in their twenties who made the Cuban Revolution.

RICARDO: *When I entered the university as a student at the School of Philosophy and Letters, I got involved in the student struggles around two main issues: the role of the student movement in opposition to Batista, especially the decisive question of armed struggle versus the peaceful mass struggle advocated by the Communists, and the university reform movement to improve the quality of education and cleaning up the corrupt politicking . . . I got involved with the activities of a group of women who were working on the second point, the moral recovery of the student association.*

University reform, one of the central strands leading to the Cuban Revolution, arose in Argentina at the time of the Rus-

sian and Mexican revolutions under the intellectual and idealistic leadership of José Ingenieros, whose writings condemned
the alleged "mediocre man" formed by capitalism—akin to the
"man in a gray flannel suit" in American fifties' cultural criticism—and extolled the "moral man" with a new revolutionary
ethos. The university reform project suggested a central role for
young students and intellectuals if they would commit to rebel
on behalf of moral incentives, a precursor, perhaps, to Ernesto
"Che" Guevara's later call for a "new man."

Deep corruption and compromise characterized Havana
at the time, reflecting the establishment of a de facto Mafia
empire operated from the United States.

The ethos of gangsterism infected the campuses. Ricardo's generation witnessed seizures of power, dictatorship, the
zoning of their island for US-based Mafia rule, and the absorp-
tion of the Left and its trade unions into the ruling regime,
leaving many young radicals feeling there was nowhere to turn.
Gen. Fulgencio Batista had led a September 1933 coup against
the weak provisional government of Carlos Manuel de Cespedes y Quesada who had come to power less than a month
before, replacing the dictator Gerardo Machado. Batista then
took control of Cuba's military, manipulated presidential elections from behind the scenes, was elected as an authoritarian
president himself in 1940, and ushered in just enough reform,
especially labor legislation, to attract the support of the Cuban
Communist Party (the Popular Socialist Party, or PSP). The
party sought shelter against anticommunist repression, and
Communist-affiliated unions benefited from concessions to
their workers. During the thirties and forties, the party adopted
a Popular Front policy of collaborating with conservative governments like Cuba's in the interest of building Western support for the Soviet Union against Nazi aggression. By 1952,
on the eve of Moncada, what Ricardo calls the "peaceful mass
struggle advocated by the Communists" had stagnated into an
understanding between the Cuban CP and the Batista dicta-

torship, while at the same time Havana was being transformed into a garish sanctuary for casinos, brothels, drugs, and money laundering on behalf of the North American Cosa Nostra. According to Robert Scheer and Maurice Zeitlin's 1963 study, "the Cuban [Communist] Party had been the first to place a member in the national cabinet, first to learn how to survive under a dictatorship, and first to achieve power in the labor movement and politics."[6]

Given their politics and alliances, the Cuban CP condemned the rebel storming of Moncada as reckless adventurism and frowned as well on conspiracies to storm the presidential palace.[7]

Of some 160 Cubans involved in the Moncada attack, eighty were captured in three days.[8] Sixty-eight were brutally tortured before being executed.[9] One of the movement's young leaders, Haydée Santamaría, was forced by her jailers to stare at her brother Abel's eye, torn bleeding from its socket, in a futile effort to break her down. Her brother dead, Haydée was one of fifty-one survivors who finally stood trial with Fidel, who smuggled out his "History Will Absolve Me" speech, scribbled in invisible lemon juice, in defense of the uprising. Especially because of Batista's killings and torture, the Moncada attackers drew the admiration of the Cuban public, further isolating the CP for its tacit support of the regime. Not all party members agreed with the accomodation with the dictator, but maintained discipline in support of the line taken by their leadership.[10]

The understanding between the CP and Batista was a contradiction, Fidel said later, which caused "many of the young people with revolutionary inclinations as well as people on the Left to stop sympathizing with the Cuban Marxist-Leninist Party."[11] Further, the Cuban party had pulled back from a general strike once before, under the Machado dictatorship in 1933, preferring to pact with the tyrant in exchange for concessions rather than push for real victories at the risk of an American intervention.[12] Scheer and Zeitlin interviewed anticommunist labor leaders who charged that the party "accepted an offer by Machado to legalize it and give it financial support if the Communists would try to stop the strike."[13] Whatever the reasons, the opportunistic alliances alienated many in Ricardo's (and Fidel's) generation sharply enough to compel a search for a *Cuban New Left*, one that would revive what historian Richard Gott calls Cuba's "long insurrectionary traditions."[14]

This insurrectionary tradition was embodied in the life of Julio Antonio Mella, a founder of the Cuban Communist Party who was exiled to Mexico where, like Fidel a generation later, he planned an invasion by sea. Mella was killed after taking two bullets to the back on January 10, 1929, using his final moments to accuse Machado of ordering his assassination. Influencing Mella was a Peruvian thinker, José Carlos Mariátegui (1894–1930), who adapted to Peru the Marxist ideas he absorbed during an Italian exile. Mariátegui's greatest relevance may lie in his early insistence on a Communist Party of Peru independent of the dictates of the Communist International's Soviet-centered leadership. Thus he helped originate the "Latin Americanization" of inherited European-centered Marxism.[15] Both revolutionaries would be deep influences on Ricardo and his generation.

RICARDO: *In every meeting of our movement, for previous generations as well, nobody ever denied that Mella was our president. He was the greatest member of our generation. Even people fighting the Communists thought so. Not long ago, Cuba published some work on Mella. He had been a most outstanding defender of the Russian Revolution in those days. But later he said he didn't want to have in Cuba what Lenin did in Russia.[16] It was one thing to follow a revolution in a different country with a different history, but it went beyond that. Mella said, "We want people who think with their own brains, not the brains of others." We don't want what he called "conducted brains." That spirit disappeared. I discovered the article by Mella many years later. It was never in any Communist Party*

*newspapers. This was by a young leader of a party that was supposed
to follow a Soviet line!*

*Mariátegui was a Peruvian theorist who was another big Bol-
shevik supporter but who advocated a different, original kind of
socialism, one that cannot be copied. "Heroic creation," he called the
process. "Creation" meant it had to be original, or originated through
an act. "Heroic" meant it would come into shape through struggle.*

That phrase—"heroic creation"—well describes the birth
experience of the Cuban Revolution. It was forged in Cuba's
long struggle for sovereignty, going back to the wars of independence against Spain (1868–1878, 1879, 1895–1898), the leadership of the exiled José Martí, who was killed in battle in 1895,
the overthrow of Machado in 1933, followed by the generation of
Fidel and Ricardo, ten years younger, in the 1950s—a continuous
ninety-year process interrupted by periodic defeats. Many say the
revolution's roots go even deeper, starting with uprisings of the
indigenous Taino people and African slaves. The point is that the
Cuban Revolution was a Cuban creation, not an event implanted
by a foreign power. Ricardo calls the revolution "heroic" because
it was literally willed into existence, and wrested from imperialists and oligarchs, by generations of dreamers who often gave
their lives crying out *Patria o Muerte*. The sovereignty of Cuba
therefore is blood sealed, not a philosophical proposition.

Creation, of course, refers only to a birth phase. Few revolutionaries back in 1960 were wondering what heroism might
look like in middle age or beyond.

From its very origins the revolution included internal "power
struggles."[17] There were sharp clashes between those believing
in institutional reform and those committed to an insurrection,
and over tactics as well among the ranks of the young revolutionaries. The fate of Ricardo's friend Fructuoso was a flashpoint
that deepened these original divisions. Ricardo and Fructuoso
had become close at the university, where they were involved in
student resistance to the regime.

RICARDO: *We were together practically every day. One day Fructuoso told me about plans to create a student Directorio* [an activist political association] *and invited me to join the new organization. I told him that I was already a member of M-26-7* [the 26th of July movement]. *At the time I worked with José Garcerán, a neighbor and friend from childhood who was responsible for the finances of M-26-7. Fructuoso told me, "It's okay, it's the same." So we continued working together in the student movement, with Fructuoso as the leader, while belonging to two different groups.*

A major difference arose over the Directorio's secret plan to attack the presidential palace and a nearby radio station, capture or kill Batista, and announce to a startled nation that they were free of the dictator. José Antonio Echeverría and Fructuoso Rodriguez were among the key leaders. Fidel, already by then in the Sierra, apparently did not know about the timing or detailed plans,[18] and later was quoted remarking that it was a "useless expenditure of blood."[19] While the attack on Batista's palace was being prepared, M-26-7 members in the Sierra were immersed in quite another plan: to smuggle a *New York Times* correspondent, Herbert Matthews, into the mountains for a clandestine interview with Fidel.[20] That took priority over any plans for the Directorio's palace attack, according to Julia Sweig. The M-26-7 members in Havana were therefore sidelined, though many of them sympathized with the palace attack.

I asked Ricardo if the palace attack was in any way meant to be another Moncada.

RICARDO: *I was not personally involved in the planning of any of those operations, but it seems to me there were substantial differences. It can be said that Moncada was an inspiration but didn't serve as a model in operational terms. There was a Directorio commitment to fight based on the earlier Mexico Pact.[21] But in the case of the palace attack, Batista was the direct personal target, coupled with an open call to popular uprising on Radio Reloj. In the case of*

Moncada, Fidel's strategic idea connected his action with a possible follow-up in the Sierra through guerrilla warfare, while the Directorio strategy was linked to an urban insurrection.

The young revolutionaries came close to shooting their way into Batista's private lair on March 13, 1957. The leader of the Directorio, José Echeverría, even announced prematurely over the captured radio that Batista was dead, before he himself was shot and killed in a street battle. At least forty Directorio activists were killed that day, along with five palace police.[22] The crackdown that followed was fierce, including rounding up, torturing, and killing an unknown number of "suspects." There were also hard feelings generated toward those revolutionary groups that refused to formally participate—among them the 26th of July movement—although M-26-7 members helped take in the wounded. Guns belonging to the Directorio left behind in a lorry were smuggled to the Sierra for M-26-7.[23]

After barely escaping the police that day, Ricardo's close friend Fructuoso Rodriguez scrambled for underground refuge.

RICARDO: *I was not involved at all in the March 13 events. But I met Fructuoso a few days later. He had taken refuge at Garcerón's house, and there we tried to organize a furthering of the struggle under those extremely difficult circumstances, and to save as much as possible what remained of the Directorio. Fructuoso and some friends had to be moved to another hiding place where we were going to discuss how the two organizations—M-26-7 and Directorio—could promote the student strikes. We got a message from Fructuoso on April 20 in the morning to meet the following day. Ironically, on April 20, 1957, my father died a natural death, and I had to go to recognize his body at the same hospital, near Humboldt Street, where the bodies of the four comrades would be carried later that same day.*

Ricardo's four comrades, including his close friend Fructuoso, were ambushed and killed by Batista's police while hiding in an apartment at Humboldt No. 7. Besides Fructuoso, the others were Joe Westbrook Rosales, José Machado Rodríguez, and Juan Pedro Carbó Serviá. One of the student militants jumped out a window, broke his leg, and was shot in the alley. The incident was made famous in a photo of a little boy looking at the blood dripping down the stairwell. The event, which became known as "the Humboldt Seven massacre," left the Directorio leaderless. As large crowds gathered for the burial, suspicions about an informant pointed to a Communist Party connection, the party at the time being the principal organizational rival in the student movement to the Directorio.

The informant who directed the police to the Humboldt safe house was indeed associated with the party, a person named Marcos Armando Rodriguez, nicknamed "Marquitos."[24] His treachery caused lasting anger and bitterness. According to a Havana University researcher I interviewed, Andrés Pertierra, "after returning to Cuba from self-imposed exile in Mexico Marquitos was discovered by the family and friends of the Humboldt 7 victims. After a brief detention he was freed and promptly sent by the CP to Czechoslovakia"[25] where "he spends from 1959 until January of 1961 on a scholarship at first and later [on] a diplomatic mission to Prague, until being recalled by the Cuban government because of his participation in Humboldt 7." During this time, Marquitos was under the de facto protection of several leading Cuban Communists, in particular PSP leader Joaquín Ordoqui and his wife, Edith García Buchaca, a screen which continued even after he was arrested and returned to Cuba, to the enduring anger of the leaders of the Directorio.[26] Marquitos's ultimate extradition from Czechoslovakia and prosecution was pursued by Fructuoso's widow, Martha Jiménez, a close friend of Ricardo's.[27] Even while being interrogated in a Cuban prison, according to Hugh Thomas, Marquitos was supported by several members of the Communist Party's Central Committee.[28] When a Cuban legal case was brought against him in 1964, "it seemed clear that he had intentionally given information to one of the worst mafiosos of the police," said Pertierra. In 1964, Marquitos was convicted of having been an informer and was executed by a Cuban firing squad.

There are indications that the CP set up the Directorio members to eliminate competition.[29] According to Pertierra, "This created an ongoing wound within the revolution's coalition because at the time Fidel's government was creating a close alliance with the Cuban Communist Party [PSP]. Why did this person give the information to the police? It was sectarianism. The CP formerly had been allies of Batista and had called Fidel a 'petit bourgeois' and a 'putschist.' They thought the same thing of the Directorio."[30]

From the earliest days of his revolutionary experience, Ricardo functioned amidst this continuous culture of rivalries, ego conflicts, warring fundamentalisms, and ideological competitions, often worsened by informants, that often undermines the potential unity of revolutionary movements. Even after the revolution's triumph in 1959, the sole leadership of the M-26-7 was "contested by other groups" including the Directorio, the Directorio Estudiantil, and the PSP.[31] Perhaps this threat of deadly disunity would shape Ricardo's evolution as a diplomat, though diplomatic mediation was not enough to paper over differences. Fidel would become the ultimate arbiter and unifier, a triumph of his charisma, courage in the Sierra, and political brilliance. But nothing was guaranteed at the time. Everything could be fragmented or lost.

RICARDO: *The relations between the Directorio and the CP have to be considered in the light of existing differences in those days. Some people in the Directorio may have had anticommunist prejudices, which were very common at the time.[32] But at our university the personal relations between the Humboldt 7 martyrs and the young Communists were pretty friendly. It was quite normal to see Juan Pedro Carbó and José Machado helping the Communists distribute their literature. Fructuoso's vice president, Anotonio Massip, was a well-known militant of the CP youth organization. At that time only two Communists had positions of leadership (the president of the philosophy school and the vice president of the agronomy school).*

Fructuoso was seen as very dangerous by the conservatives. When I was running for the elections at my school I was approached by a classmate who offered the support of the bourgeois Catholics, but he put one condition, only one: that we should break with Fructuoso. The classmate was Laureano Batista Falla, heir to one of the country's most powerful banks. Of course we refused and were defeated in the election. Surprisingly, the winner was the Communist!

I met José Antonio [Echeverría] through Fructuoso. He was a very charismatic person, a real leader, much respected by the vast majority of people at the university, including professors and employees. I am sure he would have been—like Fructuoso—in the front ranks of our people through the years ahead.

I was attracted by the radical view of the Directorio against the Batista regime, by their view of university reform, and also by their personal integrity and willingness to sacrifice themselves. They were real students too, interested in learning and cultivating themselves. We became friends.

I learned the story of Marcos Rodriguez [the informant] in 1959. I think it's not fair to blame the CP as such, but certainly some of the individuals who occupied positions of party leadership protected that person. It was a very sad story because those killed at Humboldt 7 were real revolutionaries and they never discriminated against the Communists.

I will not say that they were killed by the sectarians, but sectarianism was a factor in protecting the traitor and covering up the crime. I think sectarianism is a life-threatening disease for a revolution.

I asked Ricardo if he'd ever said something that Cuban acquaintances have attributed to him, to the effect that "Fidel united us in the present but never in the past," a reference to those submerged sectarian struggles. At a book presentation a few years ago, according to one Cuban source who was there, there was "a big debate between Directorio and 26th of July partisans, "very heated, over who betrayed whom, like it was yesterday. It was common knowledge among historians at the university. You realize that they never forget." Ricardo in retrospect took a much more diplomatic view of the clashes, though he did not deny their lingering roots:

RICARDO: *It is much more complex. I am not referring to disputes early in the revolution, much less between Directorio and M-26-7. Our entire history since the Ten Years' War was affected by divisions that were very much present during the Republic.*[33] *Fidel developed a successful strategy that got the early support of the Directorio and beyond that he was able to gain the trust of the people in a long process that led to Batista's defeat. Fidel insisted on uniting the people, the larger masses, well beyond the various organizations. "Hemos hecha una revolucion mas grande que nosotros mismos"—we made a revolution larger than us all, he would say. Also, the US threat helped to unify large sectors of the population. Unity was achieved, finally, in 1959, and maintained to the present. But when we looked to the past, differences referring to that past remained.*

CHAPTER 2

The Revolutionary War, 1956-59

Fidel and eighty other Cubans, plus the Argentine doctor Che Guevara, slipped onto Las Coloradas beach in eastern Cuba on December 2, 1956, after a turbulent, hazardous trip from Mexico aboard the battered and overloaded yacht named *Granma*.[1] The urban resistance led by Frank País launched an uprising in Santiago in expectation of the *Granma*'s arrival, but the plan went awry due to the stormy weather, when the vessel reached the shore two days later. Alerted, Batista's forces began cutting down the revolutionary guerrillas. Only twenty escaped the landing to form Fidel's guerrilla army nucleus. Fidel, Raúl Castro, Che Guevara, Juan Almeida, Ramiro Valdés, Camilo Cienfuegos, and others trekked through cane fields and ravines into the mountains, where they depended on local people and tried desperately to reconnect with the urban underground. On Christmas Day 1956, Fidel moved higher into the mountains with a sixteen-man unit.[2] This "heroic creation" was something between a triumph of the will and a miracle, not the predictable outcome of "objective conditions" or rational planning. The revolution was marked from the outset by utopian determination crossed with chance. On February 17, 1957, the *New York Times* correspondent Herbert Matthews, who had written sympathetically about the anti-Franco fighters in the Spanish

23

Civil War, found his way with his wife to the Sierra through underground connections, and interviewed Fidel. His reports were a media sensation, in the first place because Batista's office was spreading the rumor that Fidel was dead. Fidel also managed to deceive Matthews about the actual size of his miniscule "army," and was portrayed as a romantic revolutionary hero in the mainstream media.

The urban resistance suffered greatly. The disastrous March 13 attack on the presidential palace in Havana had decapitated the Directorio's leadership. Not long after, on July 30, 1957, the much-admired underground leader in Santiago, Frank País, was hunted down and killed.[3] Many thousands of people braved the repression in Santiago to gather for País's funeral, demonstrating the hidden scale of popular support in the cities. The following year, a national general strike called by the M-26-7 failed to paralyze Batista's state and deepened internal problems of morale. Che Guevara, among others, was very critical of the urban "civic resistance" movement, sharpening a strong debate between two strategies: first, the so-called foco theory of guerrilla war in which a small armed vanguard would establish a rural base in the Sierra from which to launch a war, backed with money, weapons and clandestine support networks in the cities; or second, the concept of an island-wide urban underground revolutionary movement (the Llano) employing everything from sabotage to front organizations until the moment of a climactic general strike. In early revolutionary lore, the revolution was won by the small guerrilla band in the Sierra, although in recent times the official Cuban consensus now recognizes a more balanced narrative acknowledging the role of the urban underground. Ricardo was continually underground himself, credited by historian Richard Gott with having shut down all state schools during the resistance,[4] and once he was quoted suggesting, although with great respect, that Che's theory of the Sierra vanguard was one-sided:

"I don't like to criticize Che, but on that occasion he really didn't know what he was talking about."[5]

In our 2013 conversations Ricardo did not deny the quote, but added:

RICARDO: *Che—and I myself—were both critical of some elements of the Llano leadership that were rather sectarian and generally anticommunist. Che probably was not aware of all the infighting that was going on. I entirely agreed with him regarding the role of those leaders and when we first met in 1959 we talked a lot about that and it became the basis of our friendship. As far as I know, Che was never in Havana before 1959, and his entire experience was in the Sierra.*

The Sierra turned into a military sanctuary for the expanding rebel army. During one interlude Celia Sánchez described the mountain surroundings as a "paradise." Just over two years after the *Granma* landing, after expanding the Sierra base, repelling Batista's bombings and counter-offensives, and splitting the island with several rebel offensives, just as Antonio Maceo's forces had done in 1896, on December 28, 1958, Che Guevara's column took control of Santa Clara, where the underground was led by Enrique Oltuski, posing as a Shell Oil branch manager.[6] As that New Year's Eve ended, Batista made urgent plans to flee Havana with a handful of supporters. On January 2, 1959, the army in Santiago surrendered to Fidel's column while the Batista regime crumbled. At the same time, Che and Camilo Cienfuegos led troops triumphantly into Havana. Fidel arrived one week later after a victory caravan across the island.

RICARDO: *That December the rebel army was advancing around both Santiago and Santa Clara. The leadership of the M-26-7 underground, of which I was a member, had concluded that the collapse of any of those cities would force Batista's downfall. We knew that inside Batista's army there were some trying to find a way out. Batista had sent a military convoy to Santa Clara in a train that was derailed and captured by Che's forces. We had even arranged to meet at a specific place, the FOCSA building,[7] as soon as we learned of Batista's fall,*

*which we did early in the morning of January 1. We learned through
Radio Rebelde that Batista had escaped. There were a number of
armed clashes with [Rolando] Masferrer's paramilitary group[8] as the
general strike continued. That scenario was anticipated.*

*I moved from FOCSA to the Masonic Temple, and from there
we led the occupation of the various Havana universities and high
schools with our student front and we also took over the police station in Havana near the Masonic Temple.*

*Those faithful to the Batista regime fled the country, with the
help of the United States, aboard planes and boats. Some arrived
in the United States without visas or passports since they had left
hastily on their private yachts. That happened with members of the
Batista dictatorship. Masferrer was an example. He was the boss of
one of the terrorist groups, Los Tigres. A few days after the fall of
Batista, Masferrer left on his personal boat and arrived in Florida
completely illegally. We are talking about a real gangster. I studied
his bulging file in our Ministry of Foreign Affairs in the transition
government when we asked for Masferrer's extradition.*[9]

THE ROMANCE OF REVOLUTION: RICARDO AND MARGARITA

It was during these same ecstatic times that Ricardo met the
love of his life, Margarita Perea, at the University of Havana. To
me, Margarita stands in here for the countless Cuban women
who contributed hugely to the successes of the Cuban Revolution even if history tends, wrongly, to record the revolution as a
struggle waged mostly by men.

RICARDO: *Margarita well deserves an entire book about her. We
lived in the same neighborhood but didn't know each other until we
met at the university, where we both studied at the School of Philosophy and Literature. She was born in Santiago de las Vegas, a
small town, south of and not far from Havana, where her mother*

was a schoolteacher and her father a clerk at the local court. She had some working experience as a secretary on a Cuban TV network. She was unusually well educated, with ample knowledge of literature, history, and Marxism.

She joined Juventud Socialista, the youth branch of the Cuban Communist Party. When Frank País, the main leader of the 26th of July underground, was assassinated in Santiago on July 30, 1957, a spontaneous general strike erupted there and reached Havana. Margarita was arrested on August 5 in a demonstration to pro-mote the strike. She spent several days in the BRAC [Bureau for the Repression of Communist Activities] *being interrogated and subjected to psychological torture. When she left the BRAC, her former comrades in JS said it was better to have no more contacts because she was* quemada, *"burnt out," registered by the police.*

So then she asked me if she could join the 26th of July student sec-tion that I was leading and she worked with us from then on. From January 1959 on, she was very active in the political fighting for the revolution and the process of university reform, and taught at the Workers Faculty, which was established as part of the revolution's Literacy Campaign [a flood of idealists to the countryside in 1961, led by three hundred thousand volunteer literacy teachers and administrators, which reduced the official illiteracy rate from 37 percent to 3.9 percent].[10]

Those were the beginnings of a passionate relationship sparked by the passion of the revolution itself. In life and struggle, all things seemed possible in those days. With their small child, named Margarita after her mother, the Alarcóns would eventually move to the diplomatic world of New York and the United Nations. Margarita left behind a promising career at the national art museum in Havana. In April 1980, while marching at the Peruvian Embassy in New York, Marga-rita suffered a fall which revealed that she was suffering from a rare condition, early onset Parkinson's disease.

RICARDO: *First she lost her career, then she was diagnosed with very severe glaucoma and came home very depressed. She was very young, in her twenties, and the doctor had to warn her that to avoid blindness she had to be on strict medication and never lift anything, not even our little baby. She didn't go blind until Parkinson's later attacked her eyes.*

Margarita didn't like diplomatic life at all, the cocktail parties, ceremonies, all that stuff. She only attended when it was unavoidable. The exceptions were the occasions when we socialized with diplomats who were also revolutionaries or intellectuals and she established many friendships with New Yorkers over those twelve years. Since her English was excellent, she often gave lectures on Cuban culture. Of course she had to face the travel restrictions imposed on Cuban diplomats. And we lived in a very tense atmosphere due to assassination plots and threats against me, but nothing ever appeared to intimidate her. There was no security at our small Manhattan apartment. One time, a terrorist knocked on the door and left a suspicious package. Margarita put it in the bathroom and called me at the mission. It turned out it was not a bomb, just a threat and a way to check that I lived in that particular place. The guy who brought it said it was a gift from Stokely Carmichael.

Then it was a long siege of hospitals, medical exams, and the like. In 1990 we both returned to New York, she went from the hospital to the airport. She resumed her previous activities but was limited by her deteriorated physical condition.

When they ended their New York diplomatic life in 1992, Margarita was moved into a hospital in Havana, the International Center for Neurological Rehabilitation. There for many years Ricardo spent his nights sleeping on a cot by her side, while coping by phone with diplomatic and political crises. Margarita died on February 12, 2008, twenty-eight years after the Parkinson's diagnosis.

RICARDO: *A big problem, the doctors told me, was that there was no literature on people suffering from Parkinson's for more than twenty years, which she did. The disease advances, affecting the entire body. There were two or three moments of breathing paralysis, so she had to be in the hospital because at any moment the disease could overcome her.*

After she died, an American friend told me a beautiful story. She and her little daughter were going through some papers at her home where they found a very old photo in which I appeared. They were trying unsuccessfully to identify who was that guy when the little girl interrupted to say, "Mom, I know. He is Margarita's husband."

CHAPTER 3

The Cuban Revolution and the American New Left

I n spring 1959 Fidel and his entourage blitzed the United States and entered the hearts of many in my generation. Even before the revolution, Fidel had traveled to Miami, Tampa, and other Cuban enclaves in America to raise funds and support. In April, Fidel arrived at the invitation of the American Society of Newspaper Editors.[1] President Eisenhower refused to meet him, but sent Vice President Nixon to meet and shake his hand in a famous photo op. Fidel visited Mount Vernon and the Lincoln Memorial—where he read the Gettysburg Address aloud—before being surrounded in New York by twenty thousand people at Penn Station. He dropped by the Bronx Zoo and the Empire State Building, and was given the keys to the city by Mayor Robert F. Wagner Jr. On a quick trip to Boston he spoke to ten thousand students at Soldiers Field.[2] He gave out Cuban cigars to cops and railroad porters. He had at least one affair.

These long-forgotten moments are documented in Van Gosse's comprehensive history of young Americans' enthrallment with Cuba, *Where the Boys Are*, the title borrowed from a Fifties coming-of-age novel about adventuresome young Yan-

kees and their seduction into subversion.[3] The Cuban Revolution even awakened an impulse among at least a few to join
the battle directly in solidarity. For example, Gosse cites a 1957
letter from Henry di Suvero, then at Berkeley, later an ACLU
advocate, and a close friend of mine ten years later in New
Jersey; in his letter to *New York Times* correspondent Matthews,
the young Di Suvero suggested bringing eight friends, all UC
honors students and "highly adventurous," along with two jeeps,
to "join & aid Fidel Castro."[4] Matthews discouraged them.
Instead, some of the same students went on to form SLATE,
the first independent student political party at the dawn of the
sixties.

The Fair Play for Cuba Committee (FPCC), created in 1960,
was a sharp break from the Cold War culture. Among its stu-
dent organizers was Saul Landau, soon to be the bridge between
C. Wright Mills and Fidel;[5] its cofounders included the *Nation's*
Carleton Beals and Waldo Frank[6] (the grandfather of today's
Havana-based journalist Marc Frank); and its sponsors included
many prominent intellectuals opposed to the chill of McCa-
rthyism: James Baldwin, Norman Mailer, Truman Capote, Julian
Mayfield, John O. Killens, John Henrik Clarke, Rev. Donald
Harrington, Kenneth Tynan, Dan Wakefield, and Jean-Paul
Sartre and Simone de Beauvoir.[7] In the emerging spirit of the
New Left, there was a "lack of ties to established labor, political,
or civil rights institutions, [and] hardly a fellow traveler of the
Old Left among them."[8] When Cuba nationalized US refineries
in Cuba after the companies refused to process Soviet oil (at the
insistence of the State Department), the Fair Play Committee
grew "at a dizzying pace," from three chapters and two thousand
subscribers to its *Bulletin* to twenty-seven chapters, forty student
councils, and seven thousand members in 1961.[9]

Fidel's most explosive and memorable stop during this
period came a year later in Harlem, the capital of America's
black community. Arriving for the September 1960 General
Assembly of the UN, Fidel moved into Harlem's Hotel Theresa

after experiencing what he considered a frosty reception at the deluxe downtown Hotel Shelburne.[10] In Harlem, amidst street euphoria, Fidel met with the young Malcolm X and a galaxy of black cultural and political leaders, including many who would endorse Fair Play for Cuba.

The chords of empathy between African Americans and Cubans went back long before the 1959 revolution.

RICARDO: *The nation of Cuba originated from European colonization. Historically there was immigration in both directions as a result of arriving African slaves, Haitians, and French settlers during the Haitian Revolution . . . Later, thousands fled to Cuba during the crisis in Spain* [during the Franco era]. *Where did José Martí go to organize the Cuban Revolutionary Party in the nineteenth century? To the United States, where many Cubans already lived. Between February and December of 1869, nearly one hundred thousand Cubans— seriously, one hundred thousand!—left for the United States from the port of Havana alone. That's why José Martí traveled to the United States.*[11]

Those Cubans fighting for independence from Spain in the latter half of the nineteenth century, known popularly as *mambises*, included many runaway African slaves. The recent runaways were joined by *cimarones*, known in English as "maroons": Africans who had "escaped to the Indians" beginning with slavery's introduction in 1502. The native people, facing extinction themselves, tried to form a resistance across the islands. The most famous uprising, still venerated in Cuba today, was led by a native of Hispaniola, Hatuey, who fought a prolonged guerrilla war against the Spanish before being captured, tied to a stake, and burned alive in 1512.[12] As the native people were decimated, they fled to the mountains together with newly arrived Africans, building fortified base communities, known as *palenques*. Maroon resistance communities spread across the Caribbean, including to Florida's everglade swamps. Their punishment upon capture was horrific: they were skinned, hanged, roasted alive, or decapitated so that their skulls could be impaled on stakes.[13]

In his epic history of Cuba and African Americans, Dr. Gerald Horne quotes an 1849 passage from Frederick Douglass's diaries in which the former slave and abolitionist wrote of Cuba as the "great Western slave mart of the world" and "the channel through which slaves are imported annually into the United States."[14] It was feared by American abolitionists that Confederates with their slaves would retreat to a Cuban sanctuary. Nearly a century later, in 1963, the renowned C. L. R. James wrote of the Haitian Revolution (1791–1804) that "what took place in French Santo Domingo . . . reappeared in Cuba in 1958."[15] Both revolutions were West Indian in character, James wrote, and "whatever its ultimate fate, the Cuban Revolution marks the ultimate stage of a Caribbean quest for identity."[16]

Fidel and the 26th of July movement struck a deep chord with the emerging Beat Generation too, among young bearded poets like Allen Ginsberg, who grew up in a left-wing culture, broke with the mid-century's stifling conformity, and later would be ejected from the island for his homosexuality and advocacy of marijuana.[17] The black poet LeRoi Jones, later to become the revolutionary nationalist Amiri Baraka, issued a famous essay, "Cuba Libre," in *Evergreen Review* in fall 1960, which Van Gosse calls "a gauntlet thrown down before the antipolitical ethos of the Beats."[18] A father figure of the Beats, the San Francisco poet-publisher Lawrence Ferlinghetti, was among the island's foremost enthusiasts. Robert Scheer, a Berkeley graduate student who worked at Ferlinghetti's City Lights bookstore, wrote one of the first important books defending the Cuban Revolution,[19] and later published Che's diaries in his magazine, *Ramparts*. The revolution crossed the lines between cultural and political revolt to tap the fascination of the young intellectuals and students who came to be known as the American New Left, especially through the hugely influential and best-selling writings of the sociologist C. Wright Mills.

CHAPTER 4

C. Wright Mills, Cuba, and the New Left

Ricardo and I are both lifetime students of Mills, a rebel thinker, sociologist, and writer who suffered a fatal heart attack in 1962. The founders of Students for a Democratic Society, especially those on campuses like Ann Arbor, eagerly absorbed each of Mills's books—*White Collar* (1951), about our middle-class culture; *The Power Elite* (1956), about the stifling of democracy by corporations, the military, and a bureaucratic state; *The Causes of World War Three* (1958), about the terrifying prospect of thermonuclear war; and, in 1960, *Listen, Yankee*, an impassioned attempt by Mills to awaken Americans to the challenge of third world revolutions. In those days, Mills was the intellectual parallel to Bob Dylan. Their every page and every lyric were explored like tea leaves. Mills did extraordinary empirical research on power, like virtually no one since, opening our eyes to the reality of elite dominance in a context where democratic pluralism was the conventional wisdom. He wrote in a popular, accessible style. He skewered his timid colleagues in sociology for not "thinking big." We were amazed by his lifestyle, too: a professor who rode a world-class motorcycle, designed and built a home in Nyack, and modeled himself on Ernest Hemingway. He was unquestionably macho, as was Fidel. I wrote my Michigan graduate thesis on Mills, called

Radical Nomad, so titled because I thought him a rebel in search of a cause, a movement, a party to identify with.

In 1960, just following the Cuban Revolution, Mills published a seminal "Letter to the New Left" in the London-based *New Left Review,* which managed to capture the sense that something "new" was, in Dylan's language, "blowing in the wind."[1] Mills complained of the "weariness" of the dominant "NATO intellectuals" whose complacent status quo thinking was standing "in the way of a release of the imagination." He opened the pathway to young people and students imagining ourselves as agents of social change. Decades later, it is vital to recall that youth and students then were categorized as marginal to history in both Marxist revolutionary ideology and Western liberal political theory. It was thought that there were simply too few of us enrolled in colleges, or under twenty-one years old, to make much political difference, and more important, our role in life included no "lever" to make history. That role, in radical theory, was assigned to the industrial working class who had their hands on the gears of production. Mills criticized this view as a nonempirical "labor metaphysic," an immutable truth held by the Left similar to the scriptural dogma in a religious creed.

Mills empowered our activist generation by his thesis that we were agents of social change, a phrase we imported into the 1962 Port Huron Statement. In the culmination of his 1960 essay he noted that young people were leading uprisings all over the planet, mentioning Japan, South Korea, Poland, Soviet students, the antinuclear marches in England, the sit-ins in the American South, and in Cuba, where Mills emphasized that a revolution was carried out by thirty-year-olds and where organized labor, muddled by its relationship with Batista's state, definitely was not the key agent of change.

Mills travelled to Cuba for two weeks during the summer of 1960, where he hunkered down with Fidel and many others, also bouncing in a jeep all over the island. He was accompanied by Saul Landau, a young radical graduate student who would devote his life to Cuba before he passed away in 2013. One of the key Cubans helping Mills get around was Manuel Yepe, a young intellectual who went on to become the head of Prensa Latina, the vortex of Cuba's media services. Yepe, who still lives in Havana with his wife, the social scientist and feminist Dr. Marta Núñez, recalled Mills's journey when I interviewed him in Havana in 2013.

MANUEL YEPE: *Mills was one who was prepared to understand Cuba. Everything he wrote in his book he learned in a few weeks. For his views on Cuba, he was being seriously harassed, including death threats, at home in New York, by the Miami Cubans and, it was proven, by the FBI.*[2]

We drove from Havana to the town of Viñales in Pinar Del Río for the discussions with Fidel. We arrived late at night, and Mills went to his room. I was called very early the next morning to bring Mills to Fidel's room. Fidel was still in bed, holding a machine gun. Fidel's medical doctor René Vallejo, also came by. They shut the door. Then I believe they talked for the next eighteen hours.

Mills actually talked with Fidel *eighteen hours per day for three and a half days.* The collaboration between these two over-whelming personalities seemed somehow destined. It takes nothing from Mills's talents to say that he channeled Fidel so intensely that the Cuban leader was a de facto coauthor of *Listen, Yankee.* (The same would be true, I will argue, of Fidel's role in the writing of Régis Debray's *Revolution in the Revolution?* in 1967.[3]) Mills said as much in his introduction: "I have thought the expression of my own views much less important than the statement of the Cuban revolutionaries' case. And that is why, insofar as I have been able, I have refrained from expressing a personal opinion . . . Please know, then, that as you read these letters that it is the Cuban revolutionaries who are talking to you."[4]

Mills wrote his bestseller in six weeks, worsening his serious heart condition. The stress on him was increased by the FBI. Someone sent him an anonymous letter warning that, in the words of an FBI memo on the incident, "an American agent disguised as a South American will assassinate you on your next visit to Cuba."[5] He stuffed a handgun under the bed in his New York family home. On the eve of a December 1960 nationally televised debate over Latin America with the establishment critic of Cuba, A. A. Berle, Mills fell into a coma from a severe heart attack. He recovered, but doctors discovered evidence of previous attacks. Having no health insurance increased his worries, as he wrote in a letter to the *New Left Review*'s Ralph Miliband on January 25, 1961. "What bothers me," he wrote, "is whether or not the damned heart will stand up to what must then be done" in the event of worsening times coming to America.[6]

"Fidel keeps cabling me to come on down and convalesce in Cuba, and my friend [René] Vallejo, . . . a medical man of real ability, as well as the head of INRA [Cuba's National Institute of Agrarian Reform] in the Oriente,[7] says that just to step on the island will cure me! and that he has some things to talk over anyway!"[8] But Mills wouldn't stop trying to fight "this moral anguish which is crushing me," as he put it to Landau. His heart gave out on March 20, 1962, just before the founding convention of SDS where he was invited to speak. None of us at Port Huron had known him, but all of us felt his loss. We wanted, I think, to fill his space with hope. Like many young revolutionaries the world over, we believed we would carry on to overcome what killed him.

Fifty-one years later, in 2013, sitting on an outdoor couch at Havana's Nacional Hotel, Ricardo still brought up Mills.

RICARDO: *He said he would come back in 1962. In a way we are still waiting for him. Miliband said Mills was a casualty of the Cuban Revolution. He was victimized by the Cuban Mafia with death threats and lawsuits. He wanted Saul to come ahead to get more documents for his next visit. He was trying to get documents here not just to prepare for his next visit but to prepare his defense in court where he was being accused by some gang- and Batista-related businesspeople. The State Department refused to issue the passport.*

Ricardo wrote a remembrance for *The Nation* on April 9, 2007, on the forty-fifth anniversary of Mills's death, noting that "his principal message not only retains its relevance; recent historical events vindicate it." The Soviet Union was no more; "neoliberal capitalism is global, yet its dominion is increasingly challenged by the peoples of Latin America and elsewhere." Ricardo's words in 2007 signified to me that he was resuming the search for another New Left. It was one reason that Ricardo had invited me to spend a week being interviewed about the American New Left for Cuba's archives. "We have, indeed, faced difficult times, bereft of his irreplaceable rebelliousness," Ricardo told a Montreal conference that same year, speaking of Mills.[9]

Any aging veteran of the sixties in America is likely to have Mills's books, even though they are little read or discussed in academia anymore. The pages of my two copies of *Listen, Yankee*, one a paperback, the other the original hardcover edition, are flaking and subject to tearing if underlined. Many observers might say the aging process has affected Cuba and the American New Left and in the same way. But the *content* of the pages remains truly original. The overarching themes declare the way we were or, as Ricardo said of our interviews on Cuba and the New Left in 2006, the *como éramos*, the essential ideas of the revolutions of 1960 and in the years following.

First, Mills's Cuban voice was that of *middle-class youth.* "We are new radicals. We really are, we think, a new left in the world"[10] . . . "the revolution was incubated at the university"[11] . . . "we are middle-class."[12] The voice was euphoric: "We Cubans have made the big connection between fantasy and reality, and now we are living in it."[13] Mills's Cuban voice declared that "our revolution is not a revolution made by labor unions or wage workers in the cities, or labor parties, or by anything like that. It is far from any revolution you ever heard of before."[14] The SDS document said the same: that our revolution would be led above all by young people, blacks, farmworkers, and students. Like the Cubans taking to their countryside, we would become a catalyst to awaken a moribund American liberal and labor movement.

At the time, the Cuban Revolution was neither Communist nor led by a vanguard party. Mills quotes Fidel's proclamation of 1959: "Standing between the two political and economic ideologies being debated in the world, we are holding our own position. We have named it humanism ... the tremendous problem faced by the world is that it has been placed in the position where it must choose between capitalism, which starves people, and communism, which resolves economic problems but suppresses the liberties so greatly cherished by man. ... Capitalism sacrifices man; the communist state, by its totalitarian concept, sacrifices the rights of man."[15]

Not only that: "The Communist parties in Latin America generally go for 'popular fronts' and 'national democratic coalitions' and so on ... they sacrifice immediate revolutionary action—and even [revolutionary] thought ... they are to the right of the revolution."[16]

Preferably, Mills claimed, Cuba would want to do away with the US-Soviet Cold War altogether: "We think what gives its character to our revolution is the fight between North America and Latin America. That's *our* Cold War."[17] The Port Huron Statement (PHS) issued the same denunciation. But Mills went on quoting Fidel: "Our Cuban opposition to communism doesn't mean the kind of McCarthyism and hysterical anticommunism that you've put up with in your country."[18] As the PHS said it, "An unreasoning anticommunism has become a major social problem for those who want to construct a more democratic America,"[19] leading America into expedient alliances with dictators like Cuba's Batista.[20] Written one year after the

April 1961 Bay of Pigs invasion, the PHS said that the US government was mainly interested in Cuba for commercial reasons,
and that the invasion further isolated us from Latin America.
Meanwhile, we were angered at the fact that "the world is in
transformation[,] but America is not."[21] While SDS was "in
basic opposition to the communist system,"[22] that hardly justified the Cold War's chain of American-aided dictatorships
or its permanent and growing military-industrial complex—a
memorable term given us by President Eisenhower but not until
the very end of his presidency in his 1959 farewell address. "We
should end the distinction between communist hunger and
anticommunist hunger," the Statement said, borrowing Mills's
definition of the third world as "the hungry bloc." "To support
dictators like Diem while trying to destroy ones like Castro will
only enforce international cynicism about American 'principle,'
and is bound to lead to even more authoritarian revolutions,
especially in Latin America where we did not even consider
foreign aid until Castro had challenged the status quo."[23]

While Mills identified with the Cuban Revolution, he never
abandoned his private worries about the "nightmares that
might occur in the times ahead." "It might harden into any one
of several kinds of dictatorial tyranny."[24] He noted the dangers
that Cuban society was "legally arbitrary" and expressed dislike
for "the dependence on one man as exists in Cuba today, [and]
the virtually absolute power that this one man possesses," while
emphasizing the need to "understand the conditions that have
made it so."[25] Mills didn't believe such trends were inevitable,
but due in large part to the American role. And he thought "US
policies and lack of policies are very real factors in *forcing* the
government of Cuba to align itself politically with the Soviet
bloc," instead of, as Mills hoped, "assuming a generally neu-
tralist and hence peaceful world orientation."[26] Mills believed
in a two-party electoral system for Cuba, but warned that it was
an "impossible and meaningless idea" as long as it simply meant
giving the US-backed counterrevolution an institutional form.

Besides Fidel's moral critique of communism as antihumanist, Mills quoted his Cuban narrator: "The [Communist] Party didn't play any part at all in the making of our revolution ... and were political rivals of our movement."[27]

A policy of neutralism, then arising across the third world, wasn't any longer a practical possibility for the Cubans, "as we tried to do, a year or so ago."[28] Instead, the menacing pressure of economic and military aggression from the United States made it necessary to accept a protective counterbalance that was only possible from the Soviet Union. "We are glad of their offer ... to help us if you attack us militarily."[29] Since the United States couldn't tolerate a New Left Cuba on our "doorstep," it was guaranteed that the Cubans would move into the Soviet orbit in order to survive. The 26th of July movement would be integrated with the Cuban Communist Party, humanism with Marxism, and Cuba with the Soviet-led socialist bloc.

On one key point, the future of the Soviet Union, Mills was wrong in assuming its permanence—along with even the most fervent anticommunists and "experts" on communism.

RICARDO: *I do not have a tradition of other comrades who believed in the Soviet Union. I had very limited experience with the USSR. I was in the Soviet Union once or twice, mainly in transit. My daughter was in East Germany. My main experience with them was at the UN. It showed me how much truth there was in Mills's theory of convergence of the two blocs.*

Ricardo was referring to Mills's *The Causes of World War Three*, which analyzed the threat of the raging nuclear arms race. I was surprised at how quickly he emailed me back when I asked him more about Mills's thesis.

RICARDO: *I think Mills put it in a rather prophetic manner: "These two world-dominant societies are becoming overdeveloped in a similar way; the very terms of their world antagonism are furthering their similarities ... There are many other points of convergence and coincidence between these two countries, both in dream and in reality, and as the Soviet industrial complex is further enlarged these will become more pronounced. In surface ideology they apparently differ; in structural trend and in official action they become increasingly alike. Not ideology but industrial and military technology, geared to total war, may well determine that the dreams of each will in due course be found in the realities of the other."*

Mills saw the problems raised by "hyperdevelopment," the trend both in the West and the East toward a kind of industrialization that, together with the Cold War, was the basis of their convergence. In a way Mills was also anticipating the concerns about the environment and sustainable development before the Greens were born.

Mills therefore came to a conclusion that was original for its time, and with which the New Left agreed: "And that is why I am for the Cuban Revolution. I do not worry about it. *I worry for it and with it."*[30]

Having worked and lived mainly through the chilling era of McCarthyism, Mills died before he could embrace and worry "for and with" the New Left in the United States. He never went South to the front lines of the civil rights struggle; his southern journey instead took him into the centers of Latin America's revolution. He appended a dense and cogent twenty-page appendix to *Listen, Yankee* on conditions of misery in Latin America as a whole, notes for a future study. And while strongly identifying with the potential power of "the young intelligentsia," it was impossible in 1961–1962 for Mills to see the coming of the anti-Vietnam War movement, draft resistance, student revolts, women's liberation, gay liberation, the environmental movement, and the rise of a third world movement inside the borders of the United States itself. He was a lonely prophet without a promised land. From this standpoint of isolation, however, Mills had a prophetic insight shared by few at the time, that *the domestic costs of Yankee imperialism someday might cause an armed revolutionary vanguard to rise within the United States itself,* in the belly of the very beast that Martí hated. Mills was anticipating the Black Panther Party, the Weather Underground, the Young Lords, Reies Tijerina's 1967 raid on the Tierra Amarilla courthouse, the American Indian Movement's fight for Wounded Knee, American GI mutinies during the Vietnam War, and numerous acts of violence against the state beginning in the late sixties—all occurring less than a decade after the Cuban Revolution and Mills's prophetic book. He wrote:

"In Cuba, we had to take to our 'Rocky Mountains'—you couldn't do that, could you? Not yet, we suppose. We're joking— we suppose. But if in ten years, if in five years, if things go as we think they might inside your country, if it comes to that, then know this, Yankee: some of us will be with you. God almighty, those are great mountains!"[31]

CHAPTER 5

From the Missile Crisis to Counterinsurgency

The Cuban Revolution, the American civil rights movement, and the student New Left of the sixties all shared historic similarities and bonds. They were not precisely new, though each appeared out of nowhere.

The Cuban Revolution rested on a continuous history traceable back to José Martí's generation of the mid 1800s. Both the territories of what would become Cuba and the United States were "discovered," invaded, and disrupted by Spanish conquerors. In both, indigenous tribes fought the invaders and died in great numbers. In both, slave revolts—either by indigenous people or Africans—began in the 1500s. Cuba was a desirable target for American "annexation" from the time of Thomas Jefferson and John Quincy Adams. "[Cuba is] the most interesting addition that can be made to our system of states," Jefferson once wrote.[1] Nationalist revolutionaries like Martí took exile from Spanish tyranny in New York and Florida, where they plotted their second war of independence, which started in 1895. Martí's generation was also that of W.E.B. Dubois, the leading African American revolutionary, author, academic, Marxist, and a founder of the NAACP. Martí wrote extensively about the United States for Latin American newspapers, and never doubted the US imperial goal of pretending to befriend the Cubans in order to supplant the Spanish on the island. In his final and long-remembered letter, Martí wrote that his goal was "to prevent, by [achieving] the independence of Cuba, the United States from spreading over the West Indies and falling, with that added weight, upon other lands of our America ... I have lived inside the monster and know its entrails; my sling is David's."[2] He died the next day, May 19, 1895, while fighting in Cuba, sealing his role as father of his country. True to Martí's prophecy, the United States joined the Spanish–American War, known in Cuba as the second war of independence, and emerged from the 1898 Treaty of Paris in control of Cuba, Puerto Rico, the Philippines, and Guam. Gen. Leonard Wood, fresh from pacification wars against Native Americans, became Cuba's military governor, and the 1901 Platt Amendment eliminated Cuban sovereignty, setting the stage for continuous civil rights and national liberation struggles until the 1959 revolution.[3]

RICARDO: *If you go in depth into Fidel's thinking, writing, and life, he didn't come out of the blue. He studied the Cuban revolutionary experience from 1868, the whole experience against Spain. That started in eastern Cuba. At that time, in eastern Cuba you had less slavery; it was the only place on the island with a number of black small farmers. Cespedes and his group, the Masons, didn't talk about socialism but about the exploitation of man by man.[4] They had to face the stronghold of Spanish domination, which was in western Cuba. Cespedes's idea in the Ten Years' War (1868–1878) was to invade western Cuba. What was the dream of Maceo and Gómez? Also to go and invade western Cuba. Maceo said, "Now I have to raise the torch." "Bless the torch," he once said. They wanted to burn down the sugar plantations. Some thought it was too radical or extreme to try to win a war against Spain because they didn't have support from the aristocracy.[5] Then when [General Máximo] Gómez reached Las Villas [a province immediately to the east of Havana] in the 1895–1898 war and saw the misery of a slaves, he too said, "Bendita sea la tea," more or less, "God bless the torch."[6] Others like Mella planned on going to Mexico and from there invading Cuba. The secret police killed him there.*

So Fidel knew very well what he was doing when he went to Mexico and invaded Cuba from there. His idea in the Sierra was to invade western Cuba as others had planned before. What happened in the Sierra Maestra was the fruit of that long history. It was not about a bunch of people just going to the mountains to start a war.

The Cuban Revolution unfolded while I was a student journalist in Ann Arbor. I remember being touched in an indefinable way by those guerrillas with beards. I was then preoccupied with convincing candidate John F. Kennedy to endorse a Peace Corps proposal. Before my eyes, Kennedy did so on a rain-swept Ann Arbor night, at 2:00 a.m., October 14, 1960. I wasn't sophisticated enough to quite understand that this Peace Corps was an American answer to the perceived threat of the bearded Cubans in Latin America, nor that it was the "soft power" cousin of the Green Berets being prepared for foreign jungles. The Bay of Pigs debacle in April 1961, coming so swiftly after Kennedy's inauguration, profoundly rattled my political consciousness by introducing the reality of a "deep state" where secrets were held from the voting public—and the media, my chosen profession—by a CIA-led elite of the "best and brightest," often with disastrous results. I had no idea at the time that the same CIA covertly funded the National Student Association, whose annual student conventions I attended in 1960 and 1961, and where Cuba was one of the hottest topics of controversy.

RICARDO: *During the Bay of Pigs I was at the university as vice president of FEU, and involved in defense preparations. Raúl Roa[^7] was in New York where he spent several days, maybe even weeks, denouncing the invasion at the UN. I was involved in the defense of the university area. Every building around the hill, including the Calixto García Hospital. Cubans were organized everywhere to protect their factories, neighborhoods, schools, etc. So we were at the University, all the students, workers, professors under the command of the*

FEU. We were called the Milicia Universitaria [University Militia]. In those days we were expecting an air attack or an invasion, and we were on guard watching our buildings and patrolling our area. We did not have to fight. In the end, Fidel called me to have a special broadcast on a "Universidad Popular" program. It was a Sunday TV program which I and a group of friends from the 26th, the Directorio, and the PSP ran in those years. On the program Fidel gave a long and detailed explanation of the battle that had just ended.

The Young Americans for Freedom (YAF) led the ranks of the student Right, as their cadre would continue to do for decades to come. Since the Cuban invasion was the brainchild of the CIA, the cry to "Free Cuba" aroused the YAF contingent and most student conservatives, nearly all of whom were appalled by beards—their hero Sen. Barry Goldwater disparaged Fidel as "a bum without a shave."[8] The same student activists were galvanized to resist any desegregation of lunch counters in the South, on the grounds that restaurant owners had inviolable rights to refuse service to anyone they chose. The senior voice of YAF in those years was the late William F. Buckley Jr., a former CIA agent on whose lavish Connecticut estate YAF had been founded. His magazine, the *National Review*, was editorializing in support of segregation at the time. The argument that Cubans should be freed from *their* own revolution, but not young black students from barriers to voting, eating, or riding on buses, was a contradiction few could abide. Had I known that the CIA was funding both the Cuban exiles *and* the National Student Association, that news would have shocked away all that remained of my twenty-one-year-old innocence. I wasn't old enough to vote for JFK but would gladly have done so. At the 1960 National Student Association convention I fought against the YAF proposal to liberate Cuba, not realizing that the policy was already being implemented in secret.

Ricardo was recruited by Raúl Roa to the new Cuban foreign ministry, to handle Latin American relations, at the age of twenty-four, becoming one of the youngest diplomats in the world. It was one month before the Cuban missile crisis.

Occurring shortly after the Port Huron Statement was issued in October 1962, the Cuban missile crisis fulfilled our worst nightmares and left a permanent generational scar. I personally was never more traumatized in my life, before or after those October days. The CIA was already running covert sabotage attacks and assassination efforts in Cuba, through a secret program code-named "Mongoose," with the ultimate aim of regime change. When they detected the shipment of Soviet missiles, the Kennedy brothers and their advisers secretly considered scenarios that accepted nuclear war as one possible outcome. They at least believed that the *threat* of a nuclear war was necessary to end the crisis. To be "credible," of course, it had to seem likely to an adversary that the threat was more than a bluff, that is, that nuclear weapons would be used as a last resort. In retrospect, JFK mused that the chances of Russia going "all the way" to war were "somewhere between one out of three and even."⁹ Kennedy's military advisers urged bombing the missile sites, following up with a land invasion of Cuba and, if "necessary," an attack on the Soviet Union using nuclear-armed missiles. This kind of thinking, called "crackpot realism" by C. Wright Mills, was later sensationalized in Stanley Kubrick's film, *Dr. Strangelove*, partly based on the character of Kennedy's air force secretary, Gen. Curtis LeMay. The growing Cuban-Soviet alliance was seen not only as a geopolitical threat to the Cold War power balance, not only as a violation of America's unilaterally declared Monroe Doctrine of 1823, but also as a threat aggravated by certain primordial feelings on the part of the United States that Cuba was destined to be ours. The Soviet Union's intrusion into our hemisphere by putting the missiles in Cuba represented the first time a European military power had intervened in Latin America since Napoleon III invaded Mexico in 1861.

Soviet premier Nikita Khrushchev, for his part, covertly shipped nuclear-tipped medium-range missiles to Cuba "in view of the threats of aggressive imperialist quarters," with Cuba's consent.[10] Over forty thousand Soviet troops were to be stationed in Cuba as well. Later it became known that the nuclear-tipped missiles were under the full control of the Soviets, not the Cubans, and therefore could be used or withdrawn by the Soviets at their sole discretion. Khrushchev apparently believed that this escalation would deter another US invasion and prevent, rather than provoke, a wider war. In his mind, if the Soviets could accept American nuclear warheads on the borders of the Soviet sphere of influence, for example in Turkey, then the United States could be forced into a similar position in the Western Hemisphere. The Soviet Union's stature as a protector of socialism and third world revolution would be powerfully enhanced, offsetting competition from China.

Revolutionary Cuba's position was that it had a sovereign right to defend itself against outside aggression with any kind of weapons under a deterrence umbrella. According to Gott, the idea of nuclear missiles was not at first a Cuban one.[11] "The [Soviet] desire to achieve a more equal balance of strategic nuclear forces with the United States may well have been of paramount consideration." The Cubans went along, however, despite questions about how the installation could be kept secret, and the loss of Cuban control of the weapons. As "the worst fears of the Cubans were being realized,"[12] Fidel gave an incendiary speech, which sounds today as if taped from another world, proclaiming a revolutionary willingness to face total annihilation if the war broke out: "We have the consolation of knowing that in a thermonuclear war, the aggressors, those who unleash a thermonuclear war, will be exterminated."[13] Che was penning similar sentiments which were published posthumously: "What we affirm is that we must proceed along the path of liberation even if this costs millions of atomic victims"; and he saw the Cuban people advancing fearlessly "toward the hecatomb which signifies final redemption."[14] In Cuban lore, Fidel's speech became their second Baraguá, recalling the 1878 defiant refusal by Antonio Maceo to sign a temporary cease-fire with Spain without achieving either independence or the full liberation of the slaves.[15]

In 1962, however, the question was broader than another insult to Cuban's sovereignty: the lives of hundreds of millions of people were at stake. As Kennedy noted, the range of the Soviet ICBM stretched from Hudson Bay, Canada, to Lima, Peru.[16]

Fidel and the revolution's leadership were not consulted when the Soviets quietly negotiated the dismantling of their sites and the pullout of their missiles. The Cubans felt used as pawns. According to historian Thomas, "Castro was not consulted by Khrushchev and heard the news while talking with Guevara; he swore, kicked the wall, and broke a looking glass in his fury."[17]

Decades later the world learned from Fidel that there had been forty-two medium-range missiles in Cuba, twenty with nuclear warheads and another twenty aboard a Soviet ship that was turned back. No missile launchers were yet operable, although two medium-range missiles were "ready to operate" by October 23.[18] There were forty-three thousand Soviet troops on the island.[19] "All the US nuclear and conventional forces throughout the world were now made ready for action, while a huge invasion force was massed in Florida."[20] Ninety B-52s with 25–50 megaton H-bombs were flying on Atlantic routes, while 150 ICBMs were on their launching pads.[21] On the ocean to carry out the quarantine were sixteen US destroyers, three cruisers, and an antisubmarine aircraft carrier plus backup ships.[22] JFK speechwriter Ted Sorensen recalled that "our little group seated around the Cabinet table in continuous session that Saturday felt nuclear war to be closer on that day than at any time in the nuclear age."[23] When the crisis ebbed, Fidel called on the United States to end its subversion, lift the embargo, and cease air attacks and the occupation of Guantanamo. Cuba refused to allow outside inspectors to confirm the removal of the missiles, a decision Kennedy acquiesced in. The Americans significantly promised never to invade Cuba, although hit-and-run black operations continued along with the embargo. American missiles were later removed from Turkey in a reciprocal gesture. Cuba released 1,113 Bay of Pigs prisoners in exchange for $53 million in baby food and medicines.

When the crisis suddenly emerged into public view, those of us in the New Left were involved heavily in civil rights and university reform. Concerns about the Cold War and nuclear fallout were on the rise. We generally assumed that Kennedy could be deflected away from another Bay of Pigs, reach a rapprochement with Fidel, reverse the nuclear arms race with the Soviets, and navigate toward the "new era" of our dreams. But given the Bay of Pigs invasion and now the missile crisis, it was clear that there was at least a reflexive impulse toward imperial military intervention, even including the use of nuclear weapons, under the bland surface of national security thinking. In the Cold War thinking of Secretary of State Dean Rusk, there were only two alternatives: either a US "quick strike" against Cuba or a decision to "eliminate the Cuban problem by actually eliminating the island."[24] Our rising demands for a dramatic return to domestic priorities like civil rights seemed either threatening or a diversion from the global worldview in Washington. Fighting for freedom at the University of Mississippi was less "strategic" than introducing freedom at bayonet point in Havana or in South Vietnam. The Student Nonviolent Coordinating Committee (SNCC) viewpoint of "making democracy safe for the world" was our challenge to the prevailing wisdom of Woodrow Wilson that the American mission was to make the world safe for democracy. The impulse toward military solutions was rising in 1962 toward Cuba and Vietnam, though we hardly noticed the creep until the missile crisis.

As for myself, I was wrong and naive in thinking that the only obstacle was the bitter Cuban exiles stranded in Florida, like the white segregationists in the Old South, an isolated, angry, "no surrender" minority that I believed would fade with time.

But what I hadn't figured on were the liberal, Ivy League-educated Democrats in the White House who shared the segregationists' and YAF's willingness to risk a nuclear holocaust rather than "surrender," or at the least consider a nuclear bluff.

Such stubbornness was beyond my comprehension. Even while the Dixiecrats became the Republican Party, and later the Tea Party, a bipartisan combination of politicians *still* favored the embargo of Cuba, and perhaps another military adventure. Why was this? Revenge for Fidel's repelling of the Bay of Pigs invasion? To enforce the Monroe Doctrine? To prevent the possible "export" of revolution to Latin America? To eradicate a socialist example "ninety miles from our shores"? Bertrand Russell issued an outcry to the world warning, "Within a week you will all be dead to please American madmen."[25] That said it all.

In Ann Arbor, I led an SDS protest of several hundred in response to the president's frightening speech of October 22, 1962.[26] At Harvard, an overflow crowd of over two thousand turned out; most of them, according to the SDS-affiliated journal *Common Sense*, were "more curious than partisan."[27] Thirty-five hundred turned out at the San Francisco Civic Center to hear Robert Scheer, Maurice Zeitlin, and Lawrence Ferlinghetti. Scheer's call for UN ambassador Adlai Stevenson to resign in protest drew the loudest cheers of the day. In his speech, Scheer also said that Fidel had betrayed the revolution for the first time by accepting the Soviet nuclear missiles. Fistfights broke out and protestors were attacked by young Kennedy partisans at the universities of Indiana and Minnesota. Ten thousand turned out at New York's UN Plaza on that Sunday, the day the crisis eased, bearing signs saying "We Oppose Bases and Blockades." Membership in the Student Peace Movement, Women Strike for Peace, and the Committee for a SANE Nuclear Policy grew by the hour while these groups improvised the minimal organizational structure the rising numbers needed to express their shock.

Our SDS leadership in Ann Arbor plunged into overdrive, sending a flurry of mailings trying to dissect and explain how the unthinkable had come to pass. Almost spontaneously, thousands of students from around the country began driving, bussing or hitching rides to Washington, D.C., which was ground zero for the widely expected nuclear war. I personally had been inside the White House just weeks before, to present a fresh copy of the Port Huron Statement to the president's in-house historian, Arthur Schlesinger Jr. Now the White House, gleaming on the outside while curtained within, was the center of the "hecatomb" Che wrote about in his diaries. Yet we felt drawn to be there, to protest perhaps a final time, under a shared threat with the Cuban people we hardly knew. This was the birth of the new antiwar movement of the sixties, and the turning point in the New Left's dissent from Cold War liberalism.

The protest against war with Cuba deepened a festering emotional and political divide between the New Left and the traditional liberal Democrats, then represented by Schlesinger's Americans for Democratic Action (ADA), which had led notable battles for civil rights legislation in prior years. Perhaps because they were instinctively anticommunist and pro-Kennedy, the ADA supported the administration's Cuba policy; as the liberal White House aide told the demonstrators, "You have come to the wrong address. Go see Khrushchev," completely misunderstanding why young Americans were protesting the role of *our own government*, not seeing that we were motivated by outraged patriotism. The ADA leader John Roche denounced the New Left in the *New York Times* as "morally bankrupt" adherents to an escapist "cult of survival," meaning that we should accept our nuclear fate in the name of anticommunism. We who already were on the front lines of the violent South didn't take the insult well. In interviews not long after, JFK himself would say he'd "rather my children be red than dead," as if those absurdist choices were the only ones available.[28] The late Jack Newfield, a Kennedy supporter and *Village*

Voice writer, wrote back to Roche, "You have come to the wrong generation, go see your contemporaries." It was not morally bankrupt, Newfield wrote, to "reject the Cold War's institutionalized madness, and demand a cessation of nuclear testing, abandonment of provocative bases in Turkey, cutbacks in the arms budget and other unilateral initiatives *toward* disarmament."

Just as it would polarize the once-monolithic communist world, the Cuban Revolution was causing a fundamental rethink among American liberals and the Left.

On one of those October nights, I remember being crammed into a local church listening to the great muckraking journalist I. F. Stone announce that all deadlines had passed and that missiles soon would be on their way. He, of course, was wrong, a lesson in caution about apocalyptic thinking that I would remember. It's impossible to fully reconstruct my feelings at that moment all these decades later, but it was not paralyzing fear so much as a heightened alertness, an emotional calm as we waited for Armageddon to roll itself out. Inside the White House, Bobby Kennedy talked of the "end of mankind."[29] Outside in the streets, the same unforgettable feeling was shared with one difference: we on the outside could do little about it without a movement.

With nothing left to lose, I ate a cheeseburger with two friends at a local restaurant.

I had never felt the attack of vertigo, of things falling apart in my life, until that time, and nothing resembling the feeling since. Perhaps it fortified my tendencies toward existentialism instead of the more rational expectations that come with liberalism or Marxism. It may also have caused a numbing of emotion, at least after the cloud lifted and everyday life resumed. From then forward, I never quite accepted the five-minutes-to-midnight logo of the antinuclear movement, since I would learn that near-death experiences could be escaped, the clock could be stopped. Many people today experience similar fears and depression when facing the evidence that it's "game over" due to climate change. They live permanently in the state of perpetual fear I experienced that October.

In that same issue of *Common Sense*, I published a several-thousand-word analysis with Dick Flacks in Ann Arbor, titled "Cuba and USA." The most positive outcome of October, we said, was the rise of a large-scale peace force for the first time since the fifties. But we also experienced the presence of an awesome "war lobby" ready and willing to deploy nuclear weapons in a first strike. "There was nothing we could do in the midst of this crisis to avert its extension to holocaust." Without making electoral politics "a fetish," it was clear to us that "the priority today, as never before, is power," the building of an institutional base capable of resisting the drift toward nuclear war.

That was a long time ago. There came exceptional films like *Seven Days in May* and *Doctor Strangelove*, and a few years later, peace candidates like George McGovern, Eugene McCarthy, and Robert Kennedy. All these developments can be seen, at least in part, as responses to the polarizing fear that had taken hold during and after the Cuban missile crisis. Massive popular movements played roles in ending the wars in Vietnam, Central America, Iraq, and Afghanistan, and undermining the torturers who came to power in the Americas. Along the way, Cuba continued to be embargoed and subjected to attacks from Cuban exiles sheltered in Miami. But the US government never again sent American forces to invade or bomb Cuba. That was the result of the diplomatic agreements that ended the 1962 missile crisis, and one of the factors ensuring that this resulting "cold peace" would last was the certainty that thousands of Americans would take to the streets, along with people around the world, if our government tried to invade again. Over the decades, I have learned through experience that such ambiguous victories are worth ensuring.

Largely because of Cuba, today's military doctrine of counterinsurgency gained full-fledged currency in the liberal Democratic Kennedy administration. The success of their ideological opponents in Havana inspired our leaders to want to be able to do what the Cuban insurgency had done. JFK's inaugural address warned of a "long twilight struggle" against tyranny [i.e., communism], poverty, disease, and war itself. The clandestine Green Berets would carry the spear while the humanitarian Peace Corps would win hearts and minds. Our export of the Alliance for Progress would counter Cuba's export of hemispheric revolution. Cuba, and soon South Vietnam, would be the testing grounds. The linkage was personified in Gen. Edward Lansdale who would bring a brash and unorthodox approach to campaigns against insurgencies in Vietnam and the Philippines. Lansdale argued for military action with a difference, that force could only succeed when there was a significant population that could be incited against left-wing revolutionary governments. "Winning hearts and minds" differed from a strictly humanitarian approach, however, by its integration into low-visibility military pressure—it was seen as part and parcel with a military campaign, not as an alternative to military involvement.[30] Lansdale became RFK's point man for the Cuba regime-change project.[31] Lansdale was critical of the Bay of Pigs operation for having the illusion that there was popular support for overthrowing Castro on the island. Lansdale's new strategy was summarized in an NSC memo that was later declassified: "Basically, the operation is to bring about the revolt of the Cuban people ... [by] "economic warfare to induce failure of the Communist regime ... psychological operations to turn the people's resentment against the regime, and military-type groups to give the popular movement an action arm for sabotage and armed resistance. . . ."[32] In Lansdale's view, the "climactic moment" would come from an angry reaction "sparked by an incident or from a fracturing of the leadership cadre with the regime, or both. . . ." The Lansdale proposal covered the period between March and October 1962 and was officially terminated only after the October missile crisis, which clearly demonstrated the unity of the Cuban people behind Castro's regime.

Lansdale wasn't done in his search for new laboratories of counterinsurgency. After Cuba, he returned to South Vietnam to launch the Operation Phoenix, which included coercing the peasantry into "strategic hamlets" similar to the reservations of America's nineteenth-century Indian wars. Lansdale died in 1987, becoming a legendary figure in a cult of counterinsurgency among younger officers. One of those Vietnam-era soldiers was David Petraeus, who reintroduced counterinsurgency as official doctrine in the 2006 Army-Marines *Counterinsurgency Field Manual.* The manual resurrects the legend of the Phoenix Program as a missed opportunity.[33] Counterinsurgency, which failed in Cuba in its efforts "to turn the people's resentment against the regime," in the words of Lansdale's report, continued on its path through Vietnam to the Iraq and Afghan wars of the twenty-first century. Even today, it is the key element of the US administration's programs of "democracy promotion" and "regime change" aimed at Cuba and many other countries. The Bay of Pigs invasion was seen as a fiasco because it took place *before* an organized base of anticommunist discontent could be built on the island through outside "democracy promotion." In Lansdale's thinking, repeated endlessly since then, after the precipitating "incident," which rationalized military intervention, there had to be Peace Corps-style economic development. The doctrine was recycled in the Bush Administration's 2004 and 2006 high-level reports and the Clinton era's Torricelli and Helms-Burton laws, all of which repeated Lansdale's futile dream. In Afghanistan, decades later, the US strategy was to impose military suppression followed by delivering "democracy in a box." Landsdale's legacy couldn't have been more wrong—in Cuba, in Vietnam, and in our later wars, as history has shown. Dead ideas never die.

CHAPTER 6

JFK's Assassination

. . . to some extent it is as though Batista was the incarnation of a number of sins on the part of the United States. Now we shall have to pay for those sins.
—PRESIDENT JOHN F. KENNEDY, OCTOBER 24, 1963[1]

When the murder of John F. Kennedy was announced as my plane to Minneapolis was landing, a young man behind me wearing a Goldwater button leaped up and cheered. He quickly returned to his seat amidst stony passenger silence. I deplaned long enough to make contact with some waiting students, turned around as quickly as possible, and flew back to Detroit, then spent several days huddled with close friends in Ann Arbor. One year before, the Cuban missile crisis had turned life as I knew it upside down. Now, the assassination became a second unthinkable catastrophe, and once again the subject of Cuba was in the air.

Within minutes, allegations were swirling that the shooter, Lee Harvey Oswald, was aligned with Fair Play for Cuba and was a former defector to the Soviet Union. In the confusion, rumors spread that he was connected to SDS as well. Nightmares of sudden war and domestic roundups flashed through my mind. I was twenty-three. Ricardo, then the youngest member of the Cuban foreign ministry staff, was twenty-six.

I remember being stoic, even cold, trying hard to concentrate and hold on to my mind, as my assumptions all lay shattered again. In the days after JFK's killing, I braced for a knock on the door, detentions, maybe bullets through the window. The SDS staff in New York tore through our national membership files and correspondence. No Oswald. Phone lines burned with long-distance questions, speculation, suggestions.

Shortly, a narrative took shape in the national media. Oswald was *definitely* a lone crackpot, *not a conspirator*. I wrote in *The Daily*, ostensibly reviewing a performance I'd seen, but also touching on larger issues:

> *Brecht on Brecht* was performed in a mournful Hill [Auditorium] Monday night, and must be considered ultimately in its relation to the macabre assassinations of John Kennedy and Lee Oswald.
>
> [Brecht] would attack an order which quietly assassinates meaning and new possibilities wherever they are dangerous to the current social system. [This performance's] distortion of Brecht is part of the American tendency to smother conflict for the sake of an artificial consensus, a process which generates the very parodies of protest—crime, suicide, fantasy, delinquency—that occur in Dallas and, in less spectacular ways, daily in this society.
>
> Why can't we face matters just as they are, see the real Brecht as he was? Would not a society capable of that be freer of the poisons which illusions release?"

Yes, Oswald called himself a Marxist, and yes, he visited the Cuban embassy in Mexico, and yes, he had returned from Russia with his wife, Marina. This framing of Oswald rested uneasily between two rival speculations in the public mind; first, that he was a Soviet and/or Cuban agent and, second, held by a minority of Americans, that he was an agent *of our own or of the Mafia*, who killed the president we were coming to respect, for hidden reasons of power. Either way, Cuba continued to be at the center of a global crisis, as it had been since my high school years, a potential scapegoat to be wiped from the sea.

History shows that the slightest confirmation of a Cuban hand, alone or in league with Moscow, could have triggered global war. For that reason, perhaps, the Johnson administration moved quickly to unite the country around the quickly manufactured tale of Oswald acting alone. Rumors of Mafia involvement, perhaps out of rage at Kennedy's crackdown on the Mob, Kennedy's "loss" of the Cuban casinos, perhaps in dark alliance with the Cuban exiles, were pushed off the public radar.

The truth was covered up. Even today, millions of files at the National Archive contain redactions that won't be unsealed until 2017.[2] Over one thousand records—each of them one to twenty pages in length—are held from release by the Assassinations Records Review Board (ARRB). Additionally, unknown numbers of Warren Commission documents are buried in the National Archive. Perhaps most interesting are the CIA's 295 "Joannides files"[3] sought by reporters and researchers for decades without result.

George E. Joannides was the CIA case officer who secretly organized, directed, and funded, at $50,000 a month, an anti-Castro Directorio Revolucionario Estudiantil (Revolutionary Student Directorate or DRE).[4]

RICARDO: *It was another thing completely unrelated to the DR 13 de Marzo.[5] It was organized at Havana University by some right-wing students who tried to take the name because of its strong associations, not only from the struggle against Batista but also from before, against Machado.*

Joannides failed in trying to carry out the counterrevolution. According to Jefferson Morley, a former *Washington Post* reporter whom I interviewed in 2013, "they had some support in Havana in 1959 but wouldn't support the revolution, even from within, so they moved to Miami where the CIA picked them up as articulate young people."[6] The group, whose plain purpose was to overthrow Fidel, had an estimated membership in the thousands, and members were deployed across the United States, Latin America, and international student conferences to battle the Cuban Communists. The Greek-born Joannides was transferred from Athens to the Miami CIA station by 1963, where he managed the DRE. Joannides was titled the Miami deputy director of psychological warfare operations, code-named "JM/WAVE."

The CIA was later forced to acknowledge in federal court that in August 1963 Oswald paid a friendly visit to a Directorate official in New Orleans only to be seen a short while later handing out pro-Cuba literature. A brawl and a radio confrontation ensued between Oswald and the New Orleans DRE militants. Oswald appeared to be playing a double role. According to the *New York Times*, "speculation about who might have been behind [Oswald] has never ended, with various theories focusing on Mr. Castro, the Mob, rogue government agents, or myriad combinations of the above."[7] Clearly, Morley told me, "Oswald was engaging in provocateur behavior, offering to go fight in Cuba, mentioning his Marine experience, then turning around with the pro-Cuba leaflets. That kind of political agitation is exactly what the CIA was paying the DRE to do."

When I asked Morley if he thought Oswald was working on someone's agenda or was nuts, he answered, "Those are the choices." Morley's 2003 federal lawsuit charged that Joannides had secretly financed Cuban exiles who gathered intelligence on Oswald three months before the Kennedy assassination. When Kennedy died, it was claimed, Joannides used CIA funds to help two anti-Castro militants escape the United States for Central America.[8]

Joannides's role was illuminated briefly in 1978 when the

CIA called him out of retirement and named him the agency's liaison to the US House committee investigating the Kennedy assassination, while blindsiding the legislators about Joannides's previous role of running secret operations for a violently anti-Castro organization.[9] In the same disclosure, the CIA refused to release the 295 specific documents concerning Joannides's background. Morley believes those are only administrative personnel files, not documents disclosing his career in CIA operations. In 2013, the CIA made an "amazing concession," Morley says, when the agency for the first time acknowledged that Joannides had a residence in New Orleans in the early 1960s, when Oswald and the DRE militants were skirmishing. "For thirty years they said he wasn't ever near New Orleans. Now there's powerful evidence that he knew what was going on."

Joannides went back to Athens in 1964–1968, where he participated in the military coup, then to Saigon in 1969–1970 where he reunited with his original Miami station chief, Theodore Shackley, who directed the Operation Mongoose covert operations program against Cuba with four hundred agents at his disposal.[10] He went from Miami to counterterrorism programs in Vietnam with General Lansdale. After the House assassination hearings, he faded into the shadows until dying in 1990 at age sixty-seven. His obituary identified him only as a "lawyer for the Defense Department"—"so he took the cover story right to the grave," Morley says.

This story, however incomplete, pierces one of the most confusing aspects of November 22, 1963, emphasizing the need for full disclosure of the CIA documents still held under seal, most of which may never be released in the lifetimes of anyone in the generation for whom the assassination was a pivotal trauma. There can be no "national security" claims to those documents after fifty years. Plainly the secret-keepers intended to contain and dilute the potential public reaction to those documents until later generations. In a similar way, the 1865 killing of President Lincoln by a Confederate-based conspiracy was framed as the irrational deed of a deranged actor, not as a conspiracy to defeat the Union and block Reconstruction.

The unreleased Joannides's file shows the CIA's intention to control the narrative of the Kennedy assassination in a way that *kept secret the CIA's role in or knowledge of official plots to assassinate Fidel and destroy the Cuban Revolution* (from injecting lethal poisons in his food and drink to burning cane fields and oil refineries).

There was no evidence of an invisible Cuban hand, according to the White House, the Warren Commission, and two congressional investigations.

After all, why would Fidel and the Cuban intelligence services, who conceivably deployed spies effectively in the Miami, Tampa, and New Orleans exile communities, carry out an execution of Kennedy, when the certain response would be the destruction of Cuba amidst a wider planetary conflagration? Not that Fidel lacked cause; he later provided Sen. George McGovern evidence of more than twenty US schemes to kill him.[11] However vengeful his state of mind, Fidel's constant purpose was to repel an invasion from the superpower to his north. And why would the Cuban government even take seriously an isolated ex-Marine and ex-defector showing up at their heavily surveilled Mexico City consulate with a plan to shoot a president? Why would they enter a conspiracy in which the president's last-minute November 22 itinerary *happened* to take him by a seven-story building where Oswald *happened* to have been employed *before* the president's plans were even known?

We know that Oswald's last words were: "I'm a patsy." Exactly whose "patsy" finally might be clarified if and when our government releases the remaining files.

TWO TRACKS

The Kennedy administration traveled along two tracks in its Cuba policy, which were then known in New Left thinking as the tracks of repression and cooptation. In foreign policy there was a split between those wanting to apply military force, even nuclear weapons, to "roll back" communism, and more rational minds satisfied with great power coexistence and the competition for "hearts and minds" combined with covert counterinsurgency when possible. Toward Cuba, after the Bay of Pigs humiliation, US plans were rolled out for sabotage, guerrilla war, and an invasion to topple Castro. I talked with Robert Kennedy Jr., son of the late senator, in 2014 about his childhood memories of those days:

ROBERT KENNEDY JR: *At that time there was some daylight between my father and President Kennedy on that issue. My father's focus was on freeing the prisoners that Castro took and also keeping the CIA's pressure on Castro. We had a lot of those guys* [Cuban exiles] *in our house all the time, horseback riding with us through the CIA properties and neighboring farms. My father found houses for them around our house. He found jobs for them. He had close relations with them. But the ones he was closest to were the ones who had been with Fidel against Batista. A lot of the others were Batista people. The CIA didn't like my father's friends because they wanted people who took orders. The CIA wanted the killers from Batista's circle and the mobsters. Daddy felt it was fair for us to help them fight their revolution with our training, like the French role during our revolution, but that it was their own revolution, we shouldn't be doing it ourselves.*

President Kennedy had a different attitude, especially after the Cuban missile crisis when he made friends with Khrushchev. He was wondering whether Castro was someone we could work with, and he sent many messengers to see Castro. He basically said we don't care what kind of government you have, we just don't want you to be a Soviet satellite and export revolution. His project was to change Latin American governance away from the right-wing families who just traded the presidencies among themselves. Up to that point it was to serve the mercantile interests of United Fruit and the oil companies, especially under Dulles.

If you look back, nobody knows when Castro made his choices. The history was essentially like that of [president Jacobo] *Arbenz in Guatemala, when he nationalized United Fruit. It was a similar US policy in Cuba: keep the land idle, keep the cost of labor low, keep the cost of sugar and bananas up. The invasion was Nixon's brain-child. They would get Standard Oil to shut its refinery in response to Fidel nationalizing. Fidel offered to pay them based on what their tax returns showed, just like Arbenz, same thing. In retaliation, Dulles got Standard to shut its refinery, so there was no oil coming into the country. At that point Fidel made the deal with the Soviets: Russian oil for Cuban sugar. That kind of forced him into the Soviet camp.*

Jack understood all this, and sent that message with the French journalist, Jean Daniel. His attitude was we don't care what they do as long as they aren't in the Soviet camp and export revolution, because that would screw him politically with everybody. That's what they were working toward [on the day the president was shot].

Daddy at first was only looking at how do we get rid of Castro. The story in my house was that the U-2 was shot down [on October 27] *personally by Castro, that he had taken over the Soviet SAM site. That was my father's focus.*[12]

Afterward, though, my father recommended sending down James Donovan on the [Bay of Pigs] *prisoners issues.* [Donovan, who had been the general counsel of the Office of Strategic Services, predecessor to the CIA, negotiated the release of the American U-2 pilot]. *My father sent down two of his aides, John Dolan and* [John] *Nolan, with Donovan, and they spent a lot of time with Fidel. They went to baseball games and saw how popular he was. Wherever he went, people would be cheering for him. On one of those trips, Fidel asked Donovan how diplomatic relations could be resumed, to which Donovan replied, "The way porcupines make love. Very carefully."*[13] *The view in the United States was that he was a drunken, murderous fanatic. When I met with him years later, that was still my impression too. My brother Max asked him once if he believed in God, and Fidel started talking about the stars and the planets and said anybody who studied the cosmos would be irrational if they did not believe in God.*

So they were asking can we work with this guy. Bobby wrote to the president about more aggressive Mongoose operations, and Jack didn't answer. Clearly he was reassessing Castro. When Dolan came back from Cuba in the summer of 1963 my father was aware that Jack was doing back channel with Castro. Che was going to be a problem, but you could work with Fidel. [After JFK's death] *Daddy went to Thomas Mann at State in 1964 and said we should reassess the embargo.*[14] *He went to State Department briefings on Cuba and said we should reevaluate, and was never invited to another briefing again. He was shut out. He had had a wandering portfolio over many subjects, but then he was restricted* [on Cuba].

Thus there was a tendency toward growing realism in the American elite among those who doubted whether the Cuban Revolution could be overthrown from within or without, forcing open a search for other options. Some would argue that this duality is nothing more than evidence of the "forked tongue" of the powerful at work. It is more the nature of statecraft, however, which often requires decision makers to consider the effectiveness of multiple options at the same time. Social movements and revolutionaries face the same challenges in reverse, whether to expect exclusion and coercion from the state or seize on concessions or openings on offer from the establishment. The complexity can be dizzying.

On April 21, 1963, JFK adviser McGeorge Bundy wrote a memo defining three "new initiatives" to be considered.[15] The first two had been tried before: to use "all necessary means" to force a "noncommunist" government on Cuba, or to insist on "major but limited ends." The third option was the new alternative being considered by the president: "The United States could move in the direction of gradual development of some form of accommodation with Castro." That June, the administration's "standing group" on Cuba also decided it would be useful to examine "various possibilities of establishing channels of communication with Castro."[16]

In the months before he was shot, Kennedy's administration was in a strategic reversal from its failed military policies toward Cuba. Many recent histories repeat essentially a similar story[17] of a split between Kennedy and the CIA in 1963. Kennedy felt obliged to continue supporting the Cuban exiles who had survived the Bay of Pigs, while also quietly concluding that another invasion would not be viable. Nor would hit-and-run attacks, though he authorized more of them. Nor would there be an anti-Castro coup from within the Cuban military. Kennedy also had a political reason to maintain the anti-Castro posture, "as a shield against a political uproar in the United States."[18] Only a secretive and unorthodox approach, organized outside conventional channels, could test the possibilities. *The administration had undermined its own diplomatic capacities by refusing to recognize the Castro government*, a pattern that it would repeat.

In late 1961, Kennedy aide Richard Goodwin had encountered Che Guevara at the Organization of American States summit in Punta del Este, Uruguay, and, after a late-night confidential conversation, he told the president that Che was suggesting a "modus vivendi."[19] That notion was neither explored nor acted on, Goodwin told me years later. But in April 1963, word came back from Havana through Lisa Howard, the ABC newswoman, that Fidel wanted to improve relations. Howard, described by one journalist as "sexy, stylish . . . blond and curvy,"[20] spent hours with Fidel on the night of April 21. She interviewed Fidel at length and rushed back to the United States, where she told the president of Fidel's peace initiative. White House hawks considered trying to block the ABC interview, one internal memo arguing that "public airing in the United

States of this interview would strengthen the arguments of 'peace' groups, 'liberal' thinkers, Commies, fellow travelers, and opportunistic political opponents of the present United States policy."[21] Then CIA director John McCone advised "the matter be handled in the most limited and sensitive manner," and that "no active steps be taken on the rapprochement matter at this time."[22] At this time? McCone's phrasing acknowledged that "the rapprochement matter" was being considered. The Lisa Howard interview went ahead, but there the process seemed to stall.

Shortly after, Lisa Howard sought out William Attwood, a veteran UN diplomat and former JFK classmate at Choate Rosemary Hall. Then an assistant to UN ambassador Adlai Stevenson, Attwood seized the initiative. Encouraged by an African diplomat at the UN, Attwood succeeded in gaining Cuban support for ultra-secret exploratory talks. Fidel even offered to meet Attwood at a private Cuban airfield, a plan that President Kennedy endorsed.[23] As late as November 18, four days before JFK's assassination, Fidel approved a preliminary meeting between Attwood and Cuba's UN representative, Carlos Lechuga. On the same day—November 18—Kennedy gave a major speech on Cuba before the Inter-American Press Association, in Miami, aimed at pushing the secret process along. The two sides, while far apart, clearly were moving toward formal dialogue about coexistence. Interestingly, later interviews showed that both leaders were exploring the notion of accepting Fidel as "a Tito of the Caribbean," that is, a non-aligned Communist leader.[24] On October 17, Kennedy had welcomed Yugoslavia's leader, Josef Broz Tito, to the White House, in a signal that the US government could be on friendly terms with a Communist and nationalist war hero independent of Moscow. If Tito, why not Fidel? The anger toward Kennedy rose from the Cuban right that wanted no coexistence whatsoever with Fidel. They objected sharply to the line inserted in Kennedy's October 18 speech that pledged to prevent "*another*

Cuba" in the hemisphere. The right wing realized that the president's language hid a de facto acceptance of the *existing* Cuban government while warning only against "another" one, a hint at containment rather than rollback.

In the last weeks of his life, JFK saw Jean Daniel, the French journalist at *L'Express*, who was on his way to Havana to interview Fidel. Kennedy was eager to send a message through Daniel that "US policy . . . had created, built, and manufactured the Castro movement out of whole cloth without realizing it. . . . Batista was the incarnation of a number of sins on the part of the United States [and] now we shall have to pay for those sins."[25] Kennedy invited Daniel to visit the White House on his return because "Castro's reactions interest me."[26] Daniel talked with Fidel for more than four hours late one night in Havana. Fidel indicated strongly to Daniel that Kennedy was someone he could have a dialogue with, because he was an "intimate enemy," that is, Cuba and the American mainland were too intertwined by history and geography to come to war.[27] He also hoped that Kennedy might become a great president, "the leader who may at last understand that there can be coexistence between capitalists and communists."[28]

While the hidden "track" of third-party diplomacy through Daniel was in use, so too was the traditional one of subversion and destruction. On the very day that Daniel was conveying his message to Fidel and JFK was to die in Dallas, in Paris the CIA delivered a lethal device, disguised as a fountain pen, to a Cuban asset named Rolando Cubela meant for the assassination of Fidel. The CIA emissary Desmond Fitzgerald posed as a Senate friend of Bobby Kennedy, thus conveying the impression that the Kennedys wanted Fidel finished off. Cubela, whose CIA code name was "AM/LASH," was an anticommunist former guerrilla fighter during the Cuban Revolution. He rejected the poison pen offer and, ultimately, nothing came of the plot.[29]

The November 22 meeting with AM/LASH (Cubela) in Paris was designed to leave the Kennedys in the dark. Years later, CIA director Richard Helms told Senate investigators that the Paris operation proceeded *without White House authorization* because "I [Helms] just thought this is exactly the kind of thing ... he's been asking us to do, let's get on with doing it."[30] It appears in history's hindsight that the Kennedys were unleashing demons they could not control when they chose to pursue the track of coexistence with Cuba.

The failure to officially recognize Cuba in any way also may have caused serious obstacles for any Kennedy initiative toward normalization. The contacts were essentially indirect—a casual meeting between Che and Goodwin, the encounter between Lisa Howard and Fidel, the drafting of Attwood to become involved, the suggestions of an African UN diplomat, the surreptitious visits of the Dolan, Nolan, Donovan group, the comments passed through Daniel, and so on. Few if any in the Kennedy administration had any real experience with Cuba or its revolution. Their thinking was influenced heavily by the Cuban exiles and military chieftains who wanted Fidel overthrown. Congress and the headlines at the time followed Cold War ideology in lockstep. By contrast, during the 1962 missile crisis, the Kennedys found it possible to negotiate directly, if confidentially, with the long-serving Soviet ambassador, Anatoly Dobrynin. Though the United States and the Soviet Union were Cold War enemies, they exchanged ambassadors and, after the missile crisis, even built a direct hotline. Through urgent discussions, they drew conclusions over what signals from Washington or Moscow to believe. They resolved the missile crisis behind the backs of the Joint Chiefs and Soviet generals. In the case of Cuba, by contrast, *there was no Dobrynin for Robert Kennedy to talk to.* There was Lechuga, Fidel's ambassador in New York, awaiting secret contacts about a projected discussion in the future, but one that could not be attended by any US officials directly. That was the vacuum in which James Donovan could go to ball games and fishing excursions with Fidel, in which Lisa Howard could engage him privately, all in circumvention of official channels. Over the subsequent fifty years, there repeatedly have been similar awkward efforts at *indirect* diplomacy but never a policy of *direct diplomacy* to manage the US-Cuban relationship.

The youthful Ricardo Alarcón might have made a modest contribution to conflict management through direct diplomacy during the turbulent two years between the Bay of Pigs, the missile crisis, and the assassination of John F. Kennedy. Instead Ricardo was assigned to be Cuba's liaison to a new generation of revolutionaries in Central and Latin America.

CHAPTER 7

Latin American Revolution

If Cuba succeeds, we can expect most of Latin America to fall.
—CIA DIRECTOR JOHN A. MCCONE TO PRESIDENT KENNEDY, AUGUST 23, 1962[1]

After his repeated offers for the exploring of a modus vivendi with the US—in 1961, 1963, and 1964—had been rebuffed, Castro had concluded that the best defense was offense.
—PIERO GLEIJESES, THE CUBAN DRUMBEAT, LONDON, SEAGULL BOOKS, 2009, P. 23

The mission of the present generation's revolution is getting Cuba out of this chaotic phase of the West in which we are annexed. Cuba has to convert its smallness into a continent.
—OBITUARY FOR CUBAN REVOLUTIONARY FRANK PAÍS[2]

The Cuban Revolution polarized Central and South America between ruling oligarchs and rebellious social movements. At first, the frightened and defensive governing elites rallied to the US call to isolate the new Cuban government. In late January 1962, fourteen of twenty-one governments voted to expel Cuba from the Organization of American States; Argentina, Bolivia, Brazil, Chile, Ecuador, and Mexico abstained. This was the same conference, in Punta del Este, Uruguay, where Che spoke on the sidelines with Richard Goodwin about a possible "modus vivendi" while Cuba's then-president Osvaldo Dorticós[3] called from the podium for peaceful coexistence. The Kennedy administration followed on February 3 by announcing a total trade embargo. Meanwhile, however, insurrectionary ambitions were awakened across the continent, and many insurgent leaders met in Havana on January 21 for a Peoples Assembly to plan an alternative to the OAS.[4] There, on February 4, Fidel gave the Second Declaration of Havana, calling for a global movement against US imperialism, stating for the first time that "the duty of revolutionaries is to make the revolution." His speech two years earlier—the First Declaration of Havana, on September 2, 1960, was a vision of a Latin America liberated from its role as "a zone of exploitation, a backyard in the financial and political empire of the United States, [and] a reserve supply of votes in international organizations...."[5] Now, in the Second Declaration, he gave the "green light ... to Cuban-style guerrilla movements all over the continent, to subvert the existing regimes and to help Cuba escape from its isolation."[6]

RICARDO: *It is very difficult to go back to the past. We are talking about very young people, who were all in their thirties or younger. With the aura of the victory of Cuba, people were going to the mountains.*

When I returned to New York almost thirty years later in 1990 and reread some of my old speeches, I felt how much I had matured— without abandoning my old ideals—and, of course, how much the world had changed. But in the sixties I didn't have any doubts.

I met Salvador Allende, who was probably the most important personality on the Left in Chile and elsewhere, when I was a student leader attending a conference in Venezuela organized by a front organization of the State Department, the Inter-American Association for Democracy and Freedom, led by a lady named Frances Grant. I was the only Cuban revolutionary there, and when [former Venezuelan] president [Rómulo] Betancourt came to address the meeting the security came to take me out of my room and occupied the whole floor for security reasons. So I spent a night by the pool where I met Juan Mari Brás and the Puerto Ricans who were trying to participate. We spent the evening talking, looking at the stars in the summer humidity until Allende just came walking over. He was a senator then and was a presidential candidate just before the Cuban Revolution. He found us another accommodation and we would become very good friends.

I had gone to Chile the year before, for a preparatory meeting of a Latin American youth conference. One evening I had dinner with the leader of the Chilean Trotskyites. After he criticized everyone, as a good Trot should do, he referred to the last election when Allende almost won, and to my astonishment he promised, "In the next election we will win!"

Chile at the time was a showcase of constitutional democracy, a polar alternative to Cuba.[7] I asked Ricardo if the Trotskyists believed that Chile was a unique exception to the rule that peaceful transitions were impossible.

RICARDO: *Well, at least that Chilean Trotskyist believed that.*

Nothing was foreseeable in those early moments, around 1960. The Bay of Pigs was one year away. The rapid rise and savage defeat of guerrilla wars lay ahead. The election of Allende was ten years in the future; his death in a US-backed military coup would come after three years in power. The long-term effects of these events would not be felt for thirty years when many former guerrillas led electoral coalitions to progressive victories across lands where dictatorships once had seemed secure.

RICARDO: *I was at the Latin American desk in the Foreign Ministry. And I met with many of those people* [the region's revolutionaries] *in Havana. I had nothing to do with the military training, only with political and organizational matters. Manuel Piñeiro was in charge of the* [overall] *solidarity efforts* [with the continent's guerrilla forces]. *He was more or less like Fidel, the same*

routine, working all night, sleeping in the morning. He was called
Barbarroja because of his unusual red beard.

During the early sixties, US reports estimated that some 1,500
to two thousand Latin American revolutionaries received military training or "political indoctrination" in Havana, under the
leadership of the US-educated Piñeiro, while only about forty
Cubans actually fought in other countries.[8] More than a decade
later, at least one thousand Cubans would be stationed in Nicaragua supporting the Sandinistas. Cuba was a center of resources,
training, and networking for revolutionaries. Its foremost role was
one of inspirational example, showing the world that successful
revolution was possible. But it also provided training and modest
material support. Fidel and Che assumed their places among the
legendary liberators of the continent, especially Simón Bolívar,
who provided the model for successful revolution throughout
Latin America.[9] After the CIA's crushing 1954 overthrow of
the democratically elected Guatemalan government of Jacobo
Arbenz, the Cuban Revolution offered hope that the United
States could still be held at bay by a small nation in arms. The
1954 Guatemalan CIA coup was largely the work of both President Eisenhower and Allen Dulles, on behalf of corporations
like United Fruit. The leaders in government in the United States
believed they could repeat that success five years later in Cuba.
The CIA's operations chief in Guatemala, Richard Bissell, was
charged with organizing the invasion force at the Bay of Pigs.[10]

As Piero Gleijeses notes, Fidel's vision was partly strategic—
to forge an alliance of "defense" against the "pirates" of the north
by stretching the Yankee resources too thinly to be concentrated
against Cuba. By my count, the Cuban Revolution inspired at
least twenty-four guerrilla-led organizations in a dozen countries: in Argentina, Bolivia, Chile, Colombia, El Salvador, Guatemala, Honduras, Mexico, Nicaragua, Peru, Venezuela and
Uruguay. The oligarchs, threatened by the Cuban model, fortified themselves with vicious paramilitaries, death squads, tor-

ture chambers, and token reforms; virtually all were assisted by covert American military advisers and funding.

GUERRILLAS IN VENEZUELA

"Small-scale expeditions" departed Cuba for the Dominican Republic, Nicaragua, and Panama, "freelance operations" perhaps without official blessing.[11] Che dreamt of his Argentine homeland, contemplating the bordering state of Bolivia as a step. But especially significant at first was Venezuela, a base of considerable support for the revolution against Batista. After the Cuban Revolution threatened oligarchies across the continent, Venezuela became the key to the Kennedy administration's new strategy of military intervention coupled with democratic reform. Venezuela was showcased as the American-favored alternative model to Cuba. By one estimate, 80 percent of US private and public foreign aid dollars were being invested in Venezuela.[12] The American favorite was Rómulo Betancourt, a legendary leader of long standing who had been a Communist Party leader in Costa Rica during the thirties. After the overthrow of the Marcos Pérez Jiménez dictatorship in 1958, Betancourt led the elected government of the new Venezuela, soon purging the Left and precipitating a crisis of legitimacy.

RICARDO: *Fabricio Ojeda, a Venezuelan journalist, was very important in the underground movement against Pérez Jiménez, which succeeded in defeating him in 1958, one year before our victory in Cuba. He and the* [Patriotic Junta that he led] *had a strong influence on Cuba because of our relationships and past support. In 1958, for example,* [Cuba's underground] *Radio Rebelde was broadcast on Venezuelan stations. After our victory here in Cuba, Fabricio came here, and I also met him in Caracas. He moved to organize a guerrilla front in Venezuela and became one of the first followers of Cuba's Sierra example. He was captured and killed under Betancourt.*[13]

The Venezuelan movements had succeeded in defeating the Pérez Jiménez dictatorship by a general strike and by a broad coalition in which he was the most important figure. After that, partly because of the imperialists, the Frente was split.

Ojeda was a mainstream journalist, writing dispatches from an office in the presidential palace, Miraflores. He evolved into a revolutionary as a main leader of the "Patriotic Junta" that overthrew Pérez Jiménez in 1958. Afterwards, Fabricio was elected to Venezuela's new Chamber of Deputies with the promise of a new power-sharing arrangement known as the Pact of Punto Fijo. Fabricio's party, the Democratic Republican Union (UDR), had partnered with the communist movement to overthrow the dictatorship. The US-favored Acción Democrática, led by Betancourt and symbolizing the Kennedy administration's "third way," chose to exclude the Communist way altogether, even though the CP's leaders finished second in the Caracas[14] elections of 1958. Betancourt himself had been an exiled at age twenty and a Communist Party leader in the thirties. Fabricio's UDR, which favored collaboration with the Communists, was squeezed out of the power-sharing accord by Betancourt; Fabricio ultimately resigned from his elected office and joined a new guerrilla movement supported by Fidel and Cuba, the Armed Forces for National Liberation (FALN). Fabricio was captured in October 1962, the month of the Cuban missile crisis, and sent to a prison from which he soon escaped. Meanwhile Betancourt suspended political immunity for elected deputies from the Communist and Revolutionary Left Movement (MIR), banned the parties, and had their representatives removed from the floor of Congress and taken straight to a prison. On the run, Fabricio tried unsuccessfully to consolidate his forces with the Venezuelan Communists, failed, was captured on June 21, 1966, and was found dead in a prison cell four days later. Despite the frustrations and defeats, Fabricio would be honored and revered as one of the revolution's earliest heroes when Hugo Chávez took power four decades later.

GUERRILLAS IN EL SALVADOR

But who is the enemy?
You, or your enemies?
—ROQUE DALTON, TENSE CONVERSATION[15]

The dead are growing more restless each day.
They were easy to handle before:
We gave them a starched collar a flower
We showered them with praise on a long honor list;
We buried them in a National Plot
Among the noble shades
Under the monstrous slabs of marble.

The dead man signed up with the hope of being
*   remembered:*
He joined the ranks once more
And marched to the beat of our time-honored music.
But wait a second:
The dead
Have changed since then.

They're sarcastic now
They ask questions.

I think they've caught on
That they outnumber us more every day.
—ROQUE DALTON, SOLDIER'S REST[16]

Ricardo was directly involved in supporting the Salvadoran guerrillas who took up arms after the Cuban example and, as in nearly
every insurgent struggle, were sharply divided by factions, ideology
and sectarian hatreds. The Salvador violence in the seventies and
eighties had roots, like Cuba's, in the thirties when a 1932 indigenous uprising, supported by the revolutionary Agustín Farabundo
Martí and his fledgling Communist Party, was crushed by Gen.
Maximiliano Hernández Martínez. As many as thirty thousand
Salvadorans were killed in the military's massacre,[17] known in Salvadoran history as the *matanza*, in the same era that Machado
ruled Cuba. "We all were born half-dead in 1932," the Salvadoran
revolutionary poet Roque Dalton wrote years afterward.[18] El Salvador's coffee elite, known as "the fourteen families," ruled the
small country like the sugar planters of Cuba.

Ricardo was impressed with Dalton, an intellectual and
ironic poet who felt driven to take up the gun.

Did Cuba support and train Dalton's organization, the
People's Revolutionary Army (ERP)?

RICARDO: *Yes, as well as the other groups.*

I met Dalton quite by chance in Prague in late 1967 where
he was in exile from the Salvadoran regime. He was a kindred
spirit, a skilled poet with a Beat take on life, perfect for the club
settings of Prague. He wrote of love and death as if they were
twins. But he was a man of action:

Poetry

Forgive me for helping you understand
That you're not made of words alone.[19]

A deadly split was created on the Salvadoran left when its
Communist Party leader, Salvador Cayetano Carpio, known as
"Marcial," took his faction, known as the Popular Liberation

Forces-Farabundo Martí (FPL) underground in 1970, while another group, the Ejército Revolucionario del Pueblo (ERP) appeared in 1971–1972 from dissident Christian Democrats, students, and religious people. Both favored a guerrilla approach and were prone to internal divisions. The state response to the guerrilla threat was a rapid escalation of repression.

There was perhaps an outlaw in Roque's DNA. He claimed his father was one of the Kansas Dalton brothers, a famed bank robber who took refuge in El Salvador where Roque was born in 1935. Educated in Jesuit schools and elite universities, Roque became a political outlaw at age twenty-four, inspired by the Cuban Revolution. He had already formed a University Literary Circle in the spirit of the fifties university reform currents; the military set fire to their building. Roque then joined the Communist Party, despite differences over nationalism and literary style. He was arrested for his associations and was to be executed by firing squad but the dictatorship was overthrown in a coup on the preceding day, October 26, 1960. Roque escaped to Mexico where he poured out poems while contemplating a return. He chose Cuba, where the revolutionary Casa de las Americas was a magnet for young Latin American writers.[20] He published many works during a five-year stay, also received military training, and returned to El Salvador in a clandestine role in 1965. There he was arrested while sitting in a bar, was tortured again, and sentenced to the firing squad a second time. By chance an earthquake collapsed his jail cell, and he was able to scramble free and make his way back to Cuba. From there he traveled to Prague as a journalist, poet and polemicist; his wildest free verse, written in Prague and based on overheard bar conversations, was called "Tavern (Conversatorio)":

"Good family men of the world, Unite!
"You have nothing to lose but your not wanting to!"
...
"The one sure thing I can tell you
"is that the guerrilla

"is becoming the only pure organization
"in the world of men.
"All the others show signs of going bad.
"The Catholic Church started to give off a stink
"when the catacombs were opened to the tourist trade
"and the shabbiest two-bit whores
"over ten centuries ago:
"If Christ went into the Vatican today
"a gas mask is the first thing he'd ask for.
"The French revolution was a Roquefort cheese from the start
"The international Communist movement has been weighing
    the value of
"Stalin's big shit."
...
"Okay. All that's left is to talk Zen Buddhism,
"it's in now."
"Right. Zen Buddhism is a wonderful experience,
"if and when it gradually leads you to terrorism."
...
"To choose between possible worlds: now that's
"the divine punishment."[21]

These poetic ramblings captured the unconventional and daring spirit of a whole generation of Latin American rebels who were aroused by the Cuban Revolution, crossed paths there, were published there, trained in guerrilla warfare there, and whose attitudes deeply overlapped with the New Left and the Beat Generation—not the Old Left.

RICARDO: *Roque was killed by members of his own organization, the ERP. It was so unfair and sad, a case of sectarian insanity.*

Roque's fate revealed the chaos within those same revolutionary movements. After spending five years on the Havana staff of Casa de Las Americas and helping a band of Guatemalan revolutionaries, Roque underwent plastic surgery and disappeared into El Salvador in late 1973–1974. Still writing "poemas clandestinos," he tried to join FPL and, rejected for being a poet, he turned to ERP.[22] Roque had finished eighteen volumes of poetry and prose before picking up the gun. In just over one year, days short of his fortieth birthday, Roque was killed on May 10, 1975 by his own paranoid "comrades" in a sectarian dispute. Apparently Dalton's "heresy" lay in wanting to make alliances with Salvadoran mass organizations, not to rely only on the guerrilla struggle. The faction that tortured and killed him claimed he was "a Soviet-Cuban and CIA agent."[23] His supporters then split from the ERP to form a new faction known as the Armed Forces of National Resistance (FARN). The sectarian horrors didn't end. On April 6, 1983, the second-in-command of the FPL, Melida Anaya Montes (Comandante Ana María) was murdered.

RICARDO: *She was brutally assassinated in Managua on the orders of Marcial.*[24] *Marcial had become incredibly sectarian, like Stalin. He had left the Communist Party secretary general position to create a more "pure" organization to conduct the armed struggle.*

The first reaction of the FPL to Ana María's assassination was to blame the CIA. But the Sandinista investigation showed it was done by FPL people close to Marcial. And then he killed himself when he suspected that he might be accused of the crime. The FPL went into such profound shock that it could have led to its self-destruction. It was then that "Leonel" was designated the new leader of the FPL and organized and led one of the most successful military campaigns I have ever seen, one that reversed the situation.

The *comandante* known as "Leonel González" was actually Salvador Sánchez Cerén, whose revived FPL was an organizational foundation of the Faramundo Martí Front for National Liberation (FMLN), which eventually entered El Salvador's peace negotiations, finalized in 1992. He was elected to the

National Assembly in 2000 and became the country's vice president under the FMLN's presidential candidate Mauricio Funes in 2009, heading a left-of-center coalition that defeated the right-wing party, ARENA, which was associated with death squads in the civil war of the eighties. In 2014, Sánchez Cerén was elected president of El Salvador by a narrow margin.

It must not be forgotten that seventy thousand Salvadorans died in that conflict, mostly civilians, mostly at the hands of an army armed with US weapons and taught by advisers. Even today, US counterinsurgency experts consider it a triumph that so few advisers—US congressional rules limited their number to fifty—were able to prevent a "Communist takeover." That might have been Cuba's future if the Bay of Pigs invasion had been successful. To stop "another Cuba" from emerging in the hemisphere, the United States eventually intervened in civil wars that killed hundreds of thousands in small underdeveloped nations like El Salvador and Nicaragua.

RICARDO: *Salvador Sánchez Cerén was a teacher like Ana María and had worked with her in the national teachers' union. He joined the guerrilla and became one of the best commanders. To him, Marcial and Ana María were both revolutionary leaders. Then he learned the truth of what had happened to Ana María. Imagine having to suffer that double shock in a few days. And suddenly he was obliged to substitute himself for them and assume a larger role, not just as a guerrilla chief but also as the leader of a political organization in a critical situation, and then take care of that group as it was going through its most difficult moments. I went to Managua on a number of occasions, with and without Piñeiro, to meet with them. And now he is the vice president.* [NB: Sánchez Cerén was elected president in 2014, after this interview took place.]

These movements were sometimes killing themselves. When you discover what happened in the Soviet Union or Cambodia, the extremes to which sectarianism can go, it is incredible. In Roque's case, it was partly a matter of ignorance too, not only Stalinism.

CHAPTER 8

Enter and Exit
Régis Debray

The eruption of continental urban and rural guerrilla warfare in the sixties was being intensely watched by a young
Frenchman named Régis Debray, who was on a journey to
investigate young revolutionaries across Latin America. Debray
wrote for French journals in hopes of reviving the French Left
after the dismal experiences of Algeria and Vietnam, where
the French Communists had sided with the colonial mother
country against two national liberation movements until the
last possible moment.[1] Inspired by revolutionary Cuba, Debray
searched out "revolutionary militants of every kind," spending
weeks with guerrillas in the Venezuelan state of Falcón, in
Colombia's liberated territory of Marquetalia, under police
repression in Ecuador, among Bolivia's militant tin miners, and
on the front lines of Peru, Uruguay, and Brazil.[2] His was an
audacious project, and his writings quickly caught the attention
of Fidel, Che, and many Marxist intellectuals.

In the Northern Hemisphere New Left dreamers also were
turning away from the stale politics of the West. Our new
North Star beckoned from the Global South, especially Latin
America, where Debray declared that "it was all happening."
He was a thirty-year-old, Sorbonne-educated intellectual, a
brainy protégé of the Marxist philosopher Louis Althusser, the

85

latter having been born in the Algerian colony before migrating
to French intellectual elite circles. Tired of what he considered
the failed French Left, Debray drifted from the prestigious
l'École Normale Supérieure to explore Havana. There he was
amazed during two months spent observing the revolution's literacy campaign, and he returned again immediately after the
Bay of Pigs along with many French and Spanish republicans
whose previous euphoric hopes had died in 1937. "The Spanish
Civil War and French Resistance were still alive in Cuba,"
Debray wrote.[3] Until then, Debray added, "I was ashamed of
being French."[4] Debray's writings caught the eye of Che in 1965
when the Argentine was traveling in newly liberated Algiers.[5]
Che, who read French, quickly translated Debray's essay on
Latin America and, once back in Havana, he passed it along
to Fidel, who was taken with Debray's assertion that Cuba
held up a new model of revolution, the thesis originated by C.
Wright Mills a year before. Debray, in my view, began channeling Fidel. Debray's article in *Les Temps Moderne* was written
in a literary, complex, and disciplined style that would impress
leftist intellectuals already hungry to be persuaded; the revolution, according to Debray, became exportable as a text.[6] Ideas
became weapons, and Debray was a young guerrilla using his
pen to create a liberated zone in the sectarian-ridden jungles of
Marxist political thought.

RICARDO: *There was a lot of controversy within the Latin American Left in those days, just as there had been during the revolution
here. Many people were opposed to those trying to recreate the guerrilla movement. Every country had an old guard Communist Party,
and also a split group encouraged by the Chinese, as well as others
who believed in a Cuban model. There even was an Albanian line.
Maybe it is normal when you enter a new epoch of history that you
get a large variety of interpretations. We of course had responsibility
for the Cuban Revolution.*

Debray visited several Latin American revolutionary movements then engaged in the early process of guerrilla warfare, staying for several weeks in Venezuela during the 1963 Falcón state guerrilla campaign, keeping careful diaries and writing for French journals.[7] He hitchhiked with a Venezuelan girlfriend, a militant named Elisabeth Burgos, who soon became his nominal "wife." The pair were on the road in Latin America, armed with pens in their backpacks.[8]

By 1966, Fidel transformed Debray into a disciplined "initiate" of the inner brotherhood,[9] providing the Frenchman with cover by telling the Paris Academy that he was a new "philosophy lecturer" at the University of Havana while he was being trained in Pinar del Río for active military service. Instead Debray was dispatched to a military training complex, Punto Cero, where he was immersed in the details of clandestine warfare: rifle and bazooka practice, surveillance and countersurveillance, sabotage, assassination, explosives, the fine points of mixing lethal chemical ingredients, and so on. He trained not only with Cubans, but Dominicans, Venezuelans, and Guatemalans, one of the thousands whose long march to Latin America's guerrilla fronts passed through Punto Cero. The Cuban government charged not a penny.[10]

By this time Che had disappeared on a secret military mission to central Africa, where he judged conditions were ripe for revolution, a mistaken assessment that eventually led to divisions, debacle, and retreat.[11] From there Che would secretly return to Havana and prepare himself for the Andes in 1966, his ultimate objective. "He wanted to go there [to Bolivia] almost at the very beginning," Castro recalled. "We managed to hold him until at least some preliminary work had been carried out, so he could go there with a little more safety."[12]

Now facing unremitting hostility from the United States, as Debray later wrote, the revolution was taking an alternative path to the modus vivendi with the United States proposed by Che to Kennedy aide Richard Goodwin, and broached again by the Kennedy White House just before JFK's murder.

In Debray's perceptive analysis, "Blockaded on the starting line and forced onto the defensive, the revolution takes its revenge outside, running the blockade with clandestine exports" in both Africa and Latin America.[13]

Fidel spent months tutoring Debray in the concrete mechanics, philosophical orientation, and above all, what he considered the unique strategy of the Cuban Revolution. Just as Fidel was something of a ghost writer for C. Wright Mills's 1960 book, he played a similar role on Debray's tract, *Revolution in the Revolution?*, written during 1966 and released in Havana in January 1967 with three hundred thousand first-run copies and a swelling global circulation.[14]

"The Cuban state circulated it, the air of the time gave it wings," Debray wrote.[15] Its American editors, Leo Huberman and Paul Sweezy, described the 126-page volume as a "comprehensive and authoritative presentation of the revolutionary thought of Fidel Castro and Che Guevara."[16] To *Newsweek* it was nothing less than "a primer for Marxist insurrection in Latin America."[17]

Debray was sent to Bolivia by Fidel sometime in 1964 to help explore the groundwork for Che's secret arrival in 1966.[18] According to Jon Lee Anderson, Che wanted Debray to help recruit guerrillas and assess sites in the Bolivian countryside. Familiar problems were surfacing, however. The Bolivian Communist Party, led by Mario Monje Molina, was ambivalent at best about the foco theory, especially since the party was making modest progress in Bolivian elections. But Monje worried about the attraction of guerrilla war to some of his own militants, and competition from a pro-Chinese alternative. Fidel was suggesting that Che would only use Bolivia as a platform for reaching Argentina, to put Monje's worries to rest.[19]

Debray's journey would end in him being captured, imprisoned, and lined up before a firing squad before international pressures saved his life. A letter demanding a fair trial for Debray, claiming—falsely, as it turned out—that there was no evidence of his being a Cuban agent, was published in the *New York Review of Books* on July 13, 1967, signed by Mary McCarthy, Robert Lowell, Elizabeth Hardwick, Hannah Arendt, I.F. Stone, William Styron, Dwight Macdonald, Gar Alperovitz, Murray Kempton, Andrew Kopkind, Nat Hentoff, George Plimpton, Joseph Heller, Jason Epstein, Barbara Epstein, Robert Silvers, Norman Thomas, Hans Morgenthau, and Lillian Hellman, a veritable A-list of the liberal elite. President Charles De Gaulle also called for his release, as did the Vatican.

Debray's arrest also signaled that Che was somewhere in Bolivia. Previously, American intelligence was clueless, debating whether Che was dead, somewhere in the African savannah, or the victim of a falling out with Fidel.

RICARDO: *When Debray wrote the pamphlet, there was a lot of publicity here. I told him and others that I profoundly disagreed. The book helped to spread the theory of foco, of small groups going into the mountains. In my opinion, that was wrong. In Cuba, it was not a foco in the Sierra. It was an insurrection, an armed struggle in the mountains as the center of a whole process that was based in cities. The Sierra depended on an underground movement with money, weapons, support, and a supply of many fighters. It could not have been done without a movement connected with social struggles.*

I was a member of the drafting committee for the Tricontinental, working with Foreign Minister Raúl Roa. I didn't know anything about Régis's secret activities. I met him once or twice in friendly intellectual conversations. We talked about politics, revolution, Cuba, Latin America, and the like. Remember that the main issue at that time was armed struggle versus "peaceful coexistence" and on that we entirely agreed.[20] Our differences were around the relations between the guerrilla foco and the urban struggle, and the role of the masses. We dealt with these questions as if it were a discussion on the West Bank in Paris. He was a Rive Gauche intellectual, and always drinking wine. By the way, he was a very good writer.

I asked Ricardo a natural question: But Fidel, Che, and the Cuban government were promoting the Debray thesis, no? Debray was not an independent journalist, he was working for them?

RICARDO: *Frankly, that's my impression. But it's not true that the Sierra model was the only correct way, and Che suffered the consequences of that mistake in Bolivia, which was more complicated. How can you communicate with a Quechua man who doesn't speak Spanish? In a plaza you can talk with an Indian lady in Spanish, then they will talk among themselves because you are a foreigner. Of course someday the guerrilla will establish contact, but Che didn't have time.*

Che's significance is very great. Che will be eighty-something next week. He died as a young man, forty-six years ago. Imagine if you were sitting with Che now. I am sure that he would not be saying now what he was saying then. I don't mean that he was defeated. It's not by chance that you have there in Bolivia [president] Evo Morales. You cannot take Che out of Bolivian history. But if the Bolivians were to have applied just the Debray thesis, they would have failed.

You don't find many examples in life of what Che did, putting your beliefs into life. He abandoned all comfort, the [government] ministry, [being a] big personality, and went off to train himself to fight another war. He was getting into his thirties, and to initiate a new beginning he didn't have much time to spend while conducting individual business here.

When Che died, what was the reaction of the Soviets and China? Who praised him? For the Soviets, it was embarrassing because it contradicted their line of peaceful coexistence.[21] *The Chinese were not creating another Vietnam, just criticizing the Soviets and sitting down with Kissinger to establish a new relationship. There was no peaceful coexistence for the developing countries, only right-wing dictatorships. Some in our movement started to realize that both* [Soviet and Chinese] *sides were dogmatic in their approach to*

Marxism. Che's approach was to open another front through trying to create "two, three, many Vietnams," as the way to help Vietnam. The two big powers were criticizing the Vietnam War but not putting themselves at risk. Maybe Che was rather romantic, but you can't believe in a socialist society if you ignore solidarity with others. Che's theory was to take revolution to an international level.

When Che died, it was a severe blow to the idea of armed struggle, but it went on anyway. I was ambassador in New York when the word came. I remember it very well. One Soviet colleague, probably with the best of intentions, asked if it could be said that Che was on his own, not authorized. They were concerned with its effect on détente with the United States.

I said, more or less, "Go fuck yourself."

History continues moving. Who in their right mind could advocate in Latin America for armed struggle today? Now the question should be, where would Che be now? On which side, advocating what? He would be supporting Evo Morales and trying to build this new consensus in Latin America.

REVOLUTION IN THE REVOLUTION? REVISITED

It is important today to review Debray's small book for what it actually said, what happened to Debray, and the tremendous reverberating effect on many of the New Left who turned toward foco-style violence in the late 1960s. Now that he is in France and those times are generally forgotten, it becomes difficult to resurrect the essence of Debray's thought. But it's necessary to retrieve his argument as having had a compelling logic at the time, and because revolutionary conditions such as those he was addressing may come again. Such seemingly extreme revolutionary moments have been described before, in the novels of Dostoyevsky (*The Possesssed*), André Malraux (*Man's Hope*), and others. The same impulse has appeared among some of the anarchist factions of antiglobalization protests since the nineties, and among the new clandestine cyber-guerrillas too.

One must begin by understanding what Debray and, through him, Fidel and Che, believed they were confronting in Latin America. In 1960, every Latin American country contained a Communist Party something like Cuba's, pursuing multi-class alliances with business-oriented parties, battling Cold War anticommunism, agitating for concessions for party-affiliated labor unions, and following the Soviet line of "peaceful coexistence" with the United States.

According to Debray's doctrine, this "revisionist" Marxist strategy of reform, based on protecting the Soviet bloc, could lead at best to wage concessions in the context of repressive states controlled by their militaries with US advisers and funding. Reform therefore appeared as the enemy of revolution, the latter to be deferred to a hazy Promised Land in the future.

The strategy of "peaceful transition" to socialism seemed bankrupt against military oligarchs like Batista who doomed whole generations of frustrated young idealists to "more of the same" as their common future. The Chinese stood in militant ideological opposition to these pro-Soviet parties while opening the gates to their own sectarian and violent "cultural revolution."

This latter upheaval, much romanticized by many Western intellectuals, positioned the Chinese as "revolutionary" in comparison to the Soviet Union's "revisionism," and contributed to splits across the revolutionary world. Both North Vietnam and Cuba tried to forge a path of independence while seeking support from both Communist powers. The Trotskyists, who also had a small base in Cuba and Latin America at the time, adhered to a line of uncompromising and continuous mass strikes, a strategy that was suicidal given the police and armies at the disposal of Latin America's oligarchies.

The Cuban Revolution, though led by young intellectuals often steeped in these left-wing debates, represented a sharp break. According to Debay, the Cuban model rejected the need for a vanguard party of the working class to lead the revolution, thus violating a sacred Marxist-Leninist supposition.

Instead Debray retrieved a foco theory of action by small armed vanguards—or, as he later wrote, "Bolívar revisited by [Auguste] Blanqui [1805–1881] with Lenin on the wrapper."[22] To deconstruct Debray's summary: Simón Bolívar led armies from country to country, "five times expelled from American soil within four years; defeated, ridiculed, alone, and with an obstinacy characterized as insanity,"[23] before finally hounding the Spanish Empire into retreat. Blanqui too was both glorified and abhorred for his lifetime of insurrectionary "foquism." In Latin America, romantic and hopeless idealism was enshrined in the 1605 epic Spanish tale *Don Quixote*, a favorite of revolutionaries up through Subcommandante Marcos of the current Zapatista generation.[24]

Lenin argued that a small, willful vanguard could "detonate" the czarist status quo if its force was targeted at the weakest link. Debray—and certainly Fidel and Che—believed that the immediate duty of all revolutionaries was to "make the revolution"; that the rural areas were the "weakest link" across Latin America; that the stark conditions of guerrilla existence would forge the very consciousness and links giving rise to the future revolutionary government. They believed this based on the Cuban experience and their critique of the lethargy of the traditional Communist parties of Latin America. Debray's little book didn't discount the need for an urban underground or external political alliances, but insisted that the foco—the mobile guerrilla force—was the "small motor" that would turn the "larger motor" of nationwide urban-based resistance. Further, the foco experience would "proletarianize" the middle-class revolutionaries living hand to mouth among the peasantry, and would become the embryo of a future party that could reliably lead the revolution.

Debray's own fate illustrated the extreme risks contained in carrying out such a narrow strategy. By New Year's Eve 1966,

Che's Bolivian foco consisted of just twenty-four fighters, only nine of them Bolivian, encamped in a remote farm in the country's south. The Bolivian Communist Party had withdrawn any support from the venture, and some members may have leaked his presence to his enemies. Links with an urban cell in the capital city, La Paz, were barely existent. Yet Che believed that an insurrection started in Bolivia would spread to his homeland of Argentina, and was already helping dispatch another foco of fifteen combatants to the Peruvian Andes. The ultimate "plan" was to trigger an American military intervention, which would unify the warring Soviet and Chinese governments, and create "another Vietnam in the Americas."[25]

Debray arrived in this embryonic revolutionary site in 1966 with several others. According to Anderson, Debray gave Che a copy of *Revolution in the Revolution?*, which Che immediately read and took notes on. Debray also says he expressed a desire to fight, but was advised that it would be more useful to spread the word as a writer.[26] Debray's life had become an alibi. "As only my Cuban contacts knew that I had lied throughout my trial . . . my defense was that I was an observer [who] kept Havana out of the frame. In reality I had carried a weapon and taken part in the first ambush . . . I was not there to interview people but to follow orders."[27] Debray's presence, on a secret trip one year earlier, had alerted the Bolivian Communist leadership that Bolivia, not Argentina, was the planned zone of operations, which Debray says led them to "maneuver Che toward the exit" by arranging for his location in the empty Bolivian south.[28] "My own case, while not being the determining factor, may have had an effect."[29]

On April 13, 1967 the United States openly announced it was sending military advisers to Bolivia, not acknowledging the presence of its operatives already there. On April 20, Debray and a companion were captured by the Bolivian army when they walked into a tiny village pretending to be foreign journalists.[30] Apparently buckling under harsh interrogation and torture, Debray may have confirmed that Che was in Bolivia. "When the evidence was confirmed by Debray that he really was there," said Félix Rodríguez, the Bay of Pigs veteran and CIA agent who was present at Che's execution, "that's when they really decided to move forward and put out a maximum effort in Bolivia."[31]

In high gear, the CIA selected Rodríguez, their Cuban American officer, to track Che, interrogate him after capture, and even offer him a cigarette just before a Bolivian "volunteer" executed the wounded leader on October 11, 1967, in violation of the customary rules of warfare. Rodriguez says he received an order from Washington that the decision be left with the US-funded, US-advised Bolivian authorities, who commanded that Che be shot, buried in a secret grave, his hands cut off for fingerprinting. It was death by outsourcing.

I was in Hanoi when the news of Che's death crackled over BBC Radio. A sorrowful and somber silence spread quickly. While none of them knew Che Guevara personally, every Vietnamese was aware that he was fighting to create "two, three, many Vietnams." Everyone knew that the Cuban government was the first to recognize the Viet Cong as the "legitimate representative" of the South, and that Cuba's ambassador was the only diplomat whose quarters were located amidst the guerrillas on the border of South Vietnam and Cambodia. The bonds were deep, a brotherhood unlike any I had ever seen. On their side, the Cubans believed that America's war in Vietnam was deterring the option of an American attack on Cuba, and that therefore Vietnamese blood was being shed on their behalf.

I traveled four times to Hanoi in those years, in violation of the United States, a travel ban that applied to Cuba as well. The United States threatened to take my passport, as they had actually done in the beginning of the decade to an African American journalist, William Worthy, who was reporting favorably on Cuba in US newspapers and was refused a new passport when his old one expired. Worthy finally won his protracted litigation with the State Department, but the legal threat hung over my travels in 1965, 1967, 1969, and 1973, as it would for Stokely Carmichael, whose life soon intersected with the Cuban Revolution in the late sixties. I was deeply sympathetic with the Vietnamese for the suffering they endured as a small country fighting one colonial power after another, a sympathy that carried over to Cuba too. My purpose in those Hanoi visits was as a writer who saw his task as telling the story of the "other side," the Vietnamese people who were entirely invisible behind the Cold War's Iron Curtain. I had a close sympathy for Debray, who was only slightly older, and embracing a similar challenge. I had worked with Staughton Lynd, a friend in the peace movement, to gain access to North Vietnam for Harrison Salisbury, an effort modeled on the 26th of July movement's warm welcome of the *Times'* Herbert Matthews in the Sierra Maestra. Those reporters, and the peace delegations that preceded them, broke the information blockade and gave Vietnam a somewhat more human face. I also went to Hanoi, like Debray went to Havana, because I became passionately interested in learning how a smaller power could thwart a Goliath like the United States. How were these wars waged? What were their roots in histories we didn't know? What, if any, was the role of peace movements against intervention? Unlike Debray's view of France, however, I avoided the temptation to think of the United States, and the West in general, as a dead zone for the spirit of effective protest. Neither the Vietnamese nor the Cubans took such a stark view either, even though they were targeted by the White House and Pentagon for destruction. Both Vietnam and Cuba were aware that progressive movements had arisen in "the belly of the beast." They were inviting American visitors, including solidarity activists, not to join a third world revolution but to return to America as more enlightened critics of US foreign policy. The understandable error of Debray, shared by thousands of Westerners, was born of a sense of guilt that drove him to extremes of radical alienation.

America was becoming convulsed by insurrections at home. The faces on poster images of Vietnamese and Cuban revolutionaries bore an increasing similarity to the young black people in Newark, Detroit, and Los Angeles raising Molotov cocktails against police and national guardsmen. Hundreds were killed and thousands injured in those racial uprisings in more than one hundred ghettos from 1965–1970. In America's Southwest, Chicano revolutionaries were at the barricades too, even attempting focos of their own in northern New Mexico.[32] Puerto Ricans in the Young Lords Party were on the rise in New York and Chicago, occupying buildings, training for self-defense, and identifying with the Puerto Rican independence cause. Thousands of other young men were resisting the draft for Vietnam, escaping to refuge in Canada, or going to jail against the Vietnam War. Priests, nuns, and lay Catholics were not pouring blood on draft board files, but taking the path of liberation theology across Latin America. Anger rose too within the American army barracks and US prison cells. The Black Panther Party for Self-Defense was spreading outward from its Oakland base, attracting the unemployed "brothers on the block" as many in a new generation of the best and brightest black youth in colleges, like Stokely, Angela Davis, and others whose futures arced toward Cuba. The Students for a Democratic Society would evolve, starting in 1969, into the underground Weathermen inspired by Cuba and Vietnam. After a few short years, these militant revolutionary movements would help awaken dissent within the liberal mainstream, even at the highest levels of power, in the presidential campaigns of Eugene McCarthy, Robert Kennedy, and George McGovern.

During those the most intense years of the late sixties, Che was an inspiration. Debray seemed one of us.

Yes, the differences were vast, even incomparable, between our first world and their third world. Not only were we a voting democracy with certain checks and balances, but the vast majority of Americans preferred the status quo or moderate reform to revolutionary goals that sounded vaguely communist. But in the late sixties these obvious differences were becoming blurred in our perceptions, if not disappearing fast. Yes, we lived in a durable democracy, not a police state under colonialism. But our democracy was repeatedly exposed as a subordinate part of a larger Empire whose functions were anything but democratic. It had been necessary, for example, to risk our lives in the South for the simple right to vote. When necessary, this democracy could contract itself into shadow forms: surveillance, counterintelligence (COINTEL) programs, police sweeps and shootings, informal death squads, conspiracy indictments, the targeting of such established figures as Dr. Benjamin Spock and Rev. William Sloan Coffin Jr. The Democratic Party headquarters was infiltrated by the Watergate burglars because it was seen as a shelter for New Left radicals. It was hard for young inexperienced radicals to see the difference between democracy and authoritarianism when blinded by pepper spray. The differences evaporated further during our 1969 Chicago conspiracy trial,[33] a Nixon effort to imprison symbolic leaders of the New Left, during which the Chicago police broke into an apartment at dawn to kill Black Panthers who were working on our legal defense team. The murders at Kent State and Jackson State came three months after our trial's end. I was in debates about whether to appeal the Chicago verdicts—one count of conspiracy each, carrying a five-year sentence—or join an underground resistance instead. I chose the appeal, but wondered if my faith was already outdated.

Revolution in the Revolution? was included in its entirety in SDS's *New Left Notes* in 1969. Starting around 1967, as US protests became disobedient in nature, police and prosecutors began employing more felony arrests and conspiracy charges targeting alleged "leaders." I was one of those placed on the FBI list of those to be "neutralized," a term with ominous import. In these circumstances, the natural response of many street protestors was to form "affinity groups," the political and mostly nonviolent equivalents of focos, small groups that carried out decentralized actions like blocking intersections, taking circuitous routes to evade police, throwing back tear gas canisters, treating the injured in safe houses, and so on. Mick Jagger's "Street Fighting Man" was the beat, spray-paint was the weapon for graffiti, and paste the weapon for wall postering. Many in the affinity groups lived collectively or shared revolutionary study groups. The influence of Cuba, the Panthers, and the assassinated Malcolm X led to underground networks learning to use and store weapons, mainly small arms, and build underground networks for fugitives on the run. The shared expectation of these groups was that an American police state was unfolding and Sam Cook's "People Get Ready" was prophetic.

Between 1965 and 1970, there were 1,390 "violent acts" in America, according to an analysis in *Scanlan's Monthly*.[34] Rough as the estimate was, the arc was clear, from sixteen in 1965 to 546 in 1970, and those numbers would continue growing for several more years. On campuses there were 3,463 recorded protests in 1968, one-third of them involving sit-ins, strikes, hostage-taking, and building takeovers.[35] Fueling a general restlessness were over one hundred black uprisings, spreading spontaneously despite a massive police buildup, the largest of them in Rochester, Harlem and Philadelphia in 1964, in Watts in 1965, in Cleveland and Omaha in 1966, in Newark and Detroit in 1967, and in Chicago and Washington, D.C., in 1968. By late 1967, as one hundred thousand anti-Vietnam demonstrators encircled the Pentagon, President Johnson was screaming at his advisers that "I'm not going to let the Communists take this government, and they're doing it right now!" proving that the smallest bite can cause a massive overreaction.[36] At the Pentagon a domestic war room was established to consolidate files on the New Left and prepare military options.[37]

Our capacity to actually fight the state was ludicrously small, but we couldn't help asking ourselves: didn't Fidel begin with a handful of survivors in the Sierra? Didn't Debray argue that the tiniest groups of dedicated revolutionaries could survive and grow in popularity? The "Sierra effect" was contagious, suggesting that our duty was to "start the revolution" even if the general public was uninterested. The Molotovs would wake them up. Their children would get it. And even if we couldn't win, wasn't it still useful to harass our government with resistance to the draft, mutinies in the armed forces, putting our bodies on the machinery of power, making the wars abroad more difficult by threatening instability on the home front?[38]

According to a 1969 article by SDS's Julie Nichaman, a University of Michigan anthropology student, published in Cuba's *Verde Olivo*, our role was to "destroy the imperialist monster from within."[39] Adding plausibility to this apocalyptic thinking was a too gradual thaw in the views of the public and mainstream policy specialists, which would climax with the Watergate burglaries and cover-ups, bungled by several veterans of the Bay of Pigs, provoking the constitutional crisis that would finally cause Congress to turn against Nixon. President Nixon's removal, like Lyndon Johnson's before him, would be due to the "cancer on the presidency" that would grow out of the administration's unconstitutional efforts to stop the spread of radical dissent from the margins to the mainstream.

CONSPIRING TO RELEASE RÉGIS

Toward the end of 1967, while waiting in Phnom Penh to meet three American POWs being transported over jungle trails and streams from South Vietnam, I met the Cuban ambassador-in-the-jungle, Raúl Valdés Vivo, who played a supportive logistical role in their release. Valdés Vivo, who joined the Cuban party in the 1940s and finally died in November 2013, arrived at my Cambodian hotel lobby with four unsolicited Cuban visas, one for me and three for the POWs traveling with me.[40] The American prisoners might wish to divert and defect to Cuba, the ambassador said. In that case, the paperwork was ready. The possibility had never crossed my mind and, as I naturally assumed, the three POWs desperately wanted to go home. I still have the Cuban visa in my files, evidence that another future, a very strange one, might have awaited me. I mention this anecdote only to underscore how close were the ties between Cubans and the Vietnamese, which included a Cuban willingness to risk the wrath of the United States by harboring American military defectors. The story also suggests a tendency at the time by Cuba and perhaps Vietnam to overestimate the level of antiwar militancy in America. The three POWs really wanted to go home. And go home they did.

Two months later, in January 1968, I was in Havana for the first time, sitting in an expropriated private residence talking with Fidel Castro about Régis Debray. My purpose for being in Havana was to attend an international solidarity conference, but I was drawn into the Debray case by two determined women who met me at the Hotel Nacional as soon as I arrived. One was Michele Ray, a courageous and adventurous French journalist who was captured by the Viet Cong in 1966 and subsequently spent weeks interviewing her captors for the global media. Michele was a former Chanel model who later became the wife of the Greek-born French filmmaker Costa Gavras. I was helpless before her incessant agenda, which was to introduce me to her petite and militant girlfriend, Elisabeth Burgos, the Venezuelan "wife" of the imprisoned Régis Debray. The two of them lobbied me to lobby Fidel to accept their wild proposal for a prisoner exchange—American POWs for Debray. I was skeptical, but Debray's life was in danger and it seemed worth a try. It happened that I was invited to see Fidel as part of a small American antiwar delegation, and I agreed to raise the Debray issue if the opportunity came. For a community organizer from Newark, I was in way over my head already and willing to improvise.

It was a time of great mourning in Cuba after Che's execution two months earlier. Already, however, Che had arisen from his deathbed to the status of revolutionary icon, remarkably like the resurrected Christ after his crucifixion. Huge wall murals and banners everywhere were alive with Alberto Korda's classic portrait of Che taken after the sabotage of a ship in Havana harbor, on March 5, 1960.[41]

Visitors expecting to see Fidel were required to waste several days in their hotel room waiting for The Call from a trusted aide, which could come at any time. If you were impatient, well, it was just a sign of gringo egotism. I missed much of the conference proceedings on the floors below, darting out on short trips and anxiously returning to see if the red *mensajes* button was flashing on my room's phone. Then, after several days' frustration, a caller commanded that I come to the lobby immediately. In minutes I was being driven to the dark, windy streets of Havana's Miramar district, where the vehicle pulled up to a shuttered, single-story suburban home. It was after midnight in the Cuban state, and the Fidelistas were on the move. They operated, I came to realize, as if they were still on maneuvers in the Sierra. This governance by guerrilla tactics was a reminder that the island was under siege and its leader subject to numerous assassination attempts.

I was accompanied by David Dellinger, then a veteran fifty-three-year-old pacifist from the World War II generation, and Carl Davidson, the twenty-four-year-old national secretary of SDS, a philosophy graduate student out of Nebraska, who had recently declared a new strategy, "from protest to resistance," a slogan that was inspired by the Cubans. We were asked to meet Fidel to brief him on America's swirling protest movements.

When we were seated in the empty living room of the safe house I excused myself to use the bathroom, where I found running shoes and sweatpants by a recently used shower. When I returned from the bathroom, I was face-to-face with Fidel, accompanied by his physician and close adviser, René Vallejo, and his master spy, Manuel Piñeiro, whom everyone knew as "Redbeard" or Barbarroja. Fidel's two aides had spent years in American universities and were completely familiar with US politics. We all sat down to begin one of Fidel's customary multiple-hour conversations, a habit that I found obsessive and disturbing—which at the time I considered more evidence of my gringo flaws.

I took no notes and can hardly recall all that was said that night forty-five years ago. Carl distinctly remembers that we talked about bringing thousands of Americans to visit, work, and live in Cuba for months at a time, an idea that two years later became the Venceremos Brigade. A month of cutting sugarcane by day and holding educational meetings by night would create lasting bonds in defiance of the embargo, and would build a pro-Cuba constituency in the United States, just as the 1964 Mississippi Summer Project gave thousands of northern students a serious introduction to conditions in the Deep South. Fidel was interested. Carl also remembers a discussion about hippies. My notebook, apparently quoting Fidel, says that "socialist countries view hippies as degenerate while hippies view socialist countries as uninspiring."

When I managed to raise the issue of Régis Debray, and described the notion of a swap for American POWs, Fidel shifted to a listening mode, a pensive one. He said he would take the proposal "under consideration," and nothing subsequently came of it, as far as I know. Debray was released eventually with no swaps required.

Fidel moved from discussing the antiwar movement to asking about the black uprisings in the United States, and particularly the status of the young black revolutionary, Stokely Carmichael, whose 1967 trip to Havana generated global excitement. Fidel clearly was worried for Stokely's life, and said several times that a "united front" was imperative for the Black Power militant's protection. As he repeated himself for emphasis, I saw a cloudy gravity in his eyes. My intuition was and is that he was also talking about how Che's death might have been prevented.

That was January 1968, the first month of the most volatile year of the sixties. None of us knew, except perhaps for Fidel, that Vietnam's Tet Offensive[42] was one month away. Then came the April assassination of Martin Luther King Jr. Then the uprisings at hundreds of university campuses. At Columbia the uprising was led by Mark Rudd, an SDS activist from the Jersey suburbs recently returned from Cuba. Together with other disciples of Che and Debray, he formed an "action faction" that split away from an existing SDS chapter Rudd and his allies considered too intellectual and passive. In fact the majority of SDS members voted against the action the Rudd faction was insisting upon. But the new leadership, schooled by Debray's doctrine that revolutionaries should start the revolution, stormed buildings and shut down the university in protest of the university's planned expansion into Harlem and secret military research. Like magic, the vanguard approach worked, drawing a large following of students who went to morning classes not realizing that they would be occupying buildings that night.

By chance I met Stokely that morning at the New York SNCC office. I was there to encourage him to visit Cuba. It turned out, however, that the revolution was erupting down the street at Columbia. Along with SNCC organizers, I found myself in the midst of the Columbia rebellion a few minutes later. Though only intending to observe on the first day, I was drawn in to lead one of the nighttime building occupations, taking over Mathematics Hall for five days before mass arrests by the New York police. The foco theory, transported from the Sierra Maestra to Washington Heights, somehow seemed to be applicable. The campus, the city, and even the nation were polarized and challenged by a core of SDS activists smaller than Fidel's band on the *Granma*. As campuses shut down across the country, I wrote a favorable article for *Ramparts*, titled "Two, Three, Many Columbias," that noted the complex tensions between the militant vanguard who wanted to simply shut down the campus until the war-makers were purged, and the larger number of students who wanted to reform Columbia along more liberal lines.[43]

In June, Robert Kennedy was murdered in Los Angeles. I had come to know and respect him starting in 1967 when he invited Staughton Lynd and me to discuss Vietnam and Newark at his New York condominium overlooking the East River. Staughton, a lifelong Quaker practitioner of nonviolent civil disobedience, was deeply suspicious of all politicians, especially charming ones like Bobby. So were my friends in SDS, who thought Bobby was a CIA candidate sent to co-opt the growing New Left movement. Having seen almost everything imaginable in seven short years, I had become more open to multiple paths forward, and was drawn to Bobby because of his own growing affinity with the outcasts of America since the murder of his brother. I had considered an offer from old Kennedy hands within the Democratic administration sometime in 1966 to join the Peace Corps in the Andes, where I might have plunged into guerrilla terrain on the wrong side of Che. I rejected the offer. Still, it was fascinating that Bobby Kennedy was seeking to duplicate, in establishment form, a type of community-based organizing in both Bedford-Stuyvesant and Bolivia, one that attempted to co-opt the projects sponsored by SNCC and SDS at home. President Johnson's 1964 "great society" speech also was meant to mirror and co-opt our fledgling antipoverty projects. The "'great society' speech was influenced by the Port Huron Statement," Goodwin said.[44]

I briefly wondered if we might co-opt the co-opters. And on the uppermost issue of Vietnam, Kennedy seemed altogether serious about finding a way out, his early fascination with Green Beret counterinsurgency waning before the growing evidence of its limits. I thought it was ridiculous to believe that the SDS's slogan, "Let the People Decide," could be co-opted in the service of the status quo. We were more like young Catholic Workers than the Peace Corps,[45] though we were willing to gamble on joining the War on Poverty if only from the bottom up. The difference between the Newark Community Union Project[46] and the Kennedy community service programs was that we organized poor people to fight City Hall while Sargent Shriver[47] offered incentives to city halls for "outreach," job counseling, and legal aid. As it turned out, there wasn't space for the programs of "parallel power" we envisioned, like the freedom school experiments in Mississippi. Some important reforms were achieved, like Head Start, but little was gained for participatory democracy. At that time, it certainly wasn't possible to channel any such program into Latin America under the oligarchies, even modest ones through Catholic charities. The Peace Corps raised the consciousness of its volunteers more than the hopes of the poor in the *favelas*. Che was right about the Alliance for Progress.[48]

I last saw Bobby Kennedy in a San Francisco hotel lobby on the spring night of his final debate with Sen. Eugene McCarthy. We talked briefly about the coming protests in Chicago, and I wished him well as he sought rest in his room. Saying goodbye, I noticed that his hands were swollen and covered with scratches and cuts, torn by thousands of well-wishers as his caravan passed them by. I never got to ask him whether he regretted his administration's attempts to kill Fidel. Though his family later expressed regret and became friends of the Cuban Revolution.

When Bobby was killed, I wandered in the darkness to St. Patrick's Cathedral, where his coffin was arriving from the coast. A few close friends and I were permitted to enter and sit quietly in the pews while carpenters built the funeral stage. I joined an ad hoc honor guard around the coffin while the preparations went on. I wore a green Cuban hat. I thought nothing of it. I like to believe that Bobby would have understood.

GOODBYE, DEBRAY

And what happened to Régis Debray, our generational peer whose words could be hurled like spears? The Bolivian government released him in 1970 after intervention by the French president and worldwide petitioning. According to his own account, he went back into military training in Cuba with, among others, Giangiacomo Feltrinelli, the wealthy Italian publisher of *Doctor Zhivago,* whose own life took a revolutionary turn after the Cubans sent him to meet Debray in prison in 1967. Feltrinelli apparently fantasized about creating a foco in the Alps, "until his shattered body was found at the foot of a giant pylon supplying electricity to Milan, where he had made a bungled attempt to apply our course notes," wrote Debray.[49] The publisher's death came on March 15, 1972. Italy's Red Brigades later claimed Feltrinelli had committed a "technical error" while on an operation to shut down Milan's electrical grid. Eight thousand people turned out for his funeral.[50]

Debray was soon taking in the sights of socialist Chile. "Everything was smiling, the future, the women, the eucalyptus trees. And Salvador Allende himself, who liked laughter, good Macul wine, and nice alpaca suits."[51] Debray, still based in Cuba, became close friends with Allende, and published a book of interviews with the Chilean president exploring the possibility of achieving "socialism in freedom."[52] Debray again was bonding with and channeling a great man of power. As noted, Ricardo had befriended Allende as early as 1959 and had actively helped make a peaceful transition in Chile a reality. But Fidel, while also hopeful, presented Allende with a rifle as a gift and tried to convince him that Cuba should arm and train a Chilean militia.

The US-backed coup of 1973 and the death of Allende proved Fidel's dire premonition to be correct, and profoundly shook Debray, who began to reexamine his Latin America experience. He showed up in Nicaragua in a Sandinista uniform on the

108 • *Listen, Yankee!*

last day of the 1979 revolution in Managua. That was his final
appearance as a militant.

Debray turned against the Cuban Revolution in the eighties.
His complaints—essentially about the lack of democracy—
were not without substance, but seemed as extreme and sub-
jective as his earlier desire to become an obedient instrument
of his comandante, Fidel. Where once Fidel was his unques-
tioned *Jefe*, now Debray suddenly saw Fidel as totalitarian, a
magician of power who had employed charisma to bewitch
Debray for nearly two decades. Debray returned to France to
serve his new hero, the Socialist president François Mitterrand,
becoming an official foreign policy adviser. Debray proudly
recovered his French national identity from the shame it had
once instilled in him. He became a True Believer in reverse,
with a racial, even colonial, overtone. Debray now concluded
that "my blood group was not Latino," and wrote with revulsion
of "the great Latino slaughter of those leaden years" in Latin
America."[53] Had Debray forgotten the guillotine, Robespierre,
Napoleon, and the "great French slaughters" of colonial times
in his reconversion to the Age of Reason? Debray wasn't the
only French intellectual to approve of revolutionary extremes at
the time. Sartre famously approved the thesis of Frantz Fanon
that the killing of colonizers was a necessary catharsis.[54] Others
embraced Mao Tse-tung's Great Proletarian Cultural Revolution as the way forward.[55] But in actively dismissing "objective
conditions," Debray was actively encouraging so many middle
class young dreamers toward guilt-driven deaths. "That is what
responsibility is like," he reflected on the death of Che, "the
real thing: something you cannot answer, and that you discover
twenty years afterward."[56] He began to think "that I was ready
for the funny farm myself."[57]

CHAPTER 9

The Revolutionary Flame

Cuba's socialism was the moral and political wave of the future. I was stoned on socialism!
—MARK RUDD, COLUMBIA UNIVERSITY SDS STRIKE LEADER, 1968[1]

The Tet Offensive, the Columbia student strike, the assassinations of Martin Luther King Jr. as well as Bobby and John F. Kennedy, the Soviet invasion of Czechoslovakia (which disturbingly was supported by Fidel),[2] the Chicago convention street battles, all seemed to be cascading signs of a new world. Resistance seemed logical, and revolution at least plausible to many, with no sign the Vietnam War was ending nor the dictatorships blanketing Latin America either. These conditions spurred the birth of the SDS Weather Underground in 1969. Who in those times could be completely sure of any meaningful differences between Richard Nixon, J. Edgar Hoover and the Watergate thugs with their roots in the Bay of Pigs, and the repressive Batista regime of the fifties that forced Ricardo and the 26th of July movement into underground resistance? Wasn't it only a matter of time, some of us wondered, before the US government abandoned the facade of democratic elections and expanded the roundup of dissidents? And if a repressive US foreign policy was being redeployed toward the home front,

wasn't it time to prepare the resistance? Instead of the mainstream demand to bring the *troops* home, some started calling
to bring the *war* home. I myself found it hard to distinguish
between revolutionary delusion and realism. If it could tip
either way, preparations had to begin. I was for Bobby Kennedy
and Fidel Castro at the same time.

Boatloads and planes filled with SDS people headed for their
Cuban mecca in 1968–1969. Some headed through Mexico City
in the very month that its armed forces murdered hundreds
of student democracy protestors in the plaza of Tlatelolco in
the capital.[3] Some traveled on a converted Cuban cattle boat
from Halifax, Nova Scotia, staying in Cuba for several weeks.
A briefing paper to "Cuba trippers" was signed by "your cruise
director, in struggle," Bernardine Dohrn, a University of Chicago law student who became revolutionized that year. Among
travellers were several future leaders of the Weatherman faction of SDS. Twenty-year-old Columbia student Mark Rudd,
who traveled to Cuba in January 1968 and returned to lead the
strike at his university, spelled out the impact of Cuba in a later
autobiography: "the main lesson from Columbia [was] a direct
translation of Che Guevara's strategy of revolt in Latin America
to the imperialist homeland."[4] "Like a Christian seeking to
emulate the life of Christ, I passionately wanted to be a revolutionary like Che, no matter what the price."[5]

Not all the Cuba visitors were from SDS. One of them, Phil
Hutchings of Howard University, worked with me in the SDS
Newark community organizing project as well as in SNCC. He
became SNCC chairman after Stokely's departure, and then an
early organizer of the Venceremos Brigade. As he told me in
2013:

PHIL HUTCHINGS: *The Vietnamese suggested to SDS that they help
Cuba instead of sending so many people to* [faraway and expen-
sive] *Vietnam. I went to the first organizing meeting in New York
at some rich person's house to argue for broader inclusion. At first*

*we were going to bring three hundred black, brown, and yellow
people—each!—but instead we would up with two hundred mostly
white people led by a Weatherperson, Julie Nichamin.*

*There was a decent sized group of blacks, Native Americans,
Latinos, and Asians on the second trip, 30 percent people of color,
triple the first brigade.*

Another version appears in the autobiography of the late
Carl Oglesby, a great writer and orator who became SDS president in 1964. On a trip to Cuba in 1968, Oglesby had the then-
wild idea—there were so many in the air—of thousands of
Americans breaking the travel ban to cut cane in Cuba. He met
in Havana at the home of de facto ambassador Carlos Rafael
Rodríguez[6] and several times with the same official afterward at
a New York bar before eventually winning Cuba's support. Then,
falling amidst the ruins of SDS's internal divisions, Oglesby was
purged on charges that he was proposing only a "liberal" Peace
Corps for Cuba, when the purpose should be "to bring back
more committed revolutionaries" to the United States.[7] That
was wrong, at least from the Cuban viewpoint. They wanted
more Americans schooled in the realities of the Cuban Revolution, not a training camp for American guerrillas. Despite the
sectarian tension within SDS, the Cubans welcomed the first
brigadistas in November 1969. It was "one of the most imagina-
tive enterprises ever undertaken by the American Left," in the
appraisal of historian Kirkpatrick Sale.[8]

PHIL HUTCHINGS: *One big problem was what the brigade was
supposed to do. The Cubans were nervous about interfering in US
politics. Our old enemy, Sen. James O. Eastland* [of Mississippi]
*was saying we were being trained for guerrilla warfare, that we
were studying Carlos Marighella's handbook on urban warfare.[9]
The Cubans wanted to tone it down, to get the Americans to learn
something about Cuba through their experience. The Cubans didn't
want to be flagrant and stick it in the face of the United States. Some*

of the Americans did want to take it further, and project it into a US movement for revolution.

For some of the Venceremos volunteers, the impact of Cuba lasted for a lifetime. For some, Cuba became a lifetime cause. SDS members like Michael Locker and John Frappier, my Ann Arbor roommate, formed a first-rate research center known as the North American Congress on Latin America, helping birth Cuba studies on many campuses and building a library available to many journalists. Karen Wald, who married a Cuban, wrote in her diary that the experience was "incredible, not even so much in terms of what people are learning about Cuba, as what people are learning about themselves."[10] Another example was Sandra Levinson, an SDS activist from Iowa, who went to Cuba just before the first brigade. I interviewed Sandra in 2014:

SANDRA LEVINSON: *I fell for Fidel in 1969 in a cane field, literally. It was the first day of the sugar harvest. Peter Jennings was standing there, his first trip. Fidel gave a speech and came over to a bunch of us, and asked me why I wasn't cutting. My Spanish wasn't up to it, but I told him I had polio when I was a kid. So he spent twenty minutes teaching me to cut. Then after I started cutting, something came tearing into my neck and I fell. Lionel Martin* [a pro-Cuba activist] *had thrown a piece of cane into my neck. Fidel came over, pulled me up and got me to the hospital. I had two surgeries.*

Back in New York City, Levinson founded a Cuban studies institute and a Cuban art gallery. She would promote trips to the island for many decades. In 1973 her offices were bombed by a right-wing Cuban exile.

SANDRA: *We were promoting Saul's film on Fidel. No one was there that night. A Spanish class had just left. It was a huge plastique bomb. I was lucky that it was placed in a doorjamb where there was a steel pillar, so the bomb went off in every direction but mine. The guy who did it, a Cuban with two friends, came around to case the place the night before. We gave the police a perfect description but they did nothing. The police instead showed me photos of some Puerto Rican gang members! Then the FBI came and wanted to know about leftist bombings on the West Coast! Nothing about our being bombed.*

Sandra came to know Ricardo and his wife Margarita Alarcón very well during their years at New York's Cuban mission.

SANDRA: *During the Cuban missile crisis I think Alarcón said people didn't think they were going to wake up the next morning. I thought it was a joke to be studying for my doctoral exams if we weren't going to be around. That was the moment I got involved.*

When Ricardo and Margarita were in New York, I would organize small get-togethers for him with journalists and intellectuals. It was fascinating. My friends said he was the only one who didn't have to call home for instructions. He and Fidel thought alike. They were Fidelistas, not really Communists in the old-fashioned meaning of the term. They had a very nationalist and populist ideology. Ricardo was not seen as Raúl's favorite person in those days.

I have to tell you a story Margarita told me about when she and Ricardo first started dating, that says a lot. She told her mother that Ricardo was coming over. It would have been the first time he met her mother. But Margarita had to leave the house for a meeting, and told her mother to welcome Ricardo and tell him she would be right back and give him some food. "That is a very strange young man," the mother told Margarita when she returned. He sat down at the kitchen table, she said, and while she went to get eggs he ate the whole jar of mayonnaise! He's got a very large head, I don't know why he ate it, maybe he had more important things to do than eating. Food wasn't the first thing on his agenda.

Many years later, I asked Bernardine about right-wing charges of Cuban guerrilla training of the type that Debray had secretly undergone. She waved away the question, saying, "I never favored any outside support." By contrast, she laughed, during a later trip to North Korea, she and SDS were offered weapons, training, and funding by Pyongyang. The only prerequisite, she said, was to watch a lengthy propaganda film about North Korea's revolution, which she found unbearable. She walked out of the theater and the offer.

The Weather Underground held a last conference in Flint, Michigan, in December 1969, before dispersing into clandestine collectives without public announcement. Copies of the Debray booklet were in their packets. "This is the future," one cadre said. After going underground, they successfully eluded the FBI for over five years, carrying out a score of bombings against military and corporate installations, including the Bank of America, United Fruit, Chase Manhattan, IBM, Standard Oil, Anaconda, General Motors, and even including a bathroom in the US House of Representatives—and those actions with the Weather signature were only a handful among hundreds of other bombings of ROTC buildings, induction centers, Selective Service offices, and military-related sites around the United States. During 1969–1970, according to government reports, there were six bombings per day, five thousand overall along with forty thousand threats or attempts.[11] The Weather Underground also spirited the LSD guru Timothy Leary out of a California prison, in an effort to somehow politicize the youth culture. The code name for the Leary operation was "Juju Eyeballs" from the Beatles' "Come Together."[12] True to their word, they brought the war home, or at least a skirmish, to the embarrassment of the FBI. Nearly all of the Weather people managed to surface safely by the mid- to late seventies, because the FBI was unwilling or unable to reveal the illegal surveillance methods that were employed in the attempts to capture them. The government dropped its conspiracy charges, citing the "national security" impact if their illegal surveillance methods, including wiretaps of twelve thousand separate conversations were revealed.[13]

This little-remembered attempt to create a foco in America combined both the revolutionary idealism and fatal isolation foreseen in Debray's strategy by Ricardo and others. First, the Weathermen lost three precious lives almost immediately when a bomb-in-making blew up in a Greenwich Village townhouse on March 6, 1970, killing Teddy Gold, Diana Oughton, and Terry Robbins. All three victims were like younger brothers and sisters to me, their identities cemented by the revolutionary winds of 1968–1969, when they had been convinced—by the killings of the Kennedys, King, Malcolm X, and so many Panthers—that the earlier years of nonviolence and community organizing were "reformist," naive, and in vain. Each of them wanted to live like Che and they died like him, in isolation, though by their own hands in a fiery Greenwich Village townhouse rather than a Bolivian arroyo.

Second, they were drifting beyond property damage into the shadows of terrorism. If they had carried out their fateful mission, they would have bombed a military ball, with wives, families, and civilians, at Fort Dix, New Jersey. In the new mindset, the targets were the nearest American soldiers that could be found, their families being no more innocent than countless Vietnamese civilians. It's impossible to know the state of their thinking at the moment of detonation, or whether the plans were still unsettled.

Third, they detached themselves from mass movements at just the moment that the Vietnam Moratorium of 1969–1970 and Earth Day in 1970 were drawing *millions* into public protest. The My Lai massacre revealed in 1968, the Pentagon Papers disclosure of 1971, and the evidence of the COINTELPRO surveillance (1971) were exposing the hidden horrors of the Vietnam War. The militant escalation of 1965–1970, provoked by the suffocating hopelessness of the Johnson and Nixon eras, zigzagged unexpectedly toward a new flowering of massive protest in the Watergate time. But the "small motor" of SDS, which did so much to challenge the status quo, had stalled and burned out in anonymity. The "big motor" of those mass protests was taken over by young progressives and Democratic liberals, who devoutly hoped to change the system's priorities from within. Many of them would become the Clinton Democrats.

Since SDS had either gone underground or splintered itself into sectarian feuding, there was no SDS leadership for the mass movement that, according to the Weather Underground analysis, was impossible in any event in a "mother country" so saturated with racial privilege.[14] The Weathermen could cling to their urban cells but did not dare to venture outdoors to leaflet for a mass rally. Their first—and also final—public event, the Days of Rage during the Chicago conspiracy trial, was called on October 11, 1969, the second anniversary of Che's murder. "Living like Che" consisted of raging through Chicago's Gold Coast, attacking police and the windows of elegant condominiums. Weathermen were shot and wounded that night, and dozens were injured. The corporation counsel of Chicago, Richard Elrod, suffered a broken neck. I was invited to speak briefly in Lincoln Park before the rampage began, since I knew many of the participants personally from the community organizing projects and antiwar protests only three years earlier. I was taken by surprise when I saw them that night, their heads helmeted and covered by masks, smeared with gel to counter tear gas, holding clubs and branches in their hands. I wasn't ready for the looks in their eyes. I said a few words assuring them of the Chicago conspiracy trial's defendants' general support, then left feeling old, confused and used.

The Weathermen were shocked by the townhouse deaths. They scattered everywhere, finally reassembling at a secret retreat in California a few weeks later. Realizing the total alienation from which their Weather politics was forged, and their subsequent isolation from mass political life, they purged the one individual whom they blamed for their fatal descent to pure militarism. His name was John Jacobs, though everyone called him J.J., and he had been a charismatic newcomer to their inner circle in 1968 who sailed on the fateful journey from New Brunswick to Havana in 1969. I encountered J.J. briefly at Columbia, and was struck by his hyperintense brilliant self-confidence. He could evaluate whole sections of Lenin, Mao, and Che, and excelled at ideological combat with other "tendencies" on the shrinking Left. J.J. combined this ideological skill with a competitive militancy that demanded that everyone "take it to the next level." During the Columbia strike he was among the first to seize buildings and secretly set a fire in Hamilton Hall.[15] I found his charisma to be scary and intimidating. His eyes flamed like mortars and words came in rapid fire. J.J. was the most influential voice, along with his copartner Terry Robbins, in the "New York Tribe" that plotted to make the fragmentation bombs in the townhouse.[16] After his expulsion, J.J. eventually made it across the Canadian border, assumed a fictionalized new identity, took construction jobs in Vancouver, created a patch of marijuana growth, had two children in a common-law marriage, and died a painful and premature death from cancer at age fifty in 1997. As he lay writhing on the street in a spasm of pain, a Vancouver policewoman kneeled down to try and help. He is said to have screamed and lashed out at the sight of her uniform.

Che was his hero and role model. J.J.'s family buried his ashes at the monument to Che in Santa Clara. There is a plaque there too, featuring a photo of J.J. in his prime, which thanks "the Cuban government, the Central Committee of the Cuban Communist Party, and others for the honor and respect shown him by allowing some of his ashes to be spread at the monument to Che Guevara. He wanted to live like Che. Let him rest like Che."[17]

J.J.'s thousands of pages of writings have never been published.

While a few Weathermen remain in prison today, the vast majority have returned to life above ground, where they have participated in the vast antiwar protests against Iraq and Afghanistan, or in solidarity movements with torture victims imprisoned everywhere from Baghdad to Pelican Bay, California. They include lawyers, teachers, writers, activists, parents, and grandparents. Bernardine Dohrn became an expert in family law at Northwestern University and her longtime partner Bill Ayers a noted school reformer, professor, and author of multiple books. They attended Thanksgiving parties with Barack and Michelle Obama when the president was running for a state Senate seat, and Bill served on an education foundation board with Obama, which later triggered a national uproar with Sarah Palin accusing candidate Obama of "palling with terrorists"[18] and Hillary Clinton having thrown jibes herself several months earlier.[19] It is amazing that Obama, protected by a powerful African American base, could survive charges that would have been fatal during the Cold War era. Personally, I am comforted to know that an American president has crossed paths with people who come from the radical traditions of anticolonialism and anti-imperialism long defined as taboo in the American mainstream. Obama's election and presidency are a reminder of accomplishments we thought impossible in those fugitive times. As I wrote before his December 17, 2014, decision to normalize relations, these past experiences might serve Obama well as he approaches decisions about Cuba that will be part of his legacy one way or another. If he admires King and Mandela, can he not at least understand Che or Fidel?

The period of escalating movement violence, which led also to sectarian infighting and organizational chaos, nevertheless followed a historical logic that can be charted: from the liberal default on civil rights and Vietnam in 1964–1965 and the serial killings of John and Bobby Kennedy, Martin Luther King, Malcolm X, Medgar Evers, and Fred Hampton, there was a steady upswing of antiestablishment confrontations, including civil disobedience, draft resistance, urban rebellions, GI mutinies, the formation of undergrounds of nonviolent war resisters, priests and nuns, fugitives on the run, and the creation of many autonomous revolutionary groups attempting to fight a "war of the flea," as guerrilla warfare was sometimes called.[20] In addition, millions of today's middle-aged Americans lived in their formative years amidst an outlawed drug culture. Federal repression escalated beyond the breaking point, with the deployment of a White House team of "plumbers," conspiracy indictments, political trials of antiwar activists, and lethal units of undercover police. The Vietnam War and threats to domestic civil liberties inevitably pushed a few thousand radicalized young people onto a violent path—which came to its end only when the Vietnam War ended and Nixon resigned. Similarly, the urban black rebellions declined when black mayors began to be elected in city after city. Without the revolutionary upsurge, I doubt whether those rational reforms might ever have followed.

RICARDO: *Nixon was elected in 1968 with the help of so-called crazy young people . . .*

Did he mean, I asked, hippies, blacks, and antiwar activists?

RICARDO: *I do not like at all that expression. But the point is that Nixon managed to gather a majority of voters suspicious of what appeared to them to be a too liberal Democratic candidate. The antiwar movement with its counterculture components objectively, if unwillingly, helped Nixon build such a coalition. After being elected, his China moves and the Vietnam negotiations did the rest: the "movement" got more divided and isolated. You know the story better than I do.*

In many ways, Cuba at first, followed by Vietnam, set off the domestic shock effects that awakened, rattled, and polarized America from 1960 through 1976. Even as the "long sixties" in America—1959–1976—subsided, the Cuban Revolution was far from done.

Bertolt Brecht, the German playwright who shaped the consciousness of many in SDS in its eight short years of existence, expressed it well:

To Posterity

1.

Indeed I live in the dark ages!
A guileless word is an absurdity.
A smooth forehead betokens
A hard heart.
He who laughs
Has not yet heard
The terrible tidings.

Ah, what an age it is
When to speak of trees is almost a crime
For it is a kind of silence about injustice!
And he who walks calmly across the street,
Is he not out of reach of his friends
In trouble?

It is true: I earn my living
But, believe me, it is only an accident.
Nothing that I do entitles me to eat my fill.
By chance I was spared. (If my luck leaves me
I am lost.)

They tell me: eat and drink. Be glad you have it!
But how can I eat and drink
When my food is snatched from the hungry
And my glass of water belongs to the thirsty?
And yet I eat and drink.

I would gladly be wise.
The old books tell us what wisdom is:
Avoid the strife of the world

Live out your little time
Fearing no one
Using no violence
Returning good for evil—
Not fulfillment of desire but forgetfulness
Passes for wisdom.

I can do none of this:
Indeed I live in the dark ages!

2.

I came to the cities in a time of disorder
When hunger ruled.
I came among men in a time of uprising
And I revolted with them.
So the time passed away
Which on earth was given me.

I ate my food between massacres.
The shadow of murder lay upon my sleep.
And when I loved, I loved with indifference.
I looked upon nature with impatience.
So the time passed away
Which on earth was given me.

In my time streets led to the quicksand.
Speech betrayed me to the slaughterer.
There was little I could do. But without me
The rulers would have been more secure. This was my
   hope.
So the time passed away

Which on earth was given me.

3.

You, who shall emerge from the flood
In which we are sinking,
Think—
When you speak of our weaknesses,
Also of the dark time
That brought them forth.

For we went, changing our country more often than our shoes.
In the class war, despairing
When there was only injustice and no resistance.
For we knew only too well:
Even the hatred of squalor
Makes the brow grow stern.
Even anger against injustice
Makes the voice grow harsh. Alas, we
Who wished to lay the foundations of kindness
Could not ourselves be kind.
But you, when at last it comes to pass
That man can help his fellow man,
Do not judge us too harshly.

[translation: H. R. Hays]

As Ricardo has said, a Che Guevara living today would not advocate or instigate guerrilla warfare in Latin America, but would be standing alongside Evo Morales in a much different Latin America. The focos of the sixties contributed as catalysts to the eventual demise of dictatorships and a long-term shift toward democracy in the region. The spark that the martyrs lit travelled on an unexpectedly long fuse, one that inflamed millions of people against the military repression that covered up centuries of poverty and pain. That long fuse of revolution even charged the spirit of liberation theology—a doctrine and praxis both in competition and cooperation with, and definitely in response to, the focos triggered by the Cuban Revolution. The electoral path that seemed to perish with Allende was forced open again to popular movements of the eighties and nineties, movements that always carried the banner of Che and venerated Fidel as the heroic elder of the continent. Many of the Latin American leaders elected in the nineties had roots in the guerrilla past. What began with Pinochet and Nixon's killing of democratic hopes in Allende's Chile ended in less than twenty years with a democratic plebiscite to throw the dictator out. Ignácio Lula da Silva, who was elected president of Brazil in 2002 after three failed attempts, had been a trade unionist who was imprisoned by the generals. His successor, Dilma Rousseff, Brazil's current president, was a guerrilla who suffered torture. Carlos Marighella, the author of the 1969 *Minimanual of the Urban Guerrilla*, studied by all Latin American and global revolutionaries, including the Red Army Faction in West Germany, has become an icon in today's Brazil. Lula identifies him as a "national hero" for having fought the military dictatorship, and is quoted as saying that Marighella looks down from heaven: "He would say 'it was worth dying' because we are now reaping what he and his companions sowed."[21]

Since Brazil is considered "moderate" on the spectrum of Latin American nationalism, it can be assumed that the veneration of former guerrillas is a continental consensus. On the radical end of the spectrum, Venezuela's late president Hugo Chávez was virtually a protégé of Fidel, and received boundless assistance from Cuba. Bolivia's Evo Morales finished what Che began in his country, rising from leadership of the militant coca growers' union to become the first indigenous president in five centuries. Uruguay's elected president José Mujica was a Tupamaro guerrilla leader who was shot six times and imprisoned for fourteen years. The father of Michelle Bachelet, Chile's twice-elected president, served in the Allende government, was detained, tortured, and eventually died in 1974; she, along with her mother, was also imprisoned and tortured. Nicaragua's president Daniel Ortega was the leader of the Sandinista front. The outgoing president of El Salvador, Mauricio Funes, was elected as the FMLN candidate; his brother was assassinated during the Salvadoran civil war. In 2014, as noted, a former FMLN comandante was elected president of El Salvador. The list of former guerrillas, inspired originally by Che, who came to power peacefully in the nineties is long and unexpected.

None of these democratic transitions in Latin and Central America were identical, but carried their own distinct national features. Some transitions were thwarted too: In Mexico, the Cuba-inspired student revolutionaries who had been crushed in 1968 eventually became the organizers of the Zapatistas in the state of Chiapas and narrowly lost a national referendum to include indigenous rights in Mexico's constitution. In addition, Mexico's left-wing nationalist candidates lost in presidential elections that were widely believed to have been stolen in 1988 and 2006.

The impressive roll call of recent Latin American presidents is like a family tree of the descendants of the Cuban Revolution. Che, and therefore Debray, had something to do with this line of evolutionary descent. So of course did Fidel, who will go down in history as a hero of global struggle, remembered for the scope of his impact after his beginnings in the Sierra. As Henry Kissinger would note in his diaries, Fidel "was probably the most revolutionary leader then in power."[22]

CHAPTER 10

The Cuban Revolution Goes Global

I t is rarely mentioned that Cuba is an African country almost as much as it is a Latin American one. Like Brazil and other Caribbean island-nations, modern Cuba is rooted in conquest, slavery, and antislavery rebellions. So it was a natural act, not simply a Marxist reflex, when Cuba's internationalism was cemented with an arms shipment to embattled Algeria in December 1961.[1] The vessel that brought the weapons returned to Cuba with wounded orphans, refugees, and fighters against the French. After Algeria's independence was secured, the Cubans sent fifty-five specialists to provide free health care.[2] When Algeria was threatened by Morocco in 1963, Cuba dispatched 686 armed fighters to defend the new revolutionary nation.[3]

Why and how could there be such a robust foreign policy from a poor and underdeveloped nation? From the beginning, the Cuban revolutionaries were conscious of belonging to what Mills—and SDS, in the Port Huron Statement—called "the hungry bloc," the third world instead of the first or second. Frantz Fanon, world-famous author of *The Wretched of the Earth*, was born in the Caribbean, for example, though he participated in the Algerian cause.

There was an additional strategic reason for Cuba's humanitarianism as well. According to the preeminent historian of Cuba in Africa, Piero Gleijeses, "after his repeated offers for the exploring of a modus vivendi with the US—in 1961, 1963, and 1964—Castro had concluded that the best defense was offense."[4] As one ranking Cuban officer in Africa was quoted, "Cuba defends itself by attacking its aggressor. This was our philosophy. The Yankees were attacking us from every side, so we had to challenge them everywhere, along all the paths of the world. We had to divide their forces, so that they wouldn't be able to descend on us, or any other country, with all their might. Our response had to be bold."[5]

For millions of Cubans, Africa was their mother country. Cuban blood was African blood and Cuban ancestors were from African cultures like the Yoruba and Igbo in modern Nigeria, or the Mandingo of Sierra Leone. In the twenties and thirties, Cuba experienced the rise of *Afrocubanismo*, like *négritude* in the French Caribbean, or the Harlem Renaissance, a wave of cultural nationalism across the African diaspora. It was no wonder that thousands of black Cubans would be drawn to fight for their ancient homelands—the Congo, Guinea-Bissau, Namibia—against Portuguese colonialism and South Africa's racial apartheid. As the Cuban national poet Nicolás Guillén said in 1976 as the African wars began,

> Very many slaves were brought to Cuba from Angola ... We are especially conscious of those parts of Africa from which so many of our ancestors came. It is the basis of all my poetry ... Angola is part of us.[6]

If, for the United States and the West, this was seen as communist Cuban imperialism, for the Cubans it was more akin to coming home. If, for the United States and the West, Cuba was a pawn of the Soviet Union, a majority of third world countries embraced Cuba as a leader of the tricontinental bloc known as OSPAAAL (Organization of Solidarity with the People of

Asia, Africa, and Latin America) in January 1966. The choice was remarkable because the third world conference was born in Cairo in 1957 and did not include any Latin American countries until 1965 when the Cubans were invited to join, ending any doubt about their third world roots and heritage.

At the same moment in the United States, SNCC was transforming itself into a kind of third world liberation movement on the home front. The SNCC projects among sharecroppers in the Black Belt were seen as part of a global agrarian reform movement, according to SNCC historian Clay Carson.[7]

As the integrationist impulse weakened, the black nationalism and internationalism of Malcolm X and the Nation of Islam gained sympathy. The term "Black Power" was tested for mass response by an SNCC stalwart, Willie Ricks, during the June 1966, Mississippi voting rights march where James Meredith was shot. The call was finally made by Stokely Carmichael on June 16 when Ricks told him, "Drop it now! The people are ready!"[8] The chairman of SNCC, Carmichael's explosive charisma vaulted him from left-wing community worker to global revolutionary overnight.

The term "Black Power" carried an ambiguous double meaning. For those in the Malcolm X tradition, it was the demand that mobilized young people because it terrified white people the most, implying violent retribution and a racial role reversal. For Dr. King, who at first hesitated to employ the term, it suggested that black people be organized and led toward power within the tradition of white minority immigrant groups who had come before. For Stokely, it was a bit of both. Either way, Black Power led to a sharp lessening of direct white participation in the civil rights movement, and gaining independent leverage for the black community against white-led power structures. In both its revolutionary and reformist meanings, Black Power carried a deep resonance for black people who had struggled since Montgomery in 1957 through Selma in 1965 with little to show and rising impatience.

Stokely, whom I knew through all phases of his short life (he died of cancer in 1998), was an improbable revolutionary. His future affinity for the Cuban Revolution arose from the fact that he himself was a Caribbean islander, born in Trinidad, just off the coast of Venezuela, in 1941. He joined Fair Play for Cuba while a student at Bronx High School of Science, where he grew up among left-wing Jewish radicals. Then he enrolled at the historically black Howard University in 1960 at just the moment when the student sit-in movement was unfurling across the South. Stokely joined Howard's Nonviolent Action Group (NAG) and flung himself into confrontations from Cambridge, Maryland, to Greenwood, Mississippi, where a Freedom Ride led to his being held for forty-nine days in the feared Mississippi State Penitentiary, known as Parchman Farm, and ultimately to Lowndes County, Alabama, where local people chose the symbol of a black panther in opposition to the white supremacist Democrat's rooster image. He searched the swamps of Neshoba County for the lost bodies of James Chaney, Andy Goodman, and Mickey Schwerner before they were ultimately found, mutilated, in August 1964.[9]

Stokely projected charisma to all: tall, handsome, flashing smile, heading straight into the face of death, a brilliant community organizer and speaker. We knew each other fairly well, even after Stokely broke from the white Left. He came to Newark in August 1966, one year after the Watts rebellion in Los Angeles and eleven months before Newark went up in flames,[10] spoke to eight hundred youths in our community, and on the sidelines calmly explained why white organizers like myself could no longer play leadership roles where black people were concerned. We crossed paths shortly after, when I encouraged him to go to Cuba. He already was planning to.

Within SNCC, many of Stokely's closest lifelong friends were also Caribbean born, like Courtland Cox and Michael Thelwell, whose nickname on campus was "Castro."[11] At that time, I was ignorant of any past connections between American black people and West Indian revolutionaries like Marcus Garvey, George Padmore, Aimé Césaire, or Frantz Fanon. I knew almost nothing at the time of José Martí's years in Tampa, and thought of Fidel's 1960 visit to Harlem as a sort of impromptu drop-by. My reeducation was only beginning.

During the week of the Newark uprising, on July 15, 1967, Stokely gave a London speech to a conference of left-wing luminaries, including Herbert Marcuse, R. D. Laing, Paul Goodman, Allen Ginsberg, Angela Davis, and the Caribbean historian C.L.R. James, author of the seminal text on the Haitian Revolution, *The Black Jacobins*.[12] Stokely's address, on white supremacy at home and abroad, challenged and excited the attendees. Here, after all, was a real revolutionary, life in danger, monitored by the CIA, breathing life into what might have been a stale intellectual gathering. It was provocative also because Stokely's Black Power analysis took issue with the Left's overriding Marxist emphasis on class, rather than race, in the formulation of revolutionary theory. Stokely, only twenty-five, was criticized gently[13] by his sixty-six-year old idol, C.L.R. James, whose book Stokely had studied long and hard. The criticism was muted amidst the general acclamation, though it would be raised again by the Cubans in the future. The Cubans weren't interested in a Black Power movement growing on the island. But they were very interested in young Stokely.

A Cuban diplomat attending the London conference approached Stokely immediately after his speech with an official invitation to a gathering of the Organization of Latin American Solidarity (OLAS) in Havana later that month. Dozens of third world delegations, including a rainbow of liberation movements, would be represented there, and Stokely was to be the honored guest of Fidel. He would be treated as "black America's unofficial prime minister."[14] Stokely wrote in his autobiography that "it was an excellent time for me to be going to Cuba because the revolutionary government was launching a bold initiative to counter US attempts to isolate them."[15]

For Fidel, with no modus vivendi with the United States on the horizon, it was time to throw moral and political weight behind the African Americans then rising up and often burning down American cities. Stokely readily agreed to the invitation, and was flown to Havana while Detroit was going up in smoke, occupied by US Army units back from Vietnam, with forty-three people having died in the streets.[16] Just two weeks earlier, twenty-six people were killed in six days of Newark burning. The slogan "two, three, many Vietnams" was being transferred to America's cities.

Like Mills and other revolutionary visitors previously, Stokely spent three days in conversations with Fidel, including a jeep ride in Santiago and into the former Sierra battlegrounds. He sat on the stage while Fidel spoke for two and a half hours on the fourteenth anniversary of Moncada on July 26.[17] At a four-hour closing speech, Fidel declared that "Comrade Stokely Carmichael" would be put "under my protection" to prevent any harm befalling him. For his part, Stokely gave a twenty-minute speech that drew this parallel:

> We are moving to control our African American communities as you are moving to wrest control of your countries, of the entire Latin continent, from the hands of foreign imperialist powers.[18]

The Cubans were delighted. The CIA was in overdrive. What would happen next? The right-wing American columnists Rowland Evans and Robert Novak ranted against Stokely as "Castro's arm in the US."[19] The leading *New York Times* columnist, James Reston, became unhinged at Stokely's "very surly" demeanor and described him as an arrogant peacock "strutting around" Havana, and questioned, somewhat correctly, exactly how representative Stokely was in the United States.[20] Attorney general Ramsey Clark ordered transcripts of his speeches while the State Department laid plans to take back his passport.[21]

It was impossible to know how much this global wave of solidarity was real and how much was media driven. While Stokely was becoming an American revolutionary rock star, few noticed that SNCC's organization was falling apart on the ground. Police harassment, COINTEL disruption, J. Edgar Hoover's secret pledge to stop a black "messiah" from emerging, internal feuds over race and class, centralized leadership versus base building, all these were undercutting any chance of SNCC's evolution to the leading role in unifying the African American community. Stokey himself was separating, or being separated, from the organization. While Stokely sat in the Havana spotlight, an independent delegation from SNCC was also attending the same conference. Years later, I was told by Courtland Cox, "I don't know much about that trip to Cuba, but he upset SNCC people a great deal speaking off the top of his head. He was speaking a lot for himself at that point."[22]

It isn't clear how much the Cubans knew of this tension, given their own projection of Fidel and Che as global icons coupled with a desire to avoid interference in the US movement's often confusing organizational dynamics. But when Stokely learned that his US passport would be suspended, he defiantly decided on a global odyssey that was very much paved by the Cubans. Stokely, inspired by his reception in Havana, asked if they could help introduce him to other revolutionary leaders, governments, and movements around the world. A day later, his Cuban hosts returned to his room and said, "You were invited by everyone. Where do you want to go first?"[23] He had no money and his passport was useless.

And so the trek began. A fully loaded Cubana flight through Madrid was turned back when it appeared that the FBI would take Stokely into custody upon landing. The plane refueled, the journey began again, eventually transporting Stokely to Algeria, Syria, Guinea, Egypt, and Tanzania, where Stokely was honored with meetings with Ahmed Sékou Touré of Guinea, Kwame Nkrumah (who had been ousted in a coup the year before in

Ghana), Amílcar Cabral of Guinea-Bissau, and Ho Chi Minh, among many others. There was time for hops to Sweden, Paris, and Copenhagen, where he met Jean-Paul Sartre.

Somewhere along the way Stokely developed an idea that he conveyed to the Cubans, that an African American unit should fight in *their* own African homelands, perhaps Guinea-Bissau. This, he thought, would be consistent with the Cuban strategy of expanding the third world revolution, a way to show solidarity with Africa, and, according to academic Piero Gleijeses, "to atone for [African American] participation in the war of aggression against Vietnam."[24] In 2013, I interviewed Courtland Cox, Stokely's friend and SNCC leader, and Gleijeses to understand the veracity of this story. The tale is not mentioned in Peniel Joseph's excellent biography, *Stokely* (2014), but is included in Stokely's own memoir, with Michael Thelwell, *Ready for Revolution* (2005). The evidence is compelling.

When I asked Courtland Cox in 2013, his memory was hazy. "Recruiting or arming people, that didn't come up in SNCC," Courtland Cox told me. "But it's also clear that Stokely was not opposed to armed struggle in Africa, and had no reason to hide that."

Gleijeses has interviewed the Cuban officers assigned to Stokely's trip and studied Cuban archives to confirm the proposed project. In September 1967, two Cuban intelligence officers—Víctor Dreke and Oscar Estrada—arranged Stokely's visit to Conakry, the capital of Guinea, where Stokely presented his guerrilla plan to Amílcar Cabral, leader of the popular liberation movement, who had attended the Tricontinental meetings in Havana. Cabral, according to Gleijeses, was initially wary about the possible provocation. But he agreed to a contingent of twenty or thirty African Americans, on the condition that they be trained in another country. The Cubans then accompanied Stokely to Tanzania, where Julius Nyerere agreed. By November the arrangements were made.

Why did these senior Cuban intelligence officers assist this project? "Carmichael came up with the idea, and the Cubans were sympathetic out of respect for the struggle of African Americans," Gleijeses speculated to me. "That was the only reason. Cabral didn't need these people."

After Tanzania, however, the Cuban officers said they never heard from Stokely again. "This wasn't a joke, because Cuba had very little money and they were paying for Stokely's travels with hard currency," Gleijeses told me. Why the plan fizzled is a matter of conjecture. Some scholars, like the SNCC historian Clayborne Carson, still scoff at the veracity of the whole tale. Michael Thelwell, now an emeritus professor at Amherst and coauthor of the autobiography in which Stokely twice asserts his interest in an armed African American unit, told me that, "I can very well see him saying it in a rush of revolutionary enthusiasm, some sort of fantasy," likening it to the Panthers' Huey Newton once promising regiments to fight with the Viet Cong.[25] Stokely's Pan-African thesis, with its fundamental emphasis on race consciousness, caused frictions with his Cuban hosts too.[26] The Soviet KGB began spreading false rumors that Stokely was a "CIA agent," casting a shadow over his relationships with Cuba.[27]

There is a more cynical analysis offered by Gleijeses: "Then he met the South African singer Miriam Makeba and his plans changed." According to Gleijeses, Dreke remarked of Stokely, "He dropped us." He married Makeba, became a citizen of Guinea, and settled down."[28] That is surely less than the whole story, although Stokely did marry the internationally celebrated singer and they did live in Guinea. Not only was Makeba herself a revolutionary activist, but Stokely was appointed a personal deputy to the exiled Kwame Nkrumah, joined a Pan-African party, and once took part in a risky sabotage raid over the border in Ghana.[29] Ever-present assassination rumors put Stokely's life at risk wherever he traveled. While it may never be entirely clear why the plan for an armed African American unit evaporated, it was not because Stokely settled down to married life. He himself was quite clear in his autobiography

that even after marrying Makeba, "I really wanted to participate as a frontline fighter."[30]

What would have been the geostrategic consequences of
black American guerrillas, including Stokely Carmichael,
fighting in Africa? Thirty combatants would have made no
material difference. Stokely was clearly wrong in believing that
the Black Power movement would "inevitably grow stronger
and clearer" on an international basis, meaning that his African
role would simply mean a change of location in the same
struggle.[31] But politically, reports of Stokely and American
blacks fighting against Portuguese colonialists or South African
apartheid might have exposed Washington's strong historic ties
to those white power structures, sharply highlighted Washington's hypocrisy, and further internationalized the civil rights
struggle at home. But it was not to be.

Whatever the plan, the whole global tour also suggested how
isolated Stokely had become from SNCC and the Black Power
movement he had been leading in the United States only two
years earlier. Not only was Stokely becoming detached, divisions were growing between SNCC and the Black Panther
Party over revolutionary leadership and ideology at home,
including the question of black nationalism versus united
fronts. The united front concept might have been an unachiev-
able fantasy, in the United States. The threats against him were
real. But consider what the exiled Stokely was leaving behind.
He had a mass following in the United States rivaling that of
Dr. King and was reenergizing the legacy of Malcolm X. His
thesis on Black Power was a best-selling book by that name,
coauthored with Professor Charles Hamilton.[32] Plans were
underway to organize a Black United Front under Stokely's
leadership in the nation's capital by the time of the 1968 Poor
People's March on Washington called by Dr. King. In a major-
ity-black Washington, D.C., imagine the potential impact of
a Black Power movement headquartered in a virtual colony of
the federal government, under the leadership of Stokely Car-

michael! Local marches would be "national" marches simulta-neously. The demand for congressional representation would sharpen like a spear pointed at the federal government's double standard. New relations with foreign embassies would blossom. Every federal employee and member of the government and their staffs would be impacted as they walked the streets and read the press accounts. Tourists from around the world would visit the Black Power capital of America just beyond the White House gates. It might have been too much for the American establishment to bear. Threats of assassination and counterin-telligence plots could have turned into action against Stokely. The deep tragedy lay in America's inability to accommodate a perceived threat from a black revolutionary who had been a young social-Democratic Freedom Rider only five years before. It was similar to the US failure to find a way to accommodate the Cubans from 1959 to 1966 until the revolution had become Tricontinental in scope.

The path to international media attention, however, forked far from Stokely's roots in SNCC, civil disobedience, and empowerment of local people. Stokely became an African exile at just the moment when the movements in the United States were crumbling or splintering beyond repair. SNCC faltered at home and internationally, just as SDS had in 1969 after the Weatherman faction marched toward militancy while leaving the organization behind at a key moment.

As SNCC and the Black Panthers soon faded, the more mainstream civil rights movement began successful campaigns to elect numerous black mayors and other officials and become more or less integrated into the Carter administration. Granting substantive reform—a voice and a vote—became the American way of channeling rage away from the burning barricades. Hun-dreds of blacks were elected to local offices across the South, followed by a new era of black mayors, at least twenty of them being elected between 1967 and 1979, all relative moderates who owed their victories to the civil rights movement and forerunners like Stokely.³³ The "revolution" of urban insurrections turned out to be a storm that could be contained. While the Cuban Revolution had consolidated its storms (Moncada, the Sierra) into a functioning if besieged government, in America, the uprisings left many revolutionary organizations isolated, divided, and infiltrated. In Los Angeles the post-riot promise to "Rebuild LA" became a farce. Black officials could not enforce the promised investment; instead, the reality became disinvestment from the inner city and gradual gentrification. The same happened in Newark, Detroit, and Chicago: massive white flight, corporate disinvestment, and the rise of gangs to exploit underground drug economies. Over many years, however, the insurrections of the sixties yielded up the Congressional Black and Hispanic Caucuses and, finally, the presidency of Barack Obama. One can argue that the riots in American cities led to reform but not revolution. And as I shall argue, the revolution in Cuba would lead from the heights of third world revolution back toward the necessities of reform for people living on the island. The journey was circuitous.

CUBA'S ROLE IN AFRICA

Cuba carried on with its Africa mission. Rarely had such a small third world country intervened militarily on such faraway battlegrounds, a global reach previously monopolized by the white colonial and imperial powers. This Cuban internationalism also was contrary to the mainstream political theory that nation states follow narrow state interests and hew to their geographic spheres of interest, doctrines developed from Machiavelli to Metternich. Cuba was the exception. The CIA frequently acknowledged Fidel's "sense of revolutionary mission."³⁴

RICARDO: *Africa was one of the best moments of Fidel's military and diplomatic career. He followed those battles as if he were there.*

Details. Close contacts with our people. In the same manner he followed the negotiations. We defeated the South Africans in Angola; they were humiliated. Many white South Africans were angry because their troops were being killed by black Africans and black Cubans.

The common official and media interpretation in the United States. that Cuban troops were ferried to Angola as paid tools of Soviet expansion on the African front of the Cold War. The evidence is the reverse. Cuba indeed had Soviet support, but the Cubans also were an independent revolutionary catalyst acting at times without Soviet knowledge or support. The Cubans viewed the world in a North-South context more than an East-West one. As the *New York Times'* Herbert Matthews wrote, Fidel saw the Cubans in Africa "as standard bearers for the non-aligned countries of the world."[35] As a consequence of this distorted Cold War perspective, the most significant opportunity for US-Cuban rapprochement was squandered during the well-intentioned presidency of Jimmy Carter.

Cuba's military initiatives in Africa went awry in Che's Congo mission, when tribal unity proved elusive and Cuban advisers returned home in 1965. As early as 1966, Cuba sent military trainers and doctors to Guinea-Bissau at the request of Amílcar Cabral.[36] With Cuban advisers, the forces of Guinea-Bissau defeated the Portuguese army, which provoked a revolution by left-wing generals in April 1974, bringing down the Salazar dictatorship. Immediately a struggle for power unfolded across Africa's new postcolonial battlefields. Cuba's allies were the MPLA led by Agostinho Neto, whom Che had visited in 1965[37] and who participated in the 1966 Tricontinental in Havana. A second grouping was the FNLA led by the CIA's paid ally Holden Roberto and also supported by China for Cold War reasons,[38] and the Congo's dictator Joseph Mobutu.[39] A third movement, UNITA, was headed by Jonas Savimbi, formerly allied with the colonial power and backed by the apartheid South African regime.[40] Power-sharing talks held in November 1975 deadlocked, plunging Angola into civil war. Fidel, though "preoccupied with internal developments" in Cuba (Gott, p. 252),[41] nevertheless dispatched hundreds of advisers and special forces, allowing the Neto government to declare independence on November 11.

RICARDO: *On a global level, we had Angola. It was a factor that would complicate relations with the United States. Remember too that those years were the peak of the anti–Cuba terrorist campaign. [Allende's foreign minister Orlando] Letelier was assassinated.[42] The Cubana airliner was shot down.[43] That was the last chapter of a series of sabotages against airlines. I don't know how far the US policy of attacking us would have gone.*

God, you don't have to be very analytic to figure out something was going on in Portugal. Who was doing the US analysis? In 1974 came the end of the Portuguese fascist regime,[44] which led to the decolonization process in Portugal's empire. We already had links with the MPLA in Angola and FRELIMO, the liberation movement in Mozambique. The MPLA asked for help. Mobutu was a threat on their north and South Africa from the south. It was not some arbitrary decision by Fidel or Che, but simply that the history did that. We went into Angola in 1975.

This was not "normal" behavior for a nation-state. Cuba faced violent attacks internally, remained under US pressure ninety miles away, and was allied with a Soviet Union seeking détente with Washington. Fidel, nonetheless, became preoccupied with defeating the United States and South Africa in Angola, Mozambique, Guinea-Bissau, and Namibia. That he did so was a military achievement that shook the continent. Americans were engaged in covert military operations against the transitional administration, sending weapons and trainers to the FNLA and UNITA.[45] For the racist South Africans, it was vital to shore up their border client, Namibia, then controlled by a white minority and sandwiched between Angola and the apartheid state's border. For the United States, it was important to keep American support for apartheid as discreet as possible, while framing the conflict as one of stopping the advance of the Soviet Union in Africa. Whatever the Cold War rationale, the contradiction for Washington was being on the side of Portugal and South Africa during the time of a new civil rights era at home.

On October 14, South African troops invaded Angola; on November 4, Fidel decided to intervene with Cuban troops to stop the South Africans from reaching Luanda, the Angolan capital. The South Africans had troops, tanks, and planes, and might have broken the MPLA's defense perimeters. According to official documents, Cuba made its decision without first consulting the Soviet Union; by contrast, the South African Defense official said, "We did so with the approval and knowledge of the Americans."[46]

On March 27, 1976, South African troops pulled back from Angola, rebuffed by the Cuban forces.[47] It was a stunning defeat for the white regional superpower. The war for Namibian independence now was underway, since the MPLA's Neto now could open his safe border sanctuary to the black Namibian fighters of SWAPO. The death knell also sounded for white South Africa since, for the first time, White Power had suffered military defeat. According to Gleijeses, "Cuban troops were Angola's shield against the South Africans [and] even the CIA conceded that the Cuban presence was 'necessary to preserve Angolan independence.'"[48]

The decisive battle came at a small town named Cuito Cuanavale in September 1987 when South Africa was cornering Angola's best military units. But Fidel sent his best available units to stop the South Africans in their tracks, "stripping Cuba's defenses at home down to the bone."[49] Cuba's risk taking entered history in southern Africa and among third world countries, but is missing in the mainstream American narrative of South Africa. For Fidel, according to one South African general, Angola was "South Africa's Bay of Pigs."[50]

On many occasions in coming years, Nelson Mandela would bless Cuba for the "selflessness" that he declared it showed in southern Africa.[51] Cuba also trained thousands of Angolan doctors, engineers, and schoolteachers; the Cubans carried out one million medical consultations and sixteen thousand surgeries in a nine-month period of 1977 alone.[52]

A more complex African war began with Somalia's 1977 invasion of Ethiopia, following a leftist coup that took power there with promises of land reform and literacy campaigns. The Cubans deployed twelve thousand soldiers on the rationale of protecting the sovereign Ethiopia from a cross-border invasion from Somalia. Unlike the Angolan intervention, however, this Cuban invasion was closely coordinated with the Soviet Union, ringing alarms more loudly in Washington.

In 1976 Jimmy Carter became the first American president to pledge the normalization of relations with Cuba. At the moment of celebration, it wasn't clear that Cold War considerations could cancel this bright promise.

RICARDO: *I was the UN ambassador. To me, [balancing] normalization with Cuba against the Angolan war was apples and oranges. The United States was not the colonizing power there, but Portugal was. The United States was not attacking Angola, it was South Africa that was attacking.*

According to Havana, 2,400 Cubans gave their lives in the African military campaigns.[53] Another four hundred thousand Cuban families experienced separations from the departing troops, usually under a cloud of secrecy about their destinations. The Cuban people were told the fighters were on "international missions." The campaigns—and their casualties—were little reported in the Cuban media, but eventually became a source of national pride. Veterans of the Angolan wars would include Rodolfo Reyes, head of the Cuban mission at the UN, who showed me his wooden leg when I interviewed him in 2014. Another is René González, one of the Cuban Five, who spent thirteen years in an American prison and now resides in Havana. They are experienced at both fighting and negotiating with superpowers.

RICARDO: *I was part of the team in the four-part negotiations between Angola, South Africa, Cuba, the United States, and the USSR, with the Russians there as observers. The Cuban troops withdrew, South Africa withdrew, and that led to a SWAPO victory. We met mostly in Brazzaville* [capital of the Congo], *but also in New York and Geneva. The accord of Brazzaville was then signed before the UN Security Council.*

Some of the meetings were in apartheid South Africa, in Pretoria, in Capetown, and in a resort at the Kruger National Park near the Mozambique border. We were together with the Angolans in a joint delegation. We represented SWAPO and the ANC/Mandela, not officially or formally, but in consultation with them. We tried to represent their interests [and did so] *as was proven by history.*

We also had a meeting in Namibia at Mount Etjo Safari Lodge, which I visited last year [2012]. *It was a little motel. They organized excursions to see the animals at night, tigers, lions; you sit silently looking through a wooden barricade. The Boers are a peculiar people, getting very excited at spending three or four hours a night without doing anything. I went back to the same place last year. There was the same guy, the white owner, and he says hello and invites me to go to a little shop where there was this photo of Mount Etjo Safari Lodge. He was still there after apartheid was gone.*

To be there in those days was quite an experience. For example, this sounds like a joke, but it's true. Namibia was a territory under foreign [South African] *occupation. We arrived at the airport from Luanda. We would sit down in a small protocol room, then take a small military plane to Mount Etjo.* [I went again last year by helicopter.] *We were completely isolated, didn't see Namibia. But when the meetings were over, we did a reverse trip. From Windhoek it was not possible to go to Luanda. So the South African officers invited us to make a tour around town. It was beautiful, like a post card with many flowers and trees.*

And suddenly we crossed near a low wall and saw painted there a Namibian slogan, "Long live MPLA! Long live Cuba! Long live SWAPO!" We asked them, "Can you stop for us to take a photo?" When we got out of the van, a very old man was coming, walking with difficulty, and he saw us taking photos of this completely illegal graffiti. He asked who we were, and when we said Cubans, he said, "You are Cubans from Cuba? I have a grandson in the Isle of Youth!"[54]

Another time when we were in Cape Town I needed something for my stomach, an antacid, and was accompanied by a Namibian security officer to a store. Very close to me was a black South African. When I was going to pay, the security guy said, "Don't charge him taxes, he's a diplomat." "Where is he from?" the black man asked. "Cuba," they said. "That's not true. Cuba doesn't support the apartheid regime!" It was very confusing for him, but it shows how much the local people knew.

The experience was very interesting because it wasn't formal diplomacy. Imagine the little motel, with nothing to do but walk around. Near the end we reached a compromise with South Africa and were finalizing the agreement when some SWAPO troops entered Namibia from Angola and the South Africans went mad and threatened to blow up the talks, everything. It was then that we held the emergency meeting at Mount Etjo to put the process back on track.

At the end of our negotiations, we had a good compromise after so many years of fighting each other. These people eat a lot of meat, the meat of animals they hunt. Of course there were some toasts. My friend "Pik" Botha [a moderate Afrikaner who served as foreign minister of the apartheid regime and later as a minister in the Nelson Mandela cabinet] *rose up and said, in a strong German accent, "My dear Cuban colleagues, I have devoted almost my entire life to defending my country, and demanding the withdrawal of the Cubans from Africa. And now that there finally is an agreement that will lead to the Cuban withdrawal, I want to tell my friends that we shall miss you."*

Now that we were friends, we were going. At the beginning you can imagine that we were very far apart. And we were nearing the end of the Soviet Union. The ANC and SWAPO were very wise in the way that they handled it. To our advantage, we had won the war in the field. The ANC underground leaders came to Cuba from time to time to talk, and they were always in communication with their leaders in prison. At the end it was good for everybody. The South African whites continued to have their properties, just like the guy I met again in Mount Etjo.

The American diplomat, Chester A. Crocker, signed the agreements with Ricardo, Pik Botha, and the Angolans at Brazzaville before the foreign ministers signed at the United Nations. According to Wikipedia, "Crocker, architect of the US policy of 'constructive engagement' toward apartheid South Africa, is credited with setting the terms of Namibian independence." Defeat is not admitted in this narrative, and Cuba doesn't exist.

RICARDO: *George Shultz was the US secretary of state. He came to the signing at the US Mission across from the United Nations. I shook his hand. Our delegation included a lot of generals who had participated in the Angolan war. Everybody shook hands. Crocker and I had drinks, lunch, and we talked, it was all very informal. The diplomatic relationship between the United States and Cuba never came up.*

I had interviewed the same Chester Crocker in 1981 during a visit to the new nation of Zimbabwe, formerly Rhodesia. Crocker was part of the Reagan administration, which had come to power partly in opposition to Jimmy Carter's overtures toward Cuba. He favored avoiding sanctions against South Africa in favor of constructive engagement with the apartheid government. I asked Ricardo to tell me more about his encounters with Crocker.

RICARDO: *Crocker was at the center of everything. He is a colleague of mine, but frankly, while he is better equipped intellectually than many others, he wasn't that wise a man on Africa.*

I remember one afternoon by a pool in Brazzaville, he was having a drink and, to my surprise, he asked me what I thought about this country. He says, "I see so much Russian influence." "What?" I said. "Those are French people, not Russians, by the bar."

Ricardo Alarcón proved his skills as Cuba's representative in the complex peace diplomacy that followed the battlefield losses of Portugal and South Africa. As a result of those negotiations, the internationally supervised elections in the new Namibia resulted in political victory for the liberation fighters of SWAPO. Ricardo helped hammer out an agreement that would have been unthinkable previously. While the US diplomats merely talked of constructive engagement to mask their alliance with South Africa, Ricardo actually implemented a kind of constructive engagement at the conference table, one that ended apartheid's grip instead of "constructively" reforming it. American officials like George Shultz and Chester Crocker recognized the achievement by shaking Ricardo's hand at the end of the difficult proceedings. But the US government, while recognizing Cuba's vital role, could not recognize Cuba itself. The shadow of Cold War politics prevented an opportunity for rapprochement from being realized.

CHAPTER 11

The Liberal Democrats' Default: The Carter Era

After JFK's tentative efforts toward a modus vivendi were cut short by his assassination, Lyndon Johnson "was not inclined even to probe" a new Cuba policy, according to a lead American diplomat in Havana, Wayne Smith.[1] Fifty years later in Havana, I was interviewing Smith as he relaxed with Ricardo Alarcón at the Nacional, another case of "two old guys talking" about what might have been. Smith has long acknowledged that he was often wrong in the early days; he travels to the island frequently and advocates freeing the Cuban Five. Everything has changed, it seems, except for the fundamentals of US policy.

Seeking perhaps to lessen Cuba's isolation, Fidel floated the possibility of rapprochement again through Lisa Howard and in a long interview with the *New York Times'* Richard Eder in July 1964. Fidel sent a message that he wanted a channel of communication to avert crises. In response, UN ambassador Adlai Stevenson interpreted the message as conveying "that all our crises could be avoided if there was some way to communicate."[2] In the Eder interview, Fidel went further, offering to halt assistance to Latin American guerrilla revolutionaries in exchange for the United States cutting support for the Cuban exile operations. He also agreed to release political prisoners and begin talks on fair compensation for American properties seized by the revolution.[3] His entreaties failed to prevent the Organization of American States from terminating commercial and diplomatic relations by a 15-4 vote.[4] The Cubans seemed to be undertaking the initiative with formal Soviet encouragement. Fidel offered to discontinue "material" aid to Latin American countries if they promised peaceful relations with Havana, and indicated that his political repression could be relaxed if the covert American policies of subversion ceased permanently. In retrospect, according to the administration's leading Cuba expert at the time, Wayne Smith, Fidel's offer should have been taken up.[5] But the State Department immediately rejected the idea, and when asked why the US government traded with the Soviet Union but not with Cuba, Dean Rusk said the Soviets were a "permanent fixture" and the Castro government only temporary.[6] The essence of US policy was revealed in Johnson's April 1965 invasion of the Dominican Republic to overthrow a democratically elected government amidst declared fears of "another Cuba."[7] In that same year, the United States curtailed the sale of food and medicine unless licensed by the Commerce Department, which rarely happened. Johnson also began prosecuting Americans who violate the Cuba travel ban, over the strong objections of attorney general Bobby Kennedy.[8] In 1968, a progressive State Department policy planning-paper favoring "positive containment," "the controlled relaxation of US pressures," and a modus vivendi went nowhere.[9]

One reason for the government's reluctance to engage constructively with Cuba was that the CIA and Special Forces were seeking to track and kill Che Guevara, not accommodate his "two, three, many Vietnams" agenda. Not by accident, two Cuban American exiles—Félix Rodríguez and Gustavo Villoldo—were taking part at the operations level in Bolivia.[10] Rodríguez, a cadre in the CIA's Brigade 2506 against Fidel and Che, was present at the shooting of Che and later claimed that the assassination was ordered by the Bolivian military after conferring with Washington.

Even in death and defeat, Che's strategy of "two, three, many Vietnams" served its purpose. Besieged by Vietnam in 1967, the CIA was ordered to escalate and reprioritize its covert operations toward Indochina. This meant that "it would have to close its largest and most expensive outpost in the world—the CIA station in Miami," LeoGrande and Kornbluh write.[11] Though it would drag on another five years, "the heyday of CIA-sponsored exile operations against Cuba was over."[12]

THE CARTER YEARS

When the next Democratic president, Jimmy Carter, took office in 1977, he declared normalization to be the US policy goal; but after a promising start, his effort was shut down as "impossible" by his national security adviser, Zbigniew Brzezinski.[13] When Carter left office, the politically powerful right-wing Cuba lobby positioned itself to play a domineering role in US politics under Ronald Reagan and thereafter. When Bill Clinton campaigned for president in 1992, he endorsed the so-called Torricelli law (Cuban Democracy Act) aimed at regime change in Cuba, and then, when the Cubans shot down a Miami-based exile plane that had repeatedly violated the airspace around Havana and even dropped leaflets calling for the overthrow of the government, Clinton signed the Helms-Burton Act, which toughened sanctions and effectively ceded to Congress his executive powers over the embargo and diplomatic relations. His liberalized people-to-people travel initiatives did not change the fact that once again a liberal Democrat maintained, and even hardened, the blockade.

Each of these Democratic presidencies were followed by far more hostile Republican ones: Richard Nixon after Johnson, Ronald Reagan after Carter, the second George Bush after Clinton. Whenever a Democrat was returned to the presidency, any liberal promise of normalization evaporated in the face of a recurrent Cold War anticommunism. Even after the Soviet Union's collapse, and with it the end of the rationale that the Cubans were a Soviet pawn in the hemisphere, the embargo went on.

A few standard explanations have been offered for the Democratic default: US policy seemed to be based on waiting for Fidel to die, as the Cuban leader once told a Carter adviser, the late Robert Pastor. Following the death of its leader, it was assumed Cuba would follow the fallen Eastern European socialist countries back into the US sphere of influence.

It was claimed by Carter advisers that Fidel was to blame, in one of two ways: either he was a megalomaniac or a tool of Soviet expansionism. Invading Latin America or dispatching Cuban troops to Africa were more important to Fidel that normalizing relations with the United States, they concluded.

Some said the Cuban leadership privately wanted the embargo and nonrecognition to continue because those policies provided an "external enemy" to justify the Cuban regime's tight controls on its domestic population. On its face, this was a bizarre argument: that the embargo the United States maintained in order to strangle Cuba actually was strengthening the Cuban regime. If this was so, of course, the United States could have dropped the policy at any time.

Not recognizing a Havana regime that suppressed free speech, held rigged elections and was controlled by a Communist might look like good domestic politics. The Cuba lobby had enough money and votes to decisively sway Florida politics and the Electoral College. So one after another, Democratic presidents ended up taking the easy route.

These arguments in retrospect range between laughable and obsolete. Cuba, unlike Eastern Europe, survived the dissolution of the Soviet bloc. In any case, even during the Cold War, the United States maintained diplomatic and economic relations with the Soviet Union and, since 1971, with China. Cuban troops departed Africa, and Cuba was praised by Nelson Mandela, an

American icon, for making possible the defeat of South African apartheid. Cuba developed proper diplomatic relations with every nation in Central and Latin America. Cuba continued to survive the embargo. The UN General Assembly condemned the US embargo year after year by near-unanimous votes. The United States meanwhile recognized all sorts of ghastly undemocratic regimes. The Cuba lobby, while troublesome, gradually lost its decisive role in Florida, New Jersey, and therefore the Electoral College. A majority of Cubans in the United States, while generally opposing the Castro regime, now favor normal relations, freedom of travel, lifting the embargo, and a gradual, peaceful transition to a sovereign Cuban future.

America's Cuba policy, to paraphrase Tom Paine, is a case where the weight of older generations hangs heavily on the rights of living ones. But how to remove the carcass? One must first reconsider the nature of the problem when every past rationale now seems to lack credibility.

My own explanation follows the "Superpower Syndrome" analysis of Harvard professor and author Robert Jay Lifton. A superpower is never really *all*-powerful but is cursed to think it is, which leads to two chronic corollaries: first, the inherent assumption that the world always can be bent to the superpower's will and, second, the resilience and resources of a resisting adversary are underestimated because of an assumption of superiority. A superpower cannot respect as an equal those whom it believes to be lesser. The US government even considers its closest allies, for example, to be friendly *satellites*, but never really coequals. The United States seeks in every way to retain dominance over the global marketplace and military balance of forces in the world. Of course, this arrogant pretense must remain discreet; carried on "off camera," as the neoconservative Robert Kaplan once urged.[14]

The United States is no longer a *sole* superpower, but is impelled for psychological, cultural, and political reasons to insist that we are Number One, especially in "our own backyard," to quote current secretary of state John Kerry. Presidents representing superpower status are unable to admit failure or to retreat. Backtracking from a failed policy must never be admitted, or must be covered up by techniques of "saving face." Reputation is everything.

Cuba has always been a challenge to the Superpower Syndrome. America's nonrecognition of Cuba was among the longest in our diplomatic history, exceeded only by North Korea. When we speak of normalization, does it mean the traditional "normalcy" of superpower dominance, in which Cuba becomes a satellite, or does it mean respect, acceptance, and recognition of Cuba's right to its own independent identity? Must a "solution" to the Cuban problem appear to be a superpower triumph, masked as a victory for Cuba's dissidents, and a defeat for the Cuban Revolution and its leadership? And if the superpower is delusional, how would a solution ever come? Barack Obama's answer in December 2014 was framed as abandoning a failed, counterproductive policy for one more favorable to the American goal of promoting democracy. It was a strategic retreat back toward discarded doctrines of peaceful coexistence.

Ricardo Alarcón would have been the logical choice to be Cuba's ambassador in the United States under normal diplomatic relations. In that role he would have lent greater balance to the mainstream discourse on Cuba and the region. Fidel himself would have been interviewed more frequently in the American media instead of being virtually blacklisted from legitimate dialogue. Crisis management would have been far easier too. Instead, as we shall see, Ricardo was often forced into secrecy, hidden in the backseats of cars or holding clandestine meetings in foreign hotels, to negotiate bilateral agreements on issues like immigration reforms or the return of Elián González to Cuba.

Ricardo seemed to be of several minds in our many conversations on these issues. Once, in reflecting on America's stubborn support of South Africa until the very end, he observed:

RICARDO: *The United States is an arrogant imperial power. You cannot deal rationally with someone like that. They are being educated step by step.*

On the unexpected 2013 release of René González, one of the Cuban Five, to complete his probation at home in Cuba, Ricardo criticized the US prosecutors on the case as a whole, but welcomed the return home of González after thirteen years in American prisons:

RICARDO: *At least it was a rational step, an intelligent step. You come from such a terrible country that every time there is a positive step we have to take note.*

Toward President Obama, Ricardo's feeling was definitely ambivalent. While denouncing Obama for tightening US financial sanctions, and while describing his partial lift of the travel ban as only a return to the Clinton travel policy, Ricardo also had positive things to say, including:

RICARDO: *According to tradition, presidents take bold initiatives at the end of their second term. So according to this theory a solution has to be found now, before another president takes over . . . Obama had very good advisers in his campaign. When he spoke at that theater in Miami, outside there were only a half-dozen old guards with banners saying things like "Obama Communist." Obama has an advantage. He was discovering the Caribbean, as we say.*[15] *He is the first president since Carter to take a different approach to the Miami connection; he recognizes that the Cuban American community isn't the same now as it was in the sixties.*

That was in 2013. Ricardo still harbored doubts about normalization even after the Castro era.

RICARDO: *I don't even think his* [Fidel's] *passing will create an immediate process toward normalization. The reasons and forces*

*behind the current policy are stronger than that. The Right still will
have their catastrophic* [regime change] *scenario. And it's a fundamental assumption of the Americans that they have a right to establish
conditions first, a God-given right. It's a deep-rooted idea that Cuba
belongs to them. Remember* [under Spain's rule] *only Cuba developed a political movement seeking annexation to the United States.
Before the independence movement there were Creole landowners
who preferred incorporation into America rather than losing slavery,
which would have been the consequence of our War of Independence.
The first armed struggles against Spain were seeking Cuba's statehood.
It was very important in intellectual circles in Havana, and Martí
was still fighting it at the end of the century. The Revolution of 1868*[16]
*was the breaking point with its goals of absolute independence, the
elimination of slavery, and a republic based on "perfect equality." It led
to our longest war and a terrible defeat. The United States was deeply
involved. There still is the assumption that they have something to say
about the future of Cuba.*

*I hope I live long enough to see some Chinese statement insisting
that the United States should stop drinking coffee as a condition of
diplomatic relations.*

One of the outcomes of long years fighting in the trenches,
I have come to realize, can be entrenched thinking on all sides.
From the Cuban perspective, they have seen treachery and
false promises repeatedly since 1492. With their very survival
at stake, how prepared should they be to take the risks of new
approaches, including compromises, to resolving the conflict?
Why should Cuba not believe that any overtures from the
United States are aimed at lowering their guard? Ricardo was
not alone in doubting normalization under Obama. In late 2013,
Granma, the official newspaper of the Cuban Communist Party,
published an interview with Ramón Sánchez-Parodi Montoto,
who took part in the secret talks with the Carter administration that led to the Interest Sections being established. After
an initial period of hope, Obama "has never been, in any way,

searching for a normalization of relations. His policy is a light version of the same policy of George Bush Jr."[17] Asked if normalization was near, he said, "With Obama this is not going to happen. It might happen in a future presidential term . . . It is a mistake to think it will be with the Democrats."

Now that normalization is underway, although far from complete, it is useful to revisit the past mistakes of the well-meaning liberal Democrats in hopes of not perpetuating them in Obama's next two years.

JIMMY CARTER AND COLD WAR LIBERALISM, 1977–81

Jimmy Carter rose from the Southern sixties to eradicate the wild excesses of the Nixon years. His ascent to the White House was propelled by the spirit of the civil rights and the anti-Vietnam War movements that had expanded into the popular mainstream in the early seventies as the more radical movement vanguards became exhausted, splintered, and isolated. Rev. Andrew Young, the chief lieutenant to Dr. King, became a Georgia congressman and, to my pleasant surprise, America's representative to the United Nations under Carter. Sam Brown, leader of the Vietnam Moratorium, became a US national security adviser. Hundreds of less-known sixties veterans took offices in state capitals and in Washington.

The same internal divisions remained, however, between the traditional oligarchs in the CIA and Pentagon and the fresh faces being welcomed into the Carter administration. The Cold War remained a basic political dividing line. Carter's civil rights liberalism was balanced against the anticommunist, anti-Soviet imperatives of the Cold War.

Once, in the Oval Office, I brazenly asked the president what he felt about vast and secretive multinational corporations having more power than the elected president of the United

States—himself. The cameras were clicking as Carter answered without hesitation, "I learned that my first year in office."

One of the key questions raised by this book is whether two de facto states coexist in uneasy tension in America, one more open and accountable, driven from below by progressive Democratic constituencies and democratically chosen officials; and quite another one, a secretive and permanent national security state tending to carry out reflexive policies of its own. At times these divisions are blurred or nonexistent, as when the liberal JFK embraced the Green Berets and accepted the CIA's plan for the Bay of Pigs. (He would later be heard to mutter that he wanted to "splinter" and destroy the CIA.)[18] At other times, the gulf becomes a danger to the minimum requirements of democracy, as in the CIA's secret 1954 overthrow of the democratically elected President Arbenz's government in Guatemala, which caused decades of suffering and became a misleading model for the Bay of Pigs. Often portrayed as a clash between "doves" and "hawks," the underlying collision is often over the role of secret operations implemented without the knowledge or oversight of voters or the US Congress, or coverage in the mainstream media. While the rationale given for state secrecy is often a demonized enemy with dangerous weapons, there always is another story than the official one, usually having to do with private corporate interests in markets and natural resources. JFK's CIA director Allen Dulles was a carryover from Eisenhower; he had also represented the United Fruit company's Caribbean interests.[19] From the outset, US hostility to the Cuban Revolution was influenced by the loss of the Mob's casino interests; according to the columnist Jack Anderson, the CIA even contacted mobster Johnny Roselli to aid in one of the numerous attempts against Fidel from 1961 to 1963.[20]

The liberal Democrats were ascendant after the Watergate scandal which, among other illegalities, featured anti-Castro Cuban exiles as part of the "plumbers unit" operating out of the White House. As the divide grew between the Nixon White House and the Democrats, the Senate Foreign Relations Committee actually voted in 1974 *in favor* of diplomatic relations and ending the embargo of Cuba.[21] In July 1975, when Secretary of State Kissinger was exploring normalization, the United States voted in the Organization of American States to allow its member states to lift their diplomatic and economic sanctions against Cuba, though Washington itself chose not to implement the new OAS policy. Then in December 1975, the entire Senate passed an amendment banning US assistance to the FNLA and UNITA factions who were fighting the Cubans in Angola.[22] Early in 1975, Kissinger said in a speech that there was no point in "perpetual antagonism" between Cuba and the United States. Secret talks were held in places like a cafeteria at the LaGuardia airport.[23] As my friend the late Saul Landau told me:

SAUL LANDAU: *I was hired by* [Frank] *Mankiewicz* [a former top aide to the Kennedys] *to take a note from Kissinger to Fidel. I had asked Mankiewicz to ask Kissinger to send the note, which he did, saying let's open a dialogue. So meetings were held for a year in a little hotel near La Guardia. It led finally to the Interest Sections being set up.*[24]

This liberalizing trend flowed into the era of Jimmy Carter, who became the first president to declare a policy of normal relations. Carter's secretary of state Cyrus Vance officially endorsed normalization in his 1977 Senate confirmation hearings.[25] He made a point of saying that a Cuban troop withdrawal from Angola was *not* a precondition for talks to begin. By March, Carter refused to renew the official travel ban as well as the prohibition on Americans using their dollars on the island.[26] He also suspended US surveillance flights over Cuba. Talks made progress on maritime boundaries and fishing rights. Interest Sections, then considered to be interim steps toward full-fledged embassies, were established in Havana and Washington. Encouraging statements were made from the Cuban side; for example, defense minister, now president, Raúl Castro told two US senators that "the war has ended and now we are reconstructing the bridge brick by brick, ninety miles from Key West to Varadero. It takes a long time, but at the end of the bridge, we can shake hands without winners or losers."[27]

UN ambassador Andrew Young ventured much farther than any US official before him. I was present when he told a Tulane University audience in April 1977, "I am not afraid of communism. It's never been a threat to me as it is to some folks. And I don't think we should be so worried about Cubans in Africa. The threat to me has always been racism. We've got to get beyond the capitalism versus communism, Cold War type of debate and make the issue one of oppression, wherever it exists, in whatever system."[28] Andy was quoted as saying that Cuban troops in Angola could even bring "a certain stability and order to southern Africa."[29]

I had known Andy and his associate, Coretta Scott King, since I first migrated to Atlanta and the sit-in movement. Carter, a white born-again Southerner, had been elected president with massive support from the newly empowered African American community. The year 1976 saw Ralph Nader welcomed at a Carter softball game in Plains, Georgia, as the umpire. I was running for US Senate in the California Democratic primary, where I lost but received 1.3 million votes. Carter was about to issue an amnesty for American war resisters, including those in Canada. Ranking members of the Nixon administration were on their way to jail.

For that short moment—call it the *Carter Spring*—the radicalism of the sixties appeared to be becoming the common sense of the future. I was naive. Cold War thinking would never end within the labyrinth of the national security state. It would simply find a way to regain its footing. The Cold War state being built on the fear of communism, no US ambassador to the UN could be allowed to say otherwise. Especially not an uppity newcomer like Andy Young.

Ricardo was more skeptical of change, based on his own experience, but nonetheless was pleased with Carter's new team.

RICARDO: *The new US administration was a diverse and colorful group. My American colleagues were my friends. Andy Young and I had a very good personal relationship before and during. I would tell him that he was the imperialist ambassador and I was representing his victim, a fact that had to be clear. We were friends, however.*

I said one day that if I have to argue with you I will be harsher than I am with others. So one day he made a pretty strong speech against Cuba over Africa and Angola, and I was pretty tough in my reply. And so Coretta King called me. She asked, "Did you get my invitation to the party? No? It must have been a mistake! Please come at seven tonight."

So I went to the American mission that night for a moment of relaxation. I was convinced that the last-minute invite had to do with the speech. Coretta said to me, "Andy read what you said. He's a good guy, but he has to follow instructions." Etcetera. Then Andy came over. "Listen, Ricardo," he said, "before you say anything. I read what you said, and I agree with you. I just want you to read the draft I got from the State Department." It was a far harsher statement than Andy had made.

On June 4, 2013, I flew from Miami to Havana on a plane also carrying Wayne Smith, the former head of Carter's Interest Section in the seventies, the man who most likely would have been America's first ambassador to Cuba. Now nearing eighty, and a long-time advocate of normalization, Smith was on one of the seemingly endless trips he has taken to Cuba since 1957, when he was a graduate student and budding foreign service officer.[30] As an example of his longevity, and the intractable nature of the Cuba issue, he mentioned that the elevator we rode in the Hotel Nacional was the same one he used on his first visit fifty-six years before.

I told Smith what I was writing about, and when I asked if he could point to the most important reason that the promising normalization process was terminated in 1977, he immediately blurted out a single-word expletive, "Brzezinski."

At the earlier described background briefing on November 16, 1977, for a select circle of journalists, Brzezinski not only said normalization was "impossible" but claimed that a new CIA "study" reported a frightening buildup over the summer of Cuban troops in Angola and Ethiopia as well as a spread of Cuban troops to thirteen African countries.[31]

As later generations perhaps have learned, such classified studies often are used as instruments of public perception management. In 1950, the architects of the Cold War forecast a Kremlin conspiracy to take over the world militarily. JFK hyped a Soviet missile advantage in his 1960 campaign against Richard Nixon. The same tactic of threat escalation was employed to ignite US involvement in the Iraq War; according to an infamous British document, the Bush intelligence team fixed the facts to fit their policy preference.[32]

In an identical way, Brzezinski was quashing Carter's plan to normalize relations with Cuba. Smith, in his account, told the White House that the CIA's threat estimate about Cubans in Angola wasn't true.[33] There was no "dramatic buildup" in Angola, "not a buildup but a revision in our own bookkeeping," said Smith.[34] The larger implication that Cuba was serving as Moscow's tool for taking over Africa was ludicrous. According to historian Richard Gott, Cuba began sending combat troops to Ethiopia in the autumn of 1977 and weapons in January 1978.[35] Gott concludes that "Cuba's intervention was as decisive in Ethiopia as it had been in Angola and it broke the back of the Somali advance into the Ogaden [the territory over which they had been fighting]."[36] Fidel certainly can be criticized for an irrational belief that there was a road from nomadism to socialism in Ethiopia. Valid questions can be raised about whether the deployment of Cuban troops to Ethiopia, geographically very different from their ancestral African homelands, was worth the cost in Cuban lives and resources. But the Cuban role in Africa could hardly be described as illegitimate when compared to the assumed natural rights of American, Portuguese, French, and other Western troops in propping up the status quo.

Brzezinski's "granite" resistance to any thaw with Cuba was demonstrated again in 1978–1979 when he refused to support the first major dialogue between Castro and the Committee of 75, a delegation of Cuban exiles from Miami, a process of dialogue that resulted in significant prisoner releases and increases in family visits to the island.[37]

Wayne Smith was far from being a Fidelista. His valuable book, *Closest of Enemies*, describes US policy more as a series of botched opportunities than anything deeper, and it blames Fidel for placing his global revolutionary ambitions ahead of making up with the United States at key moments. Smith's implication is that it was both necessary and right for the United States to contain Cuba's revolutionary impulses in Latin America and Africa. Fifty years later, however, we are still living with the consequences of those judgments. In a touching scene in 2013, I witnessed Ricardo and Wayne Smith shaking hands and enjoying friendly banter on the spacious outdoor patio of the Hotel Nacional, "two old guys" who might have been the ambassadors in Havana and Washington, now simply might-have-beens, reflecting on days gone by over cigars and mojitos.

When I interviewed him in 2013, the late Robert "Bob" Pastor, Carter's former lead official on Cuba and Latin America, was still defending the Carter administration's failure to normalize in 1977 as the only outcome possible. Unlike Wayne Smith, Pastor says that Carter's *entire* national security team, not simply Brzezinski, turned cold on the normalization process at the end of 1977. The reason, he said, was Cuba's intervention in Africa, particularly in Ethiopia. He seemed eager to underscore his longstanding views.

ROBERT PASTOR: *Nobody worked harder on these issues than Wayne Smith. But his answer is too simplistic. Carter leaped over a hurdle left in place by Kissinger who said we wouldn't normalize until the Cubans left Angola. Carter was the first to say the purpose was to normalize, and that a discussion of reducing their troops* [in Africa] *was necessary. Later Carter said any expansion of the troops would make it impossible to normalize. That was the difference between us and Castro, in that he questioned why he shouldn't demand that NATO troops be withdrawn. We decided the opposite, that it was more important to stop Soviet–Cuban interests in Africa with the Cubans being under a Soviet general.*[38] *Castro thought it was more important to pursue his foreign policy.*

Pastor was a heavyweight in Latin America policy circles from his days as staff director of the 1976 Linowitz Commission, which first recommended to Carter the improvement of relations with Cuba.[39] Since the Carter years Pastor tirelessly advocated for more progressive policies toward Cuba and the region as a whole. He traveled with ex-president Carter twice to Cuba. Yet he continued to justify the suspension of diplomatic progress in 1977 as inevitable and appropriate. I could sense uncertainty in his choice of words, however.

PASTOR: *I negotiated with Ricardo* [Alarcón] *ten times under Carter and fifteen times since then. I have great respect for him.*
Did we think it would take this long? Back then, I thought sixteen years was too long! It's quite upsetting. Carter himself wishes he did . . . [Pastor corrects himself] *Carter today looks back and regrets we couldn't go forward but it was politically infeasible at the moment with thousands of Cubans in Ethiopia fighting under a Soviet general. Andy Young thought I was too tough.*

Pastor described the Carter administration as unified around the Brzezinski position, starting with the president himself. In a 2012 journal article, however, Pastor said there was "a divisive debate within the Carter administration."[40] I asked Pastor again what would have happened if Carter had followed the views of Andrew Young.

PASTOR: *Well, Carter didn't get SALT II anyway,*[41] *and he lost the November election. It's tragic we haven't been able to walk back,*

*and never have had a normal relationship, but instead fifty years of
US domination and fifty years of Cuban defiance. Reagan and Bush
never lifted the Interest Sections agreement or the Panama Canal
Treaty. But Reagan's victory meant he would have broken diplomatic relations* [if Carter had achieved them].

President Carter himself, in an interview with LeoGrande
and Kornbluh, regretted his not establishing normal relations:
"I think in retrospect, knowing what I know since leaving the
White House, I should have gone ahead and been more flexible
in dealing with Cuba and established full diplomatic relations."[42]
Who could be sure that Reagan would have broken the formal
ties if Carter had succeeded in creating them? It may seem prob-
able in hindsight, although the fact that the Interest Sections
remained in place is evidence that diplomatic gains are complicated to reverse. At the least, pressure from many in Congress
and from the United Nations would have made Reagan squander
political capital to rip up diplomatic relations with Cuba.

I also asked Pastor whether he would have opted for a different approach had he known that forty years later the impasse
still would remain. Besides the half-sentence already spoken—"-
Carter himself wishes he did . . ."—there wasn't much else Pastor
could say. In his 2012 article, however, Pastor blamed Fidel for
what was essentially a timing problem. In the beginning of the
Carter era, the president had moved quickly on Panama, SALT,
China, and energy initiatives, but "Castro lost his place in the
queue."[43] That US mentality, which assumed Castro was a sup-
plicant awaiting approval, was another example of the misunderstanding of Cuban national pride that doomed the relationship.

Cold War thinking torpedoed the most promising initiative
toward normalization in decades, a policy goal that was replaced
by regime change. Even in 2012, Pastor wrote that while he didn't
think the label "Soviet proxy" was accurate, he "understood that
it had the advantage of putting Cuba in an awkward position
where it had either to acknowledge its alliance with the Soviet

Union or defend its independence."[44] In retrospect, adding an embarrassing touch to an ultra-sensitive negotiation would seem counterproductive. In addition, Pastor's 2012 essay reflected one-sided thinking inappropriate for diplomacy. He described the 1962 missile crisis as JFK's worst nightmare, which no doubt it was, without acknowledging its roots in Cuba's security nightmares after the Bay of Pigs and multiple US assassination attempts against Fidel. And Pastor readily acknowledges that the United States under Nixon began a formal détente with China without demanding democracy or regime change as a precondition. Ricardo was unusually caustic on this point—

RICARDO: *They said it was impossible to oppose the China lobby for years. But China was a very big market. The United States finally made the step. It coincided with the Cultural Revolution in China and the Gang of Four. Suddenly China things became very fashionable. The Gang of Four, who were Mao's widow and three other guys in the party leadership who launched the Cultural Revolution, put Deng Xiaoping and other reformists in jail and committed a number of "excesses" in the name of revolutionary purity. This was precisely when Washington finally recognized China.*

There are other lessons from the Carter years worth remembering. The CIA attempted to subvert the arms limitation summit with the Soviet Union by leaking a false claim about a secret Soviet "combat brigade" in Cuba.[45] The tactic worked, helping derail the arms talks and forcing Carter to resume extensive aerial surveillance of Cuba. Pastor said in hindsight that the "secret brigade" was no secret, it had been on the island since the missile crisis, and the United States had stopped monitoring it ten years before. It was all "an artificial crisis generated by a leaked news report," he wrote—and would happen again.

On a more positive note, with intriguing implications for today, Carter and Castro secretly orchestrated a major prisoner exchange, though claiming that the two events were independent of each other. In 1978, in an apparent effort to restart the dying normalization process, Fidel released about 3,900 political prisoners, plus all US prisoners and dual nationals the following year. Separately, in September 1979, Carter commuted the life sentences of four Puerto Rican nationalists three of whom had shot up the US Congress in 1954 and one of whom had tried to kill president Harry Truman in 1952.[46] Even these extraordinary developments, however, could not rehabilitate the normalization process. According to Pastor, the sequence of releases was an attempt to get normalization back on track by the Cubans trying to appeal to Carter's priority of human rights, consistent with Andrew Young's domestic and international views. But normalization was beyond reach; the Reagan era and the right-wing Cuba lobby were rising on the horizon.

Nearly all histories of the period underplay the vital role that American public opinion and congressional urgings can play in changing US foreign policy. Watergate drove the Carter election and the sharp rethinking of the US role abroad. US Senate hearings on the CIA assassination programs, including those aimed at Fidel, gained national attention in 1975, and led to the creation of the first congressional oversight committees. A 1976 Senate amendment forbade direct covert aid to mercenaries or paramilitary groups in Angola.[47] Later, on December 19, 1975, the Senate voted 54-22 against funding the CIA's covert operations, with the House following on January 27, 1977, with a huge 323-99 vote.[48] President Gerald Ford accused Congress of having "lost its guts."[49] Kissinger blamed Congress for "losing" Angola, and Daniel Patrick Moynihan, ambassador to the UN, warned that the USSR was taking over "the strategic South Atlantic," with Brazil the next domino to fall.[50] Given Watergate and Vietnam, there was little congressional support for the Congo's Mobutu (on the CIA payroll),[51] Holden Roberto (paid by China),[52] or Jonas Savimbi (Portugal's former client[53] being backed by South Africa).[54] Cuba was a convenient administration scapegoat for America's own collusion in racist and colonial African dictatorships. The key factor in shaping public and congressional opposition was the fear of another Vietnam with explosive consequences at home. Che's strategy of "two, three, many Vietnams"—straining the resources of empire across many fronts—had come to pass. That the rising international revolt against empire might turn into disorder on the home front was to be prevented at all costs. National security experts like Harvard's Samuel Huntington warned of an "excess of democracy,"[55] referring to the rise of the Left after Vietnam and Watergate. The corporate lawyer Lewis F. Powell wrote a widely circulated strategy memo to elite insiders calling for an organized effort to stem progressive change, demonizing Ralph Nader in particular;[56] Powell was nominated to the US Supreme Court by Richard Nixon two months later.

Windows open, windows close. The post-Watergate rethinking was brief. 1979 was a good year for the anticommunist lobbies. Domestic paranoia was inflamed by the 1979 Iranian Revolution, the Soviet invasion of Afghanistan, and the Sandinista victory in Nicaragua. These threats were met by the new Miami Cuba lobby, the Vatican's assault on liberation theology in Latin America, and the election of president Ronald Reagan. The Sandinista victory and a rebel offensive in El Salvador stirred talk of a "Cuban octopus" strangling Central America.[57] The Cuba lobby was a creature sponsored by the American Right as an alternative to the earlier exile generation's failed military missions and assassination plots. The Vatican's dismantling of liberation theology was coordinated with Reagan's national security team after meetings in Santa Fe, New Mexico that year, where the participants concurred on the need to deter "radical" movements thought to be inspired by Cuba.[58]

Not until 1992 would the Democrats have another chance, and they would not come close in '92 to the positions and promise of the early Jimmy Carter years.

CHAPTER 12

The Clinton Years: Yielding to the Cuban Right

ill Clinton, a former George McGovern supporter, draft
resister,[1] war opponent, New South Democrat, and
Arkansas governor, was elected president in November 1992
by moving rightward on the American political spectrum. One
of his closest friends came to me at that year's Democratic convention with a message of assurance: "Bill told me to tell you he
still believes in the sixties." So apparently did Hillary Rodham
Clinton, an early feminist and young lawyer who had interned
in a left-wing Bay Area law office that once represented Black
Panthers and other revolutionaries.[2]

But not on Cuba policy. Given their sixties backgrounds,
the Clintons should have been inclined toward solidarity with
Cuba, or at least sympathetic to the desire for rapid dialogue
toward normalization. With the dissolution of the Soviet bloc,
the poisons of anticommunism were being drained from the
American body politic. But pragmatism for Clinton dictated
making friends with the powerful Cuba lobby invented in the
Reagan era. And, not unimportantly, Clinton had suffered a
rough experience with the Cubans when he was Arkansas governor during the Mariel crisis of 1980 when 125,000 Cubans,

including many mulattoes and blacks, were pushed by Fidel to leave in rickety boats for Miami, from which several tens of thousands were relocated to Ford Chaffee, Arkansas. The help-less refugees were denounced by the Cuban regime as scum or lumpen elements, and welcomed at first by President Carter with open arms. Having normal diplomatic relations with the United States might have averted or lessened the disaster that followed. Thousands were detained for years in Atlanta, Georgia, and Arkansas, causing a political debacle for Carter and then-Governor Clinton, one that would not be forgotten.

"Through three administrations, Mas Canosa controlled access to the White House on Cuban issues, ensuring that only hard-liners participated in policymaking," wrote Ann Louise Bardach in her *Cuba Confidential* (2002).[3] The Clinton period comprised the glory years for Mas Canosa's Cuban American National Foundation (CANF), which originated among the Bay of Pigs veterans—Canosa had been a squad leader in the invasion—evolved into a terrorist group,[4] and eventually, after three decades, became a powerful lobby, dominating Miami politics through its funding of political donations, endorse-ments, and voter turnout, that could deliver Florida's vital Elec-toral College vote. Miami's Cubans voted overwhelmingly for Reagan and the first George Bush by 70 to 80 percent margins. After signing off on most of the CANF agenda, Clinton wound up with 22 percent of the Cuban American vote in 1992.[5]

Clinton was a master of what became known as wedge politics, poaching on rival political blocs while discarding his own loyal constituencies when expedient. As a liberal, Clinton would expand person-to-person contact with Cuba that Bush had shut down; expand charter flights, improve telephone and Western Union service, and so on. Clinton also was the first US president to shake Fidel's hand, during a 2000 UN summit in New York. (The White House spin was that it was only a "chance encounter" with no substance attached, and that it was Fidel who approached Clinton;[6] no photos were ever released.

Even more timid was Clinton's vice president Al Gore, who actually escaped through a doorway to avoid Fidel years later, during Nelson Mandela's inauguration in 1994.)

Using his strategy known as triangulation Clinton went after the CANF money and endorsement with a vengeance, actually winning the Miami vote in 1996, his reelection year. It was ugly. During his 1992 campaign, Clinton promised at a Miami fundraiser to "put the hammer down on Fidel Castro and Cuba"[7] and proceeded to do so.

RICARDO: *The Cuba policy was founded on American interests and traditional perceptions of superiority. The Cuban components of the policy—such as CANF—were American-created creatures, and instruments of American policy, not the other way around as American politicians love to say.*

The nineties marked a time when a wave of free-market fundamentalism washed across the world after the Soviet Union imploded. A newly free capitalist world, free of labor unions, environmental regulations, and national barriers to Western investment and resource extraction—what Fidel cursed early on as neoliberalism—was unfurled under the banner of the World Trade Organization (WTO). By the late eighties, 85 percent of Cuba's trade was with the disintegrating USSR.[8] Both exports and imports had fallen, the former by 75 percent and the latter by over 85 percent. Real Cuban wages had dropped by 25 percent and household consumption by 33 percent.[9] Cuba's long dependence on the Soviet Union as a military deterrent to US power came to an abrupt end. I was there for two weeks in 1993, and times were more than stark. This was the era—the so-called Special Period in Peacetime[10]—when the people of Cuba went hungry, electricity was rationed, and women sold their bodies to tourists when there was nothing else to offer.

Clinton as a candidate endorsed legislation by New Jersey Sen. Robert Torricelli, the Cuban Democracy Act of 1992, which then-president George Herbert Walker Bush was reluctant to sign until prodded to do so by Clinton. The law tightened the screws of the embargo by prohibiting sales of food or medicine to Cuba. It capped cash remittances. It forbade foreign subsidiaries of US companies from trading with the island, and blocked foreign ships from leaving from or entering US ports for six months if they had entered Cuban waters. Foreign investors, including European allies, were supposed to be scared off. Its Article 8 promoted a multiparty system, and Article 1705 funded the internal Cuban opposition, with the explicit goal of restoring a market economy. In the wake of the Soviet collapse, it was assumed that Toricelli's legislation would deliver the "final blow" to Havana. During that time, "experts" like the Pulitzer Prize-winning Andrés Oppenheimer wrote triumphal books with titles like *Castro's Final Hour* (1993). Twenty-one years later, the law is still on the books, having upset many European allies of the United States, while Cuba itself still remains intact.

Clinton tightened the economic embargo by cutting off the annual flow of $500 million in family remittances, limiting travel rights for family members and academics, and increaseing funding for Radio Martí, a radio station broadcasting the CANF message to Cuba where the transmissions were jammed anyway.

Clinton also signed the Helms-Burton Act, which yielded to Congress his own executive branch's power over diplomatic recognition of Cuba and the embargo. The proximate cause was the Cuban shoot-down of two Cessnas piloted by Miami exiles described below.

The Helms-Burton law remains a structural impediment to any future normalization. It crystalizes in a few paragraphs the full meaning of "regime change." A "transition government" shall be established in Cuba, according to the law, with the following elements: [a] all political activity is legalized on the island, [b] all political prisoners are freed and Cuba's prisons placed under international inspection, [c] Cuba has to dissolve its Ministry of the Interior and the dependent Department of State Security[11] as well as local Committees for the Defense of the Revolution[12] and Rapid Response Brigades,[13] [d] elections to choose a new government are held within eighteen months after the transition, [e] multiple independent political parties are given full access to media outlets, [f] interference with Radio and Television Martí is ended, [g] an independent judiciary and trade unions are established, [f] it must not include either Fidel or Raúl Castro, [g] it provides just compensation for all properties expropriated after 1959, and [h] it is "substantially moving toward a market-oriented economic system based on the right to own and enjoy property."[14]

What the law neglects to mention among its sweeping provisions is the fact that Helms-Burton could only be implemented by means of a coup or a US invasion, or both—as would happen a decade later in Iraq. It was simply inconceivable that Cubans, however oppressed, would mass in the streets to face down the Cuban security forces in order to enjoy the benefits of capitalism, multiparty elections, and welcoming home exiles returning from Miami. The delusion of "the fall of communism" was as popular in the US Congress at that time as it was surreal.

RICARDO: *Helms-Burton changed the situation by including the original Cuban exiles' claims to compensation at the same level as the American companies' whose assets were expropriated, making any resolution impossible. The rationale at first had been to give back former US properties or fully compensate the owners for their expropriation. Helms-Burton goes far beyond that. It was a victory for those Cubans who left. They changed the logic from the original point so now it is any property nationalized in Cuba after the revolution—that's absolutely crazy because it would be impossible to implement all these decades later. Octavio Paz[15] has said that arrogance and ignorance combined to define US policy. This is one example.*

Torricelli and Helms-Burton together reminded most Cubans of what they call the Annexationist Project, which was articulated by secretary of state John Quincy Adams in 1823. It was simply a law of nature, Adams wrote, that Cuba should gravitate toward a "North American Union," a process that he declared was of "transcendent importance."[16] The 1902 Platt Amendment also asserted limits on Cuba's national sovereignty by incorporating America's "right to intervene" at any time for economic and military reasons, making Cuba a neo-colony and home to the US Guantanamo naval base.

RICARDO: *In general I have the impression that the quality of the foreign policy establishment in the United States is going down.*

When I have been involved in official meetings, they typically sit in front of a huge briefing book and go to whatever the issue is. Then usually one side invites the other to lunch and vice versa. They bring along the big briefing books. There is barely space for the water. Then we go to the Cuban residency in the evening for dinner and they bring the briefing books along again. They cannot open their mouths without checking the books.

Here is an example. There was an American interpreter named Stephanie Van Reigersberg who participated in many rounds of talks. This was in the nineties under Clinton during the immigration crisis talks.[17] At some moment, the American guy, who was arrogant, spoke as if he was discovering the Caribbean, a phrase we often use. "So," he says, "instead of a piecemeal approach, let's go back to our general philosophies." Stephanie said, "Oh my God!" and broke down. She had spent hours and hours on these details.

Around 1993–1994 it became really funny. There were two parallel tracks on the US side. There was the formal State Department delegation, with the immigration service, who would meet with us at the US or Cuban mission [at the UN]. *Then on the other track I would go and see* [the State Department's] *Peter Tarnoff in secret, without allowing his American colleagues to know we were meeting separately. He was well informed.*

Meetings with Peter were on the same issues but from a different perspective. The first group only repeated the official line while Peter transmitted to me the other concerns, especially about Guantanamo with all the Cubans and Haitians who were stuck there. It was very interesting—two-track parallel discussions but compartmentalized. People in the day meetings didn't know what I was doing in the evenings. The guy who led the official track was Dennis Hays [former State Department coordinator for Cuban policy, later the executive vice president of CANF, the hardline supporter of the embargo]. *At the time of the 1996 Brothers shoot-down incident,*[18] *he traveled in one of those planes with the Brothers. The American leadership was aware that the Cuban Mafia had infiltrated their own government.*

In August 1994 when I arrived in New York, on the very first day, I got a phone call from Peter [Tarnoff] *who said, "I want to meet with you without the others knowing."*

In those days it was difficult. In the past, the US government had protective mechanisms. You were received and transported everywhere in a limousine, bullet proofed, with windows you couldn't open, a driver from US security, other cars travelling behind you, etc. But how to meet secretly with these highly visible American protective services people around?

So our people told the US security that our president would stay here in the mission the rest of the evening, so they could go home. But the mission also had barricades so it was impossible to go out without being noticed by the police. One of our people came by in a normal car, entered the garage to pick me up, and I would lie down on the back floor of the car. Then we drove to the Carlyle Hotel, and I could sit up. Going back, I would lie down in the back.

On one occasion we left the Carlyle and were surrounded by a lot of cameras, lights, and people. I was with Peter and, I believe, Wendy Sherman [a State Department official]. *All three of us froze. But then the press crowd went past us and we were happily surprised and entered the hotel. The cameras were for Woody Allen who was playing saxophone at the hotel bar. So they ignored us completely.*

Peter and I agreed once to meet secretly in the York Hotel in Toronto. I was with a Cuban parliamentary delegation. This was in April 1995. Nobody knew in Canada, not even in my own delegation, that Peter and I were meeting. Peter got a room on another floor. Enrique Nuñez Rodríguez [26th of July movement veteran, poet, humorist, and diplomat] *was with me all the time and never knew. I remember we went to Niagara Falls and returned. Enrique later said he was surprised on our return to Cuba when I was met and greeted at the Havana airport by Fidel's secretary. I went from there directly to meet with Fidel and report on my meeting with Peter.*

The lesson I learned is that the Clinton people rightly distrusted their own government representatives. This also happened with the FAA [Federal Aviation Administration] *in the shoot-down incident. It also happened when the FBI went around the local agents when they wanted to liberate Elián González. They sent a SWAT team from Washington. Why? Because they knew that those other Cuban Miami people were out of control. I knew in 1994–1995 that I was negotiating on the basis of knowing things that had to be kept from the Cuban Mafia.*

The content of the Toronto meetings with Peter was essentially that we were making an agreement on the general future of the immigration crisis. That balseros [boat people, or rafters] *would not be received automatically in the United States. That our government would get twenty thousand visas. Etcetera. The United States was concerned about what to do with the thousands at Guantanamo. We had to reach a compromise. It was problematic. There was another actor too, the Pentagon, which was angry because the Guantanamo base was being used for these other purposes. The Pentagon didn't want to become a policeman of immigrants. It was absolutely crazy. But how to deal with it?*

We had to find a settlement by which those held in Guantanamo would be admitted into US territory. Plus there was to be a very strong statement that at noon on May 1, 1995, any Cuban found departing from Cuba would be sent back by the US. So at noon [attorney general] *Janet Reno spoke with Peter from Washington and I did the same thing in Havana.*

Let me tell you another secret. On that day [May 1] *the US Coast Guard found a small boat with Cubans who had obviously departed before the date of our agreement. Fidel asked me to talk with Peter; he thought it might be best if these people were ignored. I called Peter, and he said the agreement was very clear. So the United States sent them back to Cuba.*

SHOOT-DOWN

On February 24, 1996, any possibility of normalization under Clinton was shot down along with two Cessnas carrying four Cuban American exiles dangerously close to the island's boundaries. The four Cuban Americans were killed. A third plane escaped, carrying José Basulto, the leader of Brothers to the Rescue, back to a Miami base. Brothers was an exile group that took it upon itself to rescue Cuban refugees in open waters, shower Cuba with propaganda materials urging an uprising, and engage Cuban air defenses in high-risk adventurism. The Cuban government warned the Brothers and US authorities on multiple occasions that the planes eventually would be fired on by Cuban MiGs if the provocations continued to threaten Cuban airspace.

In response to a long pattern of Miami-based attacks on Cuba, Havana sent a covert surveillance team to monitor the armed exile groups and also to gather evidence to warn Cuba prior to such flights being cleared to go by US authorities. There were even high-level confidential meetings in Havana between the FBI and Cuban intelligence to pour over the evidence of threats to Cuba being generated by the Cuban surveillance teams.

RICARDO: *Some people in the administration wanted to create conditions for the president to veto Helms-Burton. This was before the shoot-down. Sandy Berger and Anthony Lake had accepted the text of the Helms-Burton law as it was.*[19] *My contact, who showed me the document, asked if I remembered the last time Bill Clinton vetoed a law. He'd never done that. Once it got to his desk, they said, he would sign it. Then what happened when the* [shoot-down] *incident took place was that, in a show of incredible irresponsibility, Mr. Clinton— who was under pressure from the Cuban Mafia to bomb, if you read his memoir—accepted the amendment to the Helms-Burton bill relinquishing his executive authority. It was really immoral for the administration to do that because we had been warning them that an incident could take place and that if it did it would spark everything. They knew, and they promised us to stop those flights.*

I personally discussed this issue many times in secret with Peter Tarnoff. I always raised it. I also discussed it with Morton Halperin, the Latin American director of the National Security Council. I met with him secretly, through Saul Landau, at a house in Georgetown. Morton and I were alone at a dining table, and I told him I was very concerned.

The shoot-down not only led to the Helms-Burton legislation including the president ceding authority over Cuba policy to Congress. It soon led to grave conspiracy indictments against five Cuban intelligence officers operating secretly in Florida: Gerardo Hernández, Antonio Guerrero, Ramón Labañino, Fernando González, and René González. They became known in America as the Cuban spy ring and internationally as the Cuban Five. part of a much larger Cuban intelligence network. They were tried in Miami in 2000 and convicted on multiple counts of conspiracy, espionage, and in one case, contributing to the murders of the four pilots—I would follow the unfolding case closely, since one of my lifelong friends, Leonard Weinglass, became deeply involved in the Five's federal appeal of their conviction, working closely with Ricardo. Len died of cancer on March 23, 2011, shortly after returning from lengthy meetings in Havana about the case, and left me his draft notes on the shoot-down controversy:

LEONARD WEINGLASS: *Instead of following their [flight] plan . . . the planes turned sharply south, heading straight for Havana . . . in her dissent from the opinion affirming the conviction of the Five, Judge Kravitch observed that 'the Brothers to the Rescue' had repeatedly and knowingly violated Cuban airspace since 1994. . . . In 1995, [José] Basulto's use of small aircraft to challenge Cuban authorities was already well documented. . . . According to a Cuban intelligence file on Basulto, introduced at trial, he had been recruited by the CIA, participated in an action related to the Bay of Pigs invasion, and was trained to use explosives. He also admitted to having fired a cannon from a boat just off the shores of Cuba some sixteen times at a coastal hotel. . . .*

On February 23, the US State Department's Office of Cuban Affairs notified the FAA that BTTR might attempt a flight to Cuba in the coming days . . . and that "State has also indicated the government of Cuba would be less likely to show restraint in an unauthorized flight scenario this time around. . . ." On July 14, 1995, it had formally warned that any aircraft violating its airspace would be "downed."

Just prior to February 24, Cuba declared the airspace north of Havana, extending northward out for forty miles, a restricted zone. . . . February 24 was not chosen by Basulto at random. It was the 101st anniversary of the Cuban war of independence[20] and, in 1996, it fell on a Saturday. Cuban workers had the day off, and were assembling with families and friends at popular festivities celebrated along Havana's malecón,[21] facing north over the Florida Straits. . . .

Precisely at 3:20 p.m., US radar placed Basulto's aircraft 1.5 miles inside Cuban airspace. [ICAO Report, p. 12, note 14]. US radar placed the shoot-downs at 4.8 and 9.5 miles north of Cuba's territorial airspace, within the restricted zone. They also recorded the Basulto plane 2.1 miles into Cuban airspace. There was no dispute at all that all 3 aircraft had flown approximately forty miles through a restricted zone.

The US government has refused to release satellite images that might clarify exactly where the planes went down.[22]

Ricardo was the leading Cuban official who handled the Cuban Five case until 2012. By then Ricardo had become a virtual lawyer as well as a diplomat.

RICARDO: *Bill Richardson*[23] *came to Havana twice just before the shoot-down incident. He met with me alone, and then with Fidel. I have Fidel's version of who said what and what happened. Fidel asked him to please tell Clinton to do something not to permit any more of those provocations. Richardson returned to DC, then came back to Havana and met with Fidel and me. He said on behalf of Bill Clinton, don't worry because these incidents won't happen anymore. Clinton would take the proper steps.*

Now, looking back, I don't know if Bill Richardson was a liar. A few years later when Richardson came back he wanted to meet Fidel again, and Fidel told me to meet him. So I did, and I asked him one question: "What happened in January 1996? We are supposed to be friends, but now I don't know." Bill Richardson looked up at the ceiling and said something like, "Oh that was so long ago. . . ." "The lives of innocent human beings [the Cuban Five] *are hanging on your answer," I told him, "so just to help your memory, you were sitting right there and I was right here, and we discussed the planes, and we went to the presidential palace to see Fidel, and Fidel asked you to please tell Clinton to do something to stop the flights."*

At that time, the US FAA [Federal Aviation Administration] *was conducting its own investigation and threatening Balsulto with taking his license because of previous violations. I reminded Bill Richardson that Fidel offered a dinner, that he was alone with Fidel for a while, and you told him that you spoke with Clinton.*

Looking back, I don't know if Richardson really spoke with Clinton. Fidel himself actually met with this man, not depending on me to communicate the message indirectly. On the US side, perhaps many decisions are taken by people who invent names and stories. Fidel does micromanage. Richardson finally told me that maybe he met with Tony Lake or an aide to Lake, not with Clinton. So the warning was never delivered personally.[24]

Basulto and many others wanted to disrupt any rapprochement between Cuba and the United States. Clinton was taking steps in that direction.

I believe Helms-Burton was designed to reinforce the embargo in order to prevent the president from turning things in a new direction.[25]

Remember the 1994 agreement I signed with Peter Tarnoff that went into force in 1995, saying that everyone found in US waters by the Coast Guard would be returned to Cuba? Brothers to the Rescue had made a business out of helping Cuban rafters and bringing them into US territory. Once the agreement was in effect in May 1995, Brothers to the Rescue lost their business. From the moment the Coast Guard starting sending the rafters back, the Brothers had no business. So I think they intensified their flights over Cuba to provoke an incident.

That's why every time I met US friends like Peter [Tarnoff] *and Morton* [Halperin] *I told them that an incident was going to be provoked. Fidel was very active too. Basulto was an adventurer. Even the United States accused him of having entered Cuban airspace on February 24, 1996. While the others lost their lives, Basulto was able to return safely. I wonder if Basulto's pullback that day*[26] *was deliberate.*

Many Western Cuba watchers claim that the shoot-down was a deliberate Cuban attempt to stop the normalization process from happening, though they offer no real evidence. Richard Feinberg, the Clinton National Security Council's lead Cuba policy person for 1993–1996, for example, told me that he thought Cuba secretly didn't want to rush the pace of normalization.

RICHARD FEINBERG: *Overall it's true there wasn't a clear US policy. Then there were problems in our bureaucracy, like who gets to communicate to the FAA about the shoot-downs. And what was our government's relation to the Brothers? My bottom line, though, is that the blame was on Fidel Castro, he is a strategic guy, he had*

*to know that shooting down the planes would freeze normaliza-
tion. Which was more important to Fidel, allowing the annoyance
or improving US-Cuban relations? He didn't want to move too far
and too fast. Cubans who were in meetings with him told me so.
He couldn't be seen as blocking the improvement in relations. So the
shoot-down provided a golden opportunity. And at the same time he
was shutting things down internally.*

"The common wisdom within Havana's Western diplomatic
circle was that the Cubans didn't want improved relations,"
according to Marc Frank.[27] In the case of the 1996 shoot-down,
however, the Cubans felt they were drawing a clear and legal
line of defense across their own coastal boundaries and sending
ample warnings to the president of the United States. They had
reason to believe that Clinton was personally briefed about the
dangers. It is tortured reasoning to blame Fidel for trying to
block normalization through a shoot-down. If that was the
case, all the United States had to do was stop the flights out of
Miami and test the Cubans. According to Feinberg's argument,
Fidel apparently would have looked for another pretext to avert
the normalization process. But the planes were not blocked that
day from flying from American soil; instead, what Feinberg
called the "lack of clarity" in policy allowed the provocations—
what Feinberg calls the "annoyance"—to continue.

The reporter Ann Louise Bardach writes in her *Cuba Confidential* that Alarcón himself was trying to "build a case ...
hoping to dissuade Castro from just such a course of action."[28]
Bardach offers no evidence for her thesis except that Alarcón
was seeking outside counsel on the legal issues involved, and
Ricardo disputes her account in the strongest possible terms:

RICARDO: *The whole story about me is an absolute fabrication by
Ann Louise. It is based on the insistence on an invented decision by
Fidel on that day, February 24. The decision was officially commu-
nicated to the United States through diplomatic channels and also*

privately, directly and indirectly. I did not know of any lobbying trying to change the policy and certainly had nothing to do with such invented lobbying.[29]

When I told this to Bardach, she laughed and said, "Of course he would say that. Everyone winds up in the pokey down there," ignoring the fact that Alarcón had never been accused of anything. I asked Ricardo if he would clarify at what level the decision was made to shoot down the planes. Did Cuba have a "red line" and communicate it to the White House?

RICARDO: *It was a decision publicly announced and officially communicated through regular diplomatic channels and acknowledged by the State Department and FAA. The Cuban air defense forces were of course informed of that. The specific decision in a particular circumstance is made by those in command at the defense installations. We are talking about events that develop in a matter of seconds. At their regular speed those O-2s—in American propaganda referred to as Cessnas—can overfly Havana and reach the south coast of Cuba in a few minutes. I don't think there was a red line nor a role such a thing could have played. The facts are very simple and clear: the US government was perfectly informed in advance, had promised to put an end to these flights, and had indicated it was in the process of taking away Basulto's license.*

What is clear is that the US government sheltered the armed Cuban exiles and their planes, which flew from American bases, that the Cuban government believed it had given the United States specific warnings, and that the United States had agreed to deter any further flights but nevertheless allowed the Cessnas to take off on that morning.

When I interviewed Morton Halperin, Clinton's point person during these crises, in 2013, he confirmed most of what Ricardo was saying and underscored the significance of the setback that came after the shoot-down and subsequent passage of the Helms-Burton legislation. We sat at a DC Starbucks near his offices at George Soros's Open Society Foundation.

MORTON HALPERIN: *Clinton had had a big problem in Arkansas with the Cuban refugees, and thought the rafter crisis was not a good thing. Gov. [Lawton] Childs in Florida was going nuts. I always thought it was because the new ones were black. Childs told Clinton he would round them up and put them in camps. The attorney general was deeply engaged.*

I get told by the White House you are in charge, fix it. We had just started taking Haitians to Guantanamo. It was clear that the only way to stop the rafters was to take them to Guantanamo too, not the United States. President Clinton approved, and over time it stopped the rafters.

At Guantanamo I told them you can walk out the gate, but you are not coming to the United States. I started talking to Cuban Americans about improving their lives in Guantanamo, setting up coffee shops, that sort of thing. I kept saying we have to stop this. Sen. [Bob] Graham [D-FL] said we should pick them up and dump them back on the Cuban shore. That was the first indication I had that these people thought it was viable to dump them. CANF was supportive. The Coast Guard said we can't do that. I went back to Graham. There were two models, one with and one without the Cubans. Graham said it was okay to negotiate with the Cubans, and I got the presidential agreement. We would bring the rafters back [to Cuba], the Cubans would agree not to punish them, we would monitor, and we would agree on a new process to apply for exit papers in Havana and leave. Any political types would be allowed to come, and the rest were put in a lottery.

We started the process with phone calls to the president of Mexico. Clinton called [Mexican president Carlos] Salinas through [novelist] Carlos Fuentes. Clinton asked Salinas to tell Castro that he wanted him to cooperate on the immigration crisis and, if he does, we will formally move ahead to normalization. Then Salinas called back and said Castro agreed to this two-step approach.

Now that we had an opening, I had a conversation with Alarcón. I laid out our basic proposal. We made the deal [on immigration]. *I wrote the briefing book. Tarnoff negotiated it. His wife got the tickets to Canada. It's in effect to this day.*

Two things happened. One, there was an uproar among Cuban Americans. Bill [Clinton] *had close Cuban* [American] *friends, and he has a syndrome of not wanting to hurt friends. He said he had to tell them in advance. I kept telling him that they will tell other people or will be accused of having known. We agreed to tell them only on the morning of the announcement.* [Leon] *Panetta kept coming over and saying that the president is unhappy because he wants to tell his seven friends.*

On Sunday night Peter says I have the agreement. So early Monday morning I do a memo to the president on the deal, and said I needed his approval by noon. He approved, and at noon Tarnoff called the Cubans at the Interest Section in Havana. I got the attorney general and the Pentagon to tell the FBI not to distribute any of their intercepts on Alarcón between Friday and Monday. I almost didn't remember. That would have blown the whole thing. There was a code we used, like "the bird is flying" or something, meaning that Castro and Clinton had approved.

On Monday I made a round of calls to the Coast Guard. "Do you remember," I asked them, "the deal we discussed where anybody you pick up after noon on Tuesday goes back?" We contacted the Cuban coast guard too.

[Federico] *Peña* [US transportation secretary] *was giving a speech in Miami. He kept it secret. Then I briefed two Cuban Americans in our government to fly to Havana. Only six people in the US government knew the deal. I set up meetings in the morning with the White House staff and the Pentagon, and we set up a press conference with the attorney general and the Southern Command.*

The seven "friends of Bill" went crazy because they weren't consulted. Clinton promised them that I would have nothing to do with Cuba policy after that. My reward.

What happened is that the Brothers to the Rescue were out of busi-

ness. Now if they spotted anyone in the waters they would be sent back to
Cuba. So they decided to start the overflights until one of them got shot
down. If not for that plane shoot-down, I am convinced that Clinton
would have gone ahead with normalization.

I would have grounded those airplanes the Brothers said they
were trying to fly over Guantanamo. So I got an Air Force colonel
to agree to ground all private planes. He said one of them is gonna
get shot down. We still don't have the authority to ground them.
The president later asked who was the son of a bitch who wouldn't
ground the planes?

They were trying to get shot down. I knew that they didn't want
us to move forward [to normalization], *and their only way to*
intervene was to provoke a crisis. They tried it with Guantanamo. I
told them to send a shipment to Guantanamo and they said no, no,
we want to fly it in. My staff told them, "You will be shot down."

SUMMARIZING THE SHOOT-DOWN FIASCO

To summarize, in both Ricardo's version of the 1996 shoot-down,
and that of Mort Halperin as well, the incident—and the con-
sequent halt of the Clinton initiative—happened because the
Miami exiles in Brothers were aggressively trying to rupture
rapprochement. *"They wanted to get shot down,"* to use Halperin's
exact words. The American side the story is one of bureaucratic
lapses: Richardson telling the Cubans he'd conveyed the message
to Clinton when he hadn't; Halperin unable to quite get an order
grounding the doomed planes. Glitches happen but cannot possibly be the whole story. Clinton, who now expresses regret, had
simply failed to ground the planes earlier.

Those who blame the Cubans for the shoot-down first must
ask themselves if there was any point beyond which the Cubans
had a right to defend themselves. The history of many Cuban
exile surprise attacks on the island is well documented. What
if the Brothers' mission was to strafe or bomb Havana, which

Basulto had done earlier in his paramilitary career? How could the United States permit a sanctuary for armed Cuban exiles on American soil and airfields without provoking lethal countermeasures from Cuba? That question aside, it seems clear that they felt the Clinton administration had been warned.

With the signing of Helms-Burton, a second Democratic initiative toward rapprochement had been thwarted, one with serious long-term consequences. The failure of the 1977 Carter initiative also was followed for two decades by the Reagan and Bush presidencies with even harsher efforts to bring down the Cuban regime. The failure of Clinton's late-starting initiative in 1996 was followed by twelve more fruitless years until the 2008 election of Obama began to start the process again. If one includes the 1963 feelers by JFK before his assassination, that means that the efforts of three presidents—not to mention Henry Kissinger's try in 1975—have been blocked successfully over a fifty-year period. Whatever miscalculations Havana might have made, there seem to be deeper or systemic reasons on the American side. The absence of regular diplomatic channels, which caused the Cubans to go through the unreliable Bill Richardson or Lisa Howard before him, certainly has contributed to the failure.

CHAPTER 13

Rethinking Marxism, Rethinking the Americas

The dissolution of the Soviet bloc sent a triumphal wave across the West and a shudder through Cuba. The Reagan and Clinton administrations' euphoria led to greater certainty that Fidel's days were numbered. Lost in the self-congratulations, however, was any recognition of a salient contradiction: Cuba bore little resemblance to the remote-controlled Soviet satellites in Eastern Europe and thus was less susceptible to falling from within. The hawks and neoconservatives were frozen in their doctrine that communism always equaled totalitarianism, which meant that populations were oppressed entirely and that no reforms were possible from within. The anticommunist think tanks were more faith based than factual in their assessments.

Nonetheless, Cubans had good reason to worry. According to Gott, the Cuban economy, though under a depressing Stalinist influence, had benefited from Soviet aid during from a period in "the sunny uplands of economic growth"; from 1975 to 1985, Cuba's growth rate was slightly more than 4 percent, in contrast to Latin America's 1.2 percent.[1] Soviet oil flowed to Cuba, and Cuba sent back tons of sugar, all beyond the embargo's claw.

That came to a crashing end amidst the collapse of the Soviet Union and, more importantly, so did Moscow's security guarantees against an American invasion. Cuba, however, did not collapse, only quivered alone; did not surrender to the northern Colossus, but began a careful and urgent reappraisal.

RICARDO: *The economic blow we suffered was tremendous. It was like the beginning of the American blockade again. My generation has passed through the same experience twice, goods suddenly disappearing just when you'd gotten used to them.*

Ricardo had noticed a change in Soviet behavior before the fall, as they shifted heavily toward détente with the United States.

RICARDO: *The Soviets were becoming different, trying to imitate the Americans. They had lost their stamina and diplomatic skill. There were very important changes in their diplomacy; Russia could have remained the same* [after the fall of the Soviet Union] *but they abandoned socialism. During the Yeltsin period they were acting like puppets of the United States. Their behavior was not that of a big power, it was more like that of a second-class regime. (Now, by the way, they have a sense of recovering dignity.)*

Ricardo, who was the only Latin American diplomat to address the Soviet Duma (parliament) twice, observed problems early on.

RICARDO: *Even when Mills went to a Soviet sanatorium in 1962* [for heart treatment] *it was an incredibly bureaucratic process. Any Cuban who got a cold in Moscow would want to return to Cuba.*[2] *They were an advanced economy but also very backward. A peasant superpower. The result of a particular history that I respect but was not what the original revolutionaries had in mind.*

The Europeans always thought socialism would come in Germany or France. Marx would have been surprised that a socialist regime was established in his name in the Old Russia.

The last bilateral agreement between Cuba and the USSR, if you compare it to the very first in which they bought sugar and we bought oil, showed the difference. They were also buying Cuban medical equipment, pharmaceutical expertise, and Cuban advice. We were no longer the poor developing country dependent on advanced socialism. This was in 1990–1991. We had to spend lots of resources on national defense and we counted on them for weapons. We didn't have to go through the experience they did in 1919, of arming themselves without any foreign friends. That distorted their socialism. They saved us from that experience. So we could develop much more in education, health care, culture, and social services. And there was a different cultural background. We have both African and Western civilizations. Even the Cuban peasantry was different from theirs. It was more of a rural proletariat, with tens of thousands of workers in the industrial part of producing sugar and tobacco, not a traditional isolated peasantry.

What happened with our Soviet friends? I was the ambassador at the UN in 1992 and a member of the Security Council. At first you had seating labels like "USSR" and "UKRANIAN SSR," "BYLO-RUSSIAN SSR," etcetera, but according to the UN Charter there are only five permanent members. One day when I arrived there I saw "RUSSIAN FEDERATION." In the beginning they referred to me as "Tovarich" [comrade]. Then one day it was "Gaspadin," a word something like "sir." For those who were wanting to join the capitalist bloc it was amazing that still the majority of the Russian officials called me "Tovarich," because it meant they were trapped in the middle of the turnaround. The worst time of Russian diplomacy was with Gorbachev and Yeltsin. The diplomats all started speaking English! With Gromyko before, you could talk about Shakespeare in English, but this was new. I never have understood Russian. The only guys who couldn't speak Russian were the Romanians, who used French. "Bonjour, Camarade." But the meetings of Socialist ambassadors were always in Russian before.

Nothing is linear in the way it goes.

I told Ricardo about my oldest friend in Vietnam, Nguyen Xuan Oanh, a revolutionary, writer, musician, and poet whose task was to welcome, guide, and interpret events for American visitors, which required immense tolerance during visits to bombed hospitals or pagodas, or in everyday street encounters with ordinary Vietnamese. When I asked Xuan Oanh in 1965 why Vietnam drew such an absolute distinction between American government policies and the "American people" in general, he said it came from a belief that the vast majority of Americans were either innocent, or ignorant, or opposed to the war, and that he wanted to avoid hating people who might in time become friends. It was a doctrine that was Marxist, Buddhist, and Confucian in its roots, and it seems to be shared by the Cubans I ever met in Havana. And over time, the doctrine gradually proved to be essential to ending the Vietnam War and achieving reconciliation and diplomatic relations. A model both Americans and Cubans might emulate. In 2008, fifty years after Xuan Oanh and I first met, I saw him for the last time in Hanoi. He was drinking, playing the piano, and socializing with old friends, all in their eighties. When I was leaving, he held my hand at his door, looking intensely into my eyes, and said, "Nothing can be predicted." He meant that the course of history, including the rise and fall of North Vietnam's closest ally, the Soviet Union, was unknowable and ever changing. That ideologies or mechanical concepts were ultimately only dogmas. I told this story to Ricardo one afternoon in the Nacional. He listened but gave no response. I thought perhaps it was simply too murky. But the next day, Ricardo said he thought my Vietnamese friend was right.

RICARDO: *You can see more or less one hundred yards but not one hundred kilometers. Frankly, I would hesitate to anticipate anything. Today on television it is all about gay marriage. I feel lost sometimes.*[3]

I remember Bush even saying he was surprised by the fall of the

Soviet Union. The United States was not prepared. What they did was pass through euphoria, as drunk as Yeltsin. And a lot of people were lost on the side of the Left.

There was this theory that Cuba had to fall like the Soviet Union, based on certain fundamental mistaken viewpoints that were in fashion on all sides. The idea of the eternal immutability of their brand of socialism. The entire communist movement was convinced. What happened to the old guard Communists in Latin America and Europe, I feel pity for them. It was like a Catholic being told by the pope that God does not exist, that it was all a mistake. Fortunately we, certainly myself, were not coming from that tradition.

In Cuba I felt very sorry also for my people on the street, because they had an idea of the Soviet Union very far removed from the wrongdoings and faults. They thought the Soviet Union was the generous friend who came from the other side of the earth, a kind of celestial force. Many Cubans were educated and trained there, and we imported a lot of equipment. But at the same time some Cubans had their own critical approach.

In his time, Marx considered the idea of internationalism, the First International, in which the world's revolutionaries didn't really have a nationalist approach. The idea was the emancipation of the whole global working class. I have no idea what Marx would think of the events that followed. The First and Second Internationals divided, the Third came under Lenin... [and] it all got accustomed to being like a church. Obviously in a way it was correct to promote international solidarity, but it also had a very negative dimension with the idea that doctrine and orders should be issued from a central place.

At this point Ricardo looked out from our window at Havana's Easter weekend crowds. "Why do you think people here respect Good Friday?" he asked without expecting an answer. The Cuban Revolution originally penalized religion but over decades has negotiated normal relations with the Vatican, a policy that would pay crucial dividends in normalization.

Today, a modest percentage of Cubans are practicing Catholics and the official government line emphasizes nondiscrimination between the several faiths on the island. The Cuban Catholic Church, the largest institution outside the government, is a force for human rights, but also opposes the cruelties of economic neoliberalism and supports Cuban-US rapprochement. As noted, Fidel, who went to Jesuit schools, has written his own positive reflections on religion, based on his contact with revolutionaries in Latin America's liberation theology movement.[4] The papal visits to the island in 1998 and 2012 were productive ones, exactly the opposite in their effects from those of Pope John Paul II's 1989 visit to Poland, which hastened the downfall of the Communist regime. Papal diplomacy played a crucial role in the Obama-Castro December 17 announcement of normalization, and it is almost certain that Pope Francis will continue to be a major force, in sync with Latin America as a whole, in helping to move us toward a constructive Cuban-US settlement that includes lifting the embargo.

RICARDO: [Marxism] *was represented by a set of concepts from the outside. One element that is missing in conversations about the Cuban Revolution is that a fresh and highly critical approach emerged, even among the old communist movement.*

We started going back to a sort of new New Left in Latin America, a new approach to socialism. The positive dimension [of the Soviet demise] *was not having to have a point of reference like a Vatican or a Socialist Church. It made you go back to the socialist idea which was not represented by either the Soviets or the Chinese. We were fortunate that history continued, and that Latin America evolved.*

Everybody talks about the fall of the Berlin Wall, but nobody talks about Caracazo.

In 1989, the year the Berlin Wall came tumbling down, and with it the regimes of communism, a new and different dialectic was emerging in Venezuela and across Latin America, one stirred in large part by the earlier Cuba-inspired guerrilla movements that had been defined as failures at the time. In the wake of communism's demise, America's higher powers embarked on a plan to rid the world of capitalism's new enemies: third world nationalists, labor unions, and environmental and social movements that stood in the path of "free market capitalism," or neoliberalism, the rollback of any government "interference" that protected sovereignty, working people, public health, consumers, or the environment. This radical right-wing counterrevolution was inspired by Ayn Rand's individualist ideologies of the Far Right, drafted by libertarian and conservative academics, and backed by the presumed unipolar power of the United States in a postcommunist world. Adopting the neoliberal formula, the Venezuelan government imposed unaffordable hikes on bus fares and petrol, without so much as a warning to the hard-pressed public. As Gott, the author of a history of Cuba, wrote then in his book on Venezuela, "The peoples of Latin America, in spite of the surface opulence of the middle-class sectors of cities, are much closer to the breadline than their counterparts in Eastern Europe."[5]

As for the Venezuelan rich, their lives seemed scripted on the Roman Empire model, an out-of-touch, debauched elite long aligned with the United States. The "Caracazo" Ricardo is talking about—loosely translated as the "smashing" or "big one" of Caracas—began with the shantytown poor descending on central Caracas in rebellion against the higher fares. According to the official figures, security forces shot and killed at least three hundred people in five days, while independent estimates put the death toll far higher, as many as one thousand. The Caracazo reverberated across the region as suddenly and unexpectedly as the Arab Spring revolts in this generation, signaling a powerful progressive shift in continental politics. The Caracazo also inspired a young Venezuelan military officer, Hugo Chávez, to quicken his plans for a coup against the corrupt Venezuelan regime. Hugo Chávez and Fidel Castro would become the closest of friends, and powerful strategic allies.

Chávez, after time in prison for a failed progressive coup in 1992,[6] was elected in 1998 by a 56 percent margin, and succeeded electorally in eighteen of nineteen subsequent campaigns until his early death from cancer in 2013. While he was vilified by liberals and conservatives in the United States for personifying a Latin American *caudillo*—"Hugo Boss" read a sarcastic *Foreign Affairs* headline over a photo of Chávez attired in a dress suit—Chávez was deeply popular among the poor not only in Venezuela but across the continent.[7] That he and his allies were reelected on multiple occasions, under the eye of Jimmy Carter and other international election observers, only caused US security thinkers to question electoral democracy itself, not America's long alliance with privileged elites. One of their favorite formulations was that Chávez was a democratically elected "dictator." The implications were ominous: that Chávez was illegitimate despite his popular vote total, and therefore that Venezuelan-style democracy could be justifiably subverted by externally funded "democracy" programs. This mentality sent a message to Cuba that if US "democracy" programs were part of subverting an elected government in Caracas they were even more likely to be justified toward Cuba. And if a pro-Castro figure was elected in a future Cuban election, even with international observers, he or she might not be considered legitimate by the White House either.

Indeed there are authoritarian strains in Venezuelan politics from left to right, not unlike Chicago's historic politics. Hugo Chávez was a charismatic authoritarian personality whose speeches, which I listened to in Caracas, went on far longer than I could bear in my older years. But Venezuela was their country, and Chávez clearly had a majority electoral mandate and an admirable record of improving the lives of the country's long-forgotten poor.

Although in the sixties we never envisioned a charismatic strongman as a model candidate, Chávez's program nevertheless carried seeds of the participatory democracy philosophy of the SDS Port Huron Statement. In Chávez's own exaggerated rhetoric, "the concept of *participatory* democracy will be changed into a form in which democracy based on popular sovereignty constitutes itself as the *protagonist* of power. It is precisely at such borders that we must draw the limits of advance of Bolivarian democracy. Then we shall be very near to the territory of *utopia*."[8] Based on his own experience, including the masses in the streets who came to save him during the 2002 coup, he meant participatory democracy as a mobilization of "popular power," which alone could confront institutional elites. The "territory of utopia" for him was the appearance of the silent impoverished majority finally entering the stage of history. But he also endeavored to structure empowerment of the poor at the base, through community councils, cooperatives, and the frequent use of referenda.

It is far from clear, however, that Venezuela's electoral process can sustain the social and class warfare that continues within. On the Chavista side, no one forgets the 2002 coup, when the conservative Right seized Miraflores and physically spirited Chávez away. Why he was not assassinated remains unknown, but only the force of public opinion transported him back into power. That event, supported to some extent by the Bush administration, hardened the Chavistas' doubt about a constructive and peaceful transition to what they call twenty-first century socialism. A core of the Chavista opponents were anything but the "loyal opposition" typically seen in peaceful democracies, where two different party coalitions contend back and forth for the center. The right-wing core in Venezueula simply would not accept a social revolution backed by an electoral majority. Instead, many would conspire against the Chávez regime in every possible way, seeking US support directly and indirectly. In turn, the Venezuelan government would use force against those elements of the opposition they deemed "subversive," setting in motion an spiral toward chaos.

One doesn't have to accept the Chávez revolution uncritically to recognize that Chávez represented a healthy, democratically elected counterbalance to US hegemony in the region. As I write, it has been fourteen years after Chávez's original election. A new, less charismatic president, Nicolás Maduro, was elected on a Chavista slate by a slender popular majority of 1.6 percent in the 2013 election; his ticket won the December 2013 municipal elections by 10 percent. Venezuela remains sharply divided along race and class lines, with the opposition constituencies generally representing 45 percent of the vote. The country is racked by chronic inflation, crime, and corruption, which cannot be blamed entirely on North American imperialism or a decadent Caracas bourgeoisie alone. That these crises preceded the Chávez era doesn't exempt the Chavistas from their failure to lessen them. Nor can the failures erase the historically important achievements in reducing poverty, and expanding literacy, education and health care for millions of Venezuelans. Now in the wake of December 17, Obama has signed an anti-Venezuela sanctions bill promoted by Cuban American legislators in Washington. The Cuba link is troubling. The Cuban Right is shifting its anti-Havana agenda toward Caracas, in the hope of undermining Cuba by cutting off the one hundred thousand barrels of oil sent daily to Cuba. The politics are dangerous, threatening a deeper divide in Venezuela and fuel shortages in Havana. The Cuban Right, in combination with American neoconservatives, tends to favor chaos, even civil war, in their battle with Venezuela and Cuba (as they succeeded in doing in the Middle East wars). At the same time the conflict has revealed differences in the approaches of Venezuela and Cuba, with Venezuela being the more confrontational, in ways similar to an earlier phase of the US-Cuban conflict. Margarita Alarcón, for example, criticizes Hugo Chavez's 2006 UN speech comparing Bush to the Devil as "disrespectful."

The intimate ties between Cuba and Venezuela go beyond the massive quantities of subsidized oil sent from Caracas to Havana. The alliance has helped advance Cuba's role in Latin America. Tens of thousands of Cuban medical workers, education specialists, and technicians have opened facilities to improve health care, schools, and basic literacy. The Venezuelans also have been central to another Cuban dream, the greater integration of Latin American trade, economic development, security, and diplomatic policies, independent of the Big Brother to the north.

To summarize, the electoral successes of Hugo Chávez demonstrated to Latin America's Left that a twenty-first century socialism was achievable at the ballot box, reopening the strategic possibility of achieving radical change without resorting to armed struggle. It eroded the notion of single "vanguard" parties monopolizing power as a necessary defense against outside intervention.

It caused a Cuban rethinking.

Before Chávez in Venezuela, Chile under Salvador Allende was the best-known model of socialism being created through free democratic elections. Allende's 1970 mandate, after several failed campaigns for the presidency, came with only 36 percent of the votes in a sharply polarized country, and his government was destabilized immediately and overthrown by the CIA, the Nixon administration, and General Augusto Pinochet in September 1973. Those like Ricardo Alarcón, who might have preferred an electoral opening, saw any such possibilities crushed by the rise of Pinochet—and the swift killings of three thousand opposition activists that came with it. After Pinochet came a long period of military rule and death squads across the continent. Then came Chávez in 1998 (and his reelection in 2012); Ricardo Lagos, elected in Chile in the wake of Pinochet in 2000; Luiz Inácio Lula da Silva (Lula) in Brazil in 2002; Néstor Kirchner in Argentina in 2003 (his widow Cristina Fernández Kirchner in 2007 and 2011); former guerrilla leader Tabaré Vásquez in Uruguay in 2005 (followed by José Mujica); Bolivia's Evo Morales, the first indigenous president in the county's history, elected in 2005 and again in 2009; Ecuador's Rafael Correa, elected in 2006; Michelle Bachelet in Chile in 2006; Mauricio Funes in El Salvador in 2009 (and Sánchez Céren in 2014); and the return of Daniel Ortega and the Sandinistas in Nicaragua, democratically elected in 2011 (nearly three decades after their first victory at the ballot box in 1984 was contested and undermined by the US-supported Contra War). Leaders in the Caribbean nations of Antigua and Barbuda, Dominica, and the Grenadines also aligned themselves with the new direction. Several electoral victories were short lived or thwarted: Haiti's Jean-Bertrand Aristide, Honduras' s Manuel Zelaya, and Paraguay's Fernando Lugo were overthrown with US assistance. One country, Colombia, remained under full US dominance, with an expanded number of US military advisers and drug-war bases. The greatest setback for progressive Latin America occurred in Mexico, where stolen, or at least heavily disputed, presidential elections prevented the electoral success of the Left in 1988 and in 2006, and the US-backed Mexican forces blocked a revolutionary challenge from the Zapatista movement based in Chiapas.[9] Accompanying these setbacks for the Left was the imposition of an American drug war apparatus as a steel rim of counterterrorism operations on America's southern perimeter. It should be emphasized, however, that even the most conservative bloc of Latin American countries is united in recognizing Cuba, despite and contrary to US objections.

The late eighties—roughly the same time as the fall of the Berlin Wall and the end of the Cold War—was a period of remarkable transformation in Latin America, away from the previous eras of colonialism, the Monroe Doctrine, and the right-wing military dictatorships of the decades after the Cuban Revolution. Ricardo was paying close attention. Marxism itself was being reexamined.

What was profoundly new was the way in which social movements created a relatively peaceful electoral dynamic where candidates of the Left became presidents and parliamentarians. While there was a common pattern of peaceful democratic transition in all these countries throughout Latin America, they did not follow a single monolithic blueprint. Each country's political revolution exhibited its unique cultural and national qualities. None were led by a classic industrial working class, although unionized workers played important roles in some cases. None were led by vanguard Communist parties, although Communists often were integral to their success. All were based on what some called their "vernacular revolutionary traditions," meaning that respect was paid in each country to the histories of their indigenous people, descendants of slaves, original spiritual traditions, differences of gender, color and language, their own legacies of heroism, defeat and martyrdom, etcetera. The movements weren't necessarily Marxist, but a varied brew of liberation theology, revolutionary nationalism, Marxism, indigenism, and anarchism, with deep strains of environmentalism and feminism. [10] What they held in common was a belief in pluralistic participatory democracy, not simply at the ballot box, but through the greater empowerment of local people in the decisions affecting their lives. While the Marxists among them naturally sought to reclaim a universal Marxism, the founding figures of this renewal were Latin American icons differing from country to country in terms of their politics and self-identification. This was a return to the vision of José Carlos Mariátegui, the Peruvian Marxist, whose works Ricardo found so refreshing when he discovered and recovered them from dusty archives. Chávez too was influenced by Mariátegui and his rejection of carbon-copy European ideology in favor of the "heroic creation" of things to come. Bolívar was restored as an icon after having been derided historically by both Karl Marx and most Marxists. Simón Rodríguez, the Venezuelan philosopher who taught Bolivar, wrote around the year of the 1848 *Communist Manifesto* from quite a different perspective: "Spanish America is an original construct. Its institutions and its government must be original as well, and so too must be the methods used to construct them both. Either we shall invent or we shall wander around and make mistakes." [11]

CHAPTER 14

A New Model in Our Americas

In 2006 Ricardo invited me to Havana for a week of talks about the American New Left. The times were strange. After forty-five years in power, Fidel was gravely ill after a risky intestinal surgery, and had handed over the reins of power to Raúl, permanently as it turned out. George Bush's special commission was rolling out its latest plan to force regime change on Cuba and appoint a coordinator of the coming "transition" away from Fidel's rule, along the lines of Paul Bremer's mad plan to occupy and privatize Iraq. As far as I could see, Cubans were calm. Skateboards were being introduced. Hip-hop was the craze. Venezuelan tankers floated in Havana Harbor. Ricardo, who was supposed to be running the National Assembly, instead was transcribing hours of interviews with me, as well as holding discussions with an old guard of Cuban intellectuals, and meetings with the Communist Party's youth newspaper. Ricardo never told me why it was important to conduct some twenty-five hours of interviews that week. At the time he was listed by US Cuba Watchers 1 as either third or fourth in the line of succession to power in Cuba.

Looking back now, I believe Ricardo may have been sharing the opportunity to rethink Marxism and weighing the chances that another New Left might be on the horizon in the form of the antiglobalization and pro-democracy movements. Six years later, in 2013, I emailed him these questions which he answered more or less succinctly:

When we spoke in 2006, were you thinking about participatory democracy as it might apply to Cuba's political system?

RICARDO: *Yes, I think we were talking, among other things, about participatory democracy in 2006.*

Do you agree with Marta Harnecker and others who say that electoral democracy finally became a real option for the Latin American Left after Venezuela and other Latin American parties were elected to power?

RICARDO: *I agree that electoral democracy has become an option for the Left, as has been shown by recent developments. This is the result of long years of struggle, including the time of the guerrillas, the successful resistance of the Cuban people, and the relative decline of US imperialist hegemony in Latin America and the world. But there have been some setbacks also, and attempts to restore dictatorships cannot be excluded. I want to add that I do not accept the notion, however, that democracy equals an electoral party system—with one, two, or however many parties—alone. Empowering people must go far beyond elections.*

Capitalism and democracy are contradictory and antagonistic terms. Socialism, if it is genuine, should imply participatory democracy.

Hans Kelsen[1] was not a Marxist or a left-wing militant. He was one of the most important legal minds who strongly criticized "representative democracy" as a farce, following closely on Rousseau's thinking. He found the answer with the original concept of the workers' soviets [councils] in Russia, which he defined as spreading the democratic process to a "parliamentarization of society." This he thought was the ideal way to overcome the contradiction between representative democracy and direct democracy.

Do you believe that greater democracy in Cuba will be possible only when the embargo is lifted and when the United States officially abandons regime change? That's my view.

RICARDO: *Yes. It is obviously a very difficult task to develop a democratic system under conditions of economic and political warfare. Our* mambises[2] *learned that long ago. It should also be said that only when the United States abandons its imperial policies and nature will the American people be in a position to initiate a process of* [further] *democratization of their own society.*

The problem is to agree on what "greater democracy" means. If in the Cuban case that means to evolve toward a system closer to the American version of "democracy," then by abandoning the embargo and its aggressive policies the United States would have achieved its original goal. That has been the dream of liberals in your country.

I believe in greater democracy everywhere, and to be very frank and candid, that is needed especially in the United States. And democratization means overcoming capitalism and establishing some sort of socialism as Joseph Schumpeter forecast would happen in the United States.

Originally the socialist ideal was not associated with a nationalist project but had a more universal aim and motivation. Remember the split of the Second International around World War I. Later came the "socialism in one country" thesis and Stalin's claim that such a socialism fit the model. Then the Cold War, the arms race and the threat of mutually assured destruction with the Bomb, which closed the possibilities of creative thinking and reduced the alternatives to the dominant models of each bloc.

So the end of the Soviet model opens new possibilities for socialism. The roots of the socialist ideals—equality, solidarity, freedom—go back to long before the steam engine. They came by way of figures and movements that included Jesus, Rousseau, the Jacobins, the Indians, the maroon communities, our mambises, etc.

With the corporate neoliberal trend now backfiring, for the first time in Latin America we are seeing social movements that would

*have been condemned by the old guard Left. Like catechists, the old
guard followed their Book. The problem has always been thinking
about a model. Socialism, almost by definition, should not have a
single model, but contain something coming from the will of the
people according to their own authentic traditions. Except for the
indigenous communal traditions, you will not find a "socialist" tradition in Latin America. It developed in Europe.*

*You need a definition of socialism. Just being the reverse of cap-
italism is too narrow. Does it have other roots than in Europe and
Marx? For example, with Christianity you have communal and
solidarity traditions long before Karl Marx. Traditions of working
together and sharing benefits were here long before Columbus
discovered America. We don't have a different source of socialism
based in a pre-Columbian tradition. That's why Mariátegui spent
a lot of time studying the pre-Hispanics, the Incas. He found some
elements of collectivism. Those Indians shared the ownership of the
land for generations, for example. Some Marxists were critical
of him because the Incas had an Inca. The Indians here in Cuba
have disappeared.[3] You can't really refer to a Taíno tradition.
But in these countries that tradition is more important than the
1848 Revolution in Paris! So leaders like Evo have a tremendous
advantage.*

*On the one hand, the dissolution of the USSR was the biggest
blow my country ever suffered. No one would say it was salutary.
But someday historians will ask what would have happened to us
if the Soviets hadn't disappeared. It would have been what Mills
predicted, a bureaucratic convergence.[4] In the East, state capitalism;
in the West, market mechanisms of capitalism.*

*I was invited to speak in 2006 at an international gathering
of intellectuals on Marxism, here in Havana. I don't know if it's
because I am an intruder on this specialty, not a professional philosopher, you know, I quote you, you quote me, that sort of thing. I
used to be a philosopher in a university. Then I became a diplomat.
Because of the way I lived, I did not have enough time to concentrate
on matters of philosophy. I would have liked to devote more time to*

them, but if you are president of the National Assembly you cannot imagine how many hours there are spent reading and attending meetings on issues you might not feel interested in. Now I feel relief.

The paper I gave was not written against anyone in particular, but maybe it was written to everybody. From a Cuban or Latin American perspective, what happened was this. Marx was a genius, a guy who did what he did, I really don't think he could have imagined what would happen with his writings. He would be surprised. The first problem is that his theory that inspired so many people started in Europe, but was extended to Latin America because of the number of European immigrants who came here bringing it with them.

I don't have the tradition of other comrades who believed in the Soviet Union. I had a very limited experience there, mainly in foreign policy. Knowing some Soviet comrades at the UN, I had a very depressing image of what that kind of socialism was all about. Bureaucratic and dogmatic. I experienced what Che had reported in speeches long before. It became difficult to see a difference between Eastern and Western Europe. Just bureaucrats representing a state interest. What surprised me was the way they disappeared like a leaf in the wind.

The speech Ricardo gave at the conference in 2006 is titled "Marx After Marxism, The Global Fight for Immigrant Rights in a Neoliberal Economy." More than anything I was reading at the time, it explained and predicted the new New Left model that he envisioned arising to confront neoliberalism's ascendant moment. What should be appreciated about the text is that Ricardo was still the president of the Cuban National Assembly, a leader and diplomatic face of the Cuban Revolution to the world. The speech is not the renunciation of Marxism and the communist model demanded by the Right, and even by most liberals in the West. But neither could it have drawn much support from orthodox communist cadres anywhere. It was philosophical, diplomatic, elegant, and prophetic.

Ricardo opened with the same distinction he made in our

many interviews, and in a voice I found not unlike the Port Huron Statement, which we had offered as a "living document." Here is how Ricardo began his speech that day in 2006:

I take as a starting point the warning, not always heeded, of Rosa Luxemburg: "The work Capital, *of Marx . . . is not gospel in which we are given Revealed Truth, set in stone and eternal, but an endless flow of suggestions." Self-critical reflection is called for on our side.*[5]

He goes on to say that corporate globalization is entering a new phase of triumphalism that masks its inner weaknesses and contains "new, unsuspected possibilities for revolutionary action." The most important of these are seen in the swell of confrontations against neoliberalism then (in 2006) sweeping the world, from Latin America to antiglobalization protests in Seattle. "For the first time, anticapitalist malaise is manifested, simultaneously and everywhere, in advanced countries and among those left behind and is not limited to the proletariat and other exploited sectors." Ricardo names "those that demand the preservation of the environment, or work for the rights of women and discriminated people and those excluded because of gender, ethnicity, or religion." In a key passage, Ricardo redefines the class struggle in a way that bears close reading:

A diverse group, multicolor, in which there is no shortage of contradictions and paradoxes, grows in front of the dominant system. It is not yet the rainbow that announces the end of the storm. Spontaneity characterizes it; it needs articulation and coherence that need to be stimulated without sectarianism, without being carried away with wildness. The great challenge of revolutionaries, of communists, is to define our part, the place that we should occupy in the battle. For that, we need a theory.

The world has changed since Marx developed his theory. Alarcón points out, for example, that every twenty-five years global population growth adds in one generation the total number that lived on earth when Marx was writing. "Irreversible climate change" is already upon us, due to capital's devouring of resources. Equally important:

The third world penetrates the first. The latter needs the former and at the same time rejects it. In Europe and North America [the third world] *appears to be an undesirable protagonist, a mute guest that demands its rights. The US Congress continues discussing what to do with those who number at least eleven million people—that is, the size of the Cuban population—the so-called undocumented— searching for formulas that allow for them to continue to be exploited while access to that society is closed.*

These observations, made in 2006 during the first moments of the so-called antiglobalization movement, and one year after an historically unprecedented one million immigrants gathered to demand their rights in Los Angeles, were extremely prescient, creatively turning certain elements of Marxist orthodoxy upside down. Whereas in nineteenth- and twentieth-century Marxism, the undocumented, the lumpen, the unemployables were defined as a threat to the wage standards and protections of industrial workers, in this new twenty-first-century scenario, the third world immigrants were seen as "penetrating" the North and changing the nature and composition of the working class itself. It was true, Ricardo noted, that the new immigrants still represented a pressure to lower wages and were a stimulant to right-wing xenophobia. But capitalism itself had invited them as cheap laborers, and they weren't going home. In addition, few if any American workers thought of themselves as members of Lenin's worker "aristocracy" living happily above the underclass either; they were being threatened by the outsourcing of their jobs to *maquiladoras* in the third world while at the same time immigrants were being pulled into the deindustrialized low-wage service economy of the United States.

We saw them both converge, united, in Seattle, both forces

opposing neoliberal globalization.[6] *One must help them to converge.
To struggle also so that the antiwar and antiglobalization movements flow into the same great stream and that all those discriminated against, all the marginalized, be included. That is the main
duty of revolutionaries today. It is the way to create a better world.
It is the road to take in advancing toward socialism. To achieve
socialism in this century there must be "heroic creation," one that is
authentic, independent, and therefore diverse and unique.*

It seemed as if the New Left that attracted us in 1960 was
beginning all over again. Spontaneous uprisings and social
movements were challenging the status quo, with the key
difference of having a broad electoral mandate everywhere
in Latin America. Was the time of the dictators over? Could
neoliberalism—with its ideological claim that no alternatives
were possible—offer enough concessions to alleviate the popular anger? Could a Barack Obama change the global mood
toward the United States, and become a multiracial face of the
old empire or a president creating real openings for the future?
Would unrelenting greed plus America's unconscious assumption of entitlement toward Latin America continue to unite
the continent toward independence and integration? At home,
would the issue of immigrant rights be the spearhead of a
broad new civil rights and labor movements led perhaps by the
Dreamers movement, a reminder of the early Freedom Riders?
Would Ricardo's prediction of the third world's "penetration"
into the first world come true, assuring a new popular majority
of Latinos, African Americans, Asian Americans, women, and
LGBT activists that could be mobilized inside and alongside the
traditional labor movement in a new majority coalition against
rampant inequalities in the United States? The demography
alone pointed toward a permanent progressive majority. And
as of December 2014 Obama had taken bold executive action
to protect about five million new immigrants from deportation
while removing most restrictions on Cubans becoming more

able to influence America from within. The number of undocumented people in America was about eleven million, the same as the number of unrecognized Cubans ninety miles away. The result of his two executive orders—one on the undocumented, the other on Cuba—will enlarge a Latino diaspora and enrich America's multicultural character.

It remains to be seen what happens, but on one point Ricardo has been adamant since our interviews in 2006: that reform is possible and desirable. The use of the word "reform" may at first seem utterly prosaic in the context of American politics, but coming from a Cuban revolutionary it deserves careful reflection. First, "reform" was the doctrine of the social-democratic rivals of the Marxists in the twentieth century. The term "reformist," even today, is dismissed by most radicals and anarchists—who are a strong force in Latin America and throughout the antiglobalization and environmental networks—as an approach that only reinforces the mass illusion that meaningful change is possible within a capitalist democracy. Reform is precisely what Ricardo spoke of that day in 2006:

I will go farther. I do not believe that capitalism cannot be reformed. The Great Society in your country is an example. The most important task of the Latin American left is to reelect President Lula in Brazil. Notwithstanding his faults, if Lula is defeated, all of Latin America will be worse off.

Perhaps the Cuban Revolution itself was entering a state of reform, a "stage" its founders once believed they could bypass.

I was in Porto Alegre for the historic meeting of the World Social Forum in January 2003 where Brazil's newly-elected president Lula spoke to a large crowd unaccustomed to supporting politicians. The scene was an extraordinary one, with well over one hundred thousand people participating and networking, at least twelve thousand of them said by the organizers to be from around the world. The city of Porto Alegre itself was then an experimental laboratory for participatory democratic budgeting, a model city watched with interest in other countries. I visited agrarian cooperatives that had originated with seizures and defense of vacant lands by a militant peasants' union, Via Campesina (Way of the Peasant).

Lula's Workers Party arose as a parliamentary arm of these social movements, but electoral politics at the Forum was itself a contentious issue. Many if not most of the delegates there believed that electoral politics sapped the vitality and coopted movements from civil society. Lula took up the challenge directly, announcing that he intended to fly from Porto Alegre straight to Davos, Switzerland, to the snow-covered retreat of the World Economic Forum, an invitation-only gathering of the financial and corporate elite. Since Porto Alegre had been constituted as the counterpoint to Davos, many were stunned at Lula's decision to attend both. There was nothing wrong, he argued, with challenging the bankers in their lair. And he promised the throng that day that while change would come in small steps only, that in eight years people might be surprised by all that he predicted would be accomplished.

As it turned out, Lula did achieve a kind of grand bargain, committing to pay Brazil's debts to the international financial institutions and strengthening Brazilian state capitalism while also establishing a "Great Society" for the poor, resulting in a huge reduction of poverty and an expansion of education and jobs. Lula's key reform was the *bolsa familia* (family allowance), a grant to millions of poor families made on the condition that they send their children to school and receive vaccinations. The redirection of national income stimulates consumption and purchasing power, though without a radical redistribution of power and wealth. Under Lula and Brazil's Workers Party, the Left gained ground in local and state elections. Modest progress was made in legitimizing the land reform. Lula indeed spoke up in Davos and other global forums in favor of taxing financial capital and weapons sales to fund social programs. He denounced the 2008 Wall Street Crash as resulting from the "irrational behavior of some people that are white [and] blue eyed. Before the crisis they looked like they knew everything about economics, and they have demonstrated they know nothing about economics."[7] His strategy, as described by one of his Brazilian advisers to me, was to avoid an "ideological confrontation" with the United States, preferring instead to drive the hardest bargains possible. For a moment, he became President Obama's favorite politician in the world, illustrated by such presidential accolades as "Here's my man, right there" and "Love this guy,"[8] and a global advocate for peaceful resolution of conflicts beyond Latin America, such as the in Middle East. When he was listed by Western pundits as the leader of Latin America's "good Left" versus Cuba, Venezuela and the "bad Left" in the region, he refused to succumb to the game of divide and conquer.

While there were clear differences between Cuba, Venezuela and Brazil, Lula acted as if they were all part of a single and newly emerging Latin American bloc. He accepted Brazil's huge corporate sector as fundamental to his national development strategy, not simply as rivals in a class struggle over wages. He was, in short, in favor of state capitalism, social democracy, and an independent and democratic Brazil where the country's poor—over half the population—were assured wages above poverty levels, health care, and schools for their children. Where Lula performed poorly, as in protecting the Amazon rainforest from destruction, new social movements and elected officials entered the field of politics hoping to tip the balance in their direction. This was a huge improvement over the military dictatorship that had imprisoned Lula, then a trade union leader, in the seventies. His was a government that could not have happened without social movements, liberation theology, rainforest campaigners, Afro-Brazilians, and landless peasants. But it was also a country with a powerful business sector, moving through the kind of "national democratic" phase of struggle that good Leninists, anarchists, and original Fidelistas traditionally opposed as co-optive corporate capitalism. The difference in Brazil and the rest of Latin America in the nineties was that the new nationalist elites were largely *anti*-imperialists wanting to control their *own* manifest destinies in a time when US global power was beginning to wane. One key example is Brazil's projected role in Cuba's mega-development at the one-billion-dollar container port of Mariel, designed to facilitate Cuba's position as a hub in trade with Latin America and East Asia.

By any measure, Brazil—and most of Latin America—represented in the nineties a region of economic and social progress while most countries on other continents stagnated or were devastated by military conflicts. Ricardo was correct in his estimate of Lula. Like his successor, Dilma Rousseff, an ex-guerrilla who'd suffered torture, Lula was not an ideological soul-mate with Hugo Chávez, but both were kindred Latino spirits on nationalist paths to a new multipolar world. Cuba was becoming integrated fully into this new Latin America, constructing a counterbalancing power that opened up creative new ways—economic, political, and diplomatic—to make the Yankee listen.

What began as an effort in 1960 by the United States to isolate Cuba was ending in 2014 with a complete reversal, an America isolated in the world when it came to Cuba. The 2013 UN General Assembly vote to lift the US embargo was 188-2, with only Israel supporting the United States. No one—not even America's dependable regional allies like Mexico and Colombia—agrees with the White House on its nonrecognition and embargo policies.

One symbol of Cuba's stature in the world came at the December 2013 funeral of Nelson Mandela in South Africa, where Raúl Castro and Barack Obama were among five leaders chosen to speak. A courteous, globally televised handshake occurred between the two leaders, much to the consternation of the diminishing Cuba lobby. It is said that during the six-second handshake Raúl leaned toward Obama to say, "Mr. President, I am Castro." Under US law, the president is forbidden to "recognize" the Cuban government as long as either Fidel or Raúl Castro is in power.

President Obama simply smiled.

The long vision and diplomatic skills of Ricardo Alarcón have been indispensible to this gradual transformation of Cuba's place in the world to one of recognition and respect. He is too experienced, however, to think the struggle is over for good.

RICARDO: *Nothing can be predicted, as your Vietnamese friend said. In the eighties, for example, they talked about the "Japanese Miracle," but now the Asian tigers don't play the role that was predicted. Today everything seems to be going in the direction of Latin American integration independent of American rule, but you don't know. It appears this will be in Cuba's favor, in allowing the necessary space to develop. I would hesitate to anticipate. But change is here. The 1961 Alliance for Progress promised $20 billion over ten years, and now China spends as much in one country. Latin America is becoming an exceptional place. When Latin American leaders meet with European leaders, the Europeans ask for help now. Cuba has very strong links with the main countries. Dilma and Lula both are close friends. What is missed by foreign analysts is that some countries are counted as US friends, but they are no longer dependent on the United States. They are trading partners, no more. Now there are not only [Cuban] embassies in Brasília and Havana, but Brazil is the strategic investor in the super-port being built at Mariel.[9] Havana Harbor will be for tourism. Mariel will be the seaport. The reason is the expansion of the Panama Canal. The big containers can't enter our harbor. We spent lots of effort bringing cargo through Jamaica to Cuba, but now we will have the economic zone at Mariel. The Brazilians are very active. Lula loves soybean harvesting, for example. What this means is that it's not just support* *from the leftist president and the Workers Party, but you also have the Brazilian business community involved. In the past, we used to have a lot of blah, blah, blah, but it wasn't very concrete. Now everywhere you see a different approach for the first time. We are more or less moving like the Europeans were moving a few decades ago, toward integration. We'll see.*

This involves capitalist production, and to deny it is absurd. In the good old days some thought there was only one form of socialism with strong state control over all the economic activities. You will see people competing, the seeds of capitalism being planted, but also you have to face the realities and adapt them to the social goals you establish for yourself. In Latin America in the seventies it was normal for the state to play an active role in the economy, before Pinochet and neoliberalism. Now most countries in Latin America have the state regulating different aspects of the economy, and that's our case. We admit foreign investment, even 100 percent ownership, but the key is our approval.[10] *It's an open market but with certain state norms and regulations.*

[Sen. Jesse] *Helms actually was trying to close every door to international capitalist influence* [in the name of anticommunism], *it was really crazy. He wanted to close any possibility of foreign investment in Cuba with threats against anybody "trafficking" with expropriated property—that included the entire Cuban economy. If Helms-Burton had been successful, the Cuban state would have been the only investor in Cuba. Also by strengthening and expanding the sanctions against trade with Cuba, Helms-Burton created more obstacles to implementing within Cuba the very changes that were in themselves promoting new economic actors like private farms and restaurants.*[11]

The future for Cuba and the United States may be uncertain. But one thing that is certain is that our past policy of containment and isolation has failed completely. Cuba is a fully integrated partner in the new Latin America. How the United States will adjust is the main question for the future.

CHAPTER 15

Rescuing
Elián González,
Losing Al Gore

A fierce tempest arose in 1999 about a controversial other, a boy named Elián González, who had washed ashore. The drama was intense, day after day, as the Clinton administration, Cuba, and the anti-Castro Cubans conveyed their passions to millions of Americans watching on television from late 1999 until June 2000. More than ever, the irrational wrath of the anti-Castro exiles was on full display across the United States. The tide of opinion rolled heavily against the exiles as the weeks wore on. The US government stood firmly on the side of the same Cuban government that it refused to recognize. Elián González, seven years old, was returned to his father in Cuba after being treated to the delights of Disneyland by his exile great-uncle. Shortly afterwards, Vice president Al Gore, who broke for cold political reasons with his own president to support the Miami exiles in the Elián controversy, lost the presidency anyway in the 2000 election in Florida, which involved massive irregularities by the Republican Party and their new right-wing Cuban American allies.

It was one of the more abnormal episodes in the long history of the American-Cuban dysfunctional relationship. As often before, Ricardo Alarcón was at the center of things, yet unable to play any open diplomatic role. When it ended, Ricardo stood at José Martí International Airport to welcome Elián González home, ninety miles from the scene of drama.

Little Elián and two other Cubans had survived the horrific drowning of his mother, Elizabeth Brotons, and eleven others trying to float to Miami where they could automatically receive permanent legal status in the United States. It is assumed in the United States, of course, that the *balseros* (rafters) are in flight from communist tyranny when in fact they also resemble the hundreds who die every year trying to illegally cross the Sonoran Desert for jobs cleaning American yards and toilets. America's policy of "saving" little ones from communism, in the case of Cuba, began with the "Peter Pan" exodus of 1960–1962 when the Catholic Church arranged for fourteen thousand young-sters, under the age of sixteen, to be flown out of Cuba, leaving their parents behind, in order to protect the children from com-munist "indoctrination." Naturally, the exiles, Brothers to the Rescue, Florida right-wingers, and the Republican Party saw another chance to revive the narrative of Peter Pan in the Elián González case. They turned out to be as wrong about Elián as they were about the reality of modern Cuba.

Elián's mother was estranged from his father, Juan Miguel, who worked as a waiter in a Veradero tourist center. After the drowning, the Cuban American National Foundation (CANF) proclaimed Elián a "child victim" of Castro's regime, a story that soon crumbled when Juan Miguel held a press conference demanding that Elián be returned to him, as justified by both US and Cuban law. The Miami relatives orchestrated press con-ferences of their own, even taking Elián off to Disneyland as an example of the American Way of Life.

RICARDO: *Gregory Craig became [Juan] Miguel González's lawyer. He was very close to the Clintons, a student activist in the sixties who rose to be presidential assistant and White House counsel under*

Clinton, whom he defended against impeachment, and in the same capacity he also served for one year under Obama.

When Greg came here he was at a big law firm with many connections. He was suggested to us by the National Council of Churches' Joan Campbell Brown. He came several times, and met with us for hours and again for hours more by phone. He took a very good position as both a lawyer and as a human being.

After weeks of internal discussion, the US immigration service under Doris Meissner ruled in favor of Juan Miguel's rights as a father. But the anti-Castro relatives immediately appealed and a Florida court ruled that Elián could stay with the Florida family faction during the appeal. Meissner was a Clinton liberal whose husband Chuck, assistant secretary of commerce for international economic policy, was killed in a freak plane crash during the Irish peace process. (I had worked as a temporary adviser to Chuck Meissner during that period.) In addition to Meissner and Craig, attorney general Janet Reno, a former Florida prosecutor, was directing the legal strategy through her deputy, Eric Holder. Theirs was a determined team who knew what they were up against. The US administration's tough position came as something of a surprise, given Clinton's connections to the Miami Cuban Right. Politically, the more expedient move might have been to keep Elián with his Miami exile relatives, though that would have been a violation of US law. Was Clinton attempting to do the right thing after having squandered the possibilities of rapprochement during his eight years? The answer may never be known.

RICARDO: *There was a very difficult and aggressive lady in the US Interests Section in Havana, Vicki Huddleston. Wendy Sherman[1] was our secret channel to Madeline Albright.*

It became very personal for Greg Craig, I think. Greg is very much a family man, so it was not just a legal job but also a case where he was motivated personally.

The Miami Cubans played it very stupidly. It was a moment when the completely different perceptions of the Cuban Right and the American mentality were most clearly shown. They were saying they were the "real Americans" but they were un-American. It was one of the most publicized cases of child abuse in history.

I used to be friends with Diane Sawyer in New York. She came down here, then went to Miami, and had a camera interview with Elián when he said he wanted to stay in Miami. The boy was six years old. She should have been sued, and the network too, because you cannot do that to a little boy. Both Greg and I had been in touch with her hoping she would do something in a better direction, but she didn't.

Ricardo received many urgent messages from US officials while staying in the Havana hospital with his wife Margarita.

RICARDO: *One time Greg called me and said, "Listen, I have a message from Doris Meissner. It is very sensitive. She wants to ask you what is the blood type of Elián." Imagine what goes through the mind! Why is Doris Meissner interested in Elián's blood type? Did they want us to believe they were going to do something dangerous to recover the child? Another time Greg called at night to relate a conversation with Eric Holder. He'd had a strong discussion with Eric Holder. Juan Miguel was getting desperate, he wanted to go to Miami personally. Greg said he would go with him if he decided to go. What finally happened? Janet Reno made a strange proposal to have both families living more or less in the same quarters in a complex in Miami. When Juan Miguel was told this he was very angry, and I am sure the Miami groups didn't like it either.*

That night Greg transmitted to Holder how angry Miguel was. Holder said something like, "It's easy to swim outside the swimming pool." Then he asked, "Where will you be tonight?" So then Greg called me to say something might happen and to ask where would I be. At the hospital with my wife, I told him. I was sleeping with the TV on CNN, and in the middle of the night Greg called again and asked, "Are you watching CNN?"

*Suddenly the Miami Cubans were interrupted by an FBI SWAT
team, not from Miami but from the federal government, who were
taking over houses, a classic secret operation that could have led to
some injury, which is why Doris wanted to know Elián's blood type.
It made us stand still. But it turned out to be an excellent operation
to return Elián. Can you imagine what might have happened?*

Greg Craig was representing Juan Miguel in a custody
case over his son, not the Cuban government, and he advised
Juan Miguel of that fact. The Justice Department was moving
slowly, attempting to placate the Cuban relatives, which proved
impossible. The department even wanted to draw in a team of
psychiatrists for family counseling. When Craig complained
about the dilatory and unnecessary tactic, it was Ricardo who
counseled patience, even noting that the Cubans would have
done the same thing if the situation were reversed. In the event,
the three shrinks met for hours in Miami with Juan Miguel and
his wife, and concluded that they constituted a "wonderful little
family," according to an individual close to the process.

One evening in Washington, Juan Miguel came to dinner
at Hickory Hill, the home of Ethel Kennedy. This was the very
place where Bobby, Ethel, and family sheltered the anti-Castro
exiles in the early sixties, and where angry exiles once broke
in to retrieve their banner from the Bay of Pigs debacle. The
dinner for Juan Miguel started very formally, but ended with
everyone singing around the table.[2] Times had changed.

At a key moment in the drama, Craig drove Juan Miguel to
the Justice Department building for a direct meeting with Janet
Reno. The meeting was closed. Juan Miguel was advised by
Greg to tell Reno what he truly wanted to do. If Juan Miguel's
answer was to become an American citizen, the naturalization
process would have been immediate. The INS general counsel
was waiting in the building. Or, if Juan Miguel wished to take
Elián back to Cuba, that would be arranged immediately as
well.

The Justice Department premise apparently was that anyone in their right mind would accept a hero's welcome in America and turn their back on Cuba. Two members of Congress were called in to the proceedings to repeat the offer to Juan Miguel. It would have been simple for Miguel to choose America. He was "completely independent," Ricardo said. Juan Miguel wasn't a Cuban ballplayer seeking to make millions, nor a dissident fleeing prison. He was a father of a traumatized child, who wanted to take his son home. For one of the Americans attending, however, it was astonishing "that Cuba had become so demonized that it was impossible to believe anyone would want to raise his son there." So far from Disneyland.

After the SWAT raid, Elián and Juan Miguel were placed on a plane from Andrews Air Force base and flown to Havana, where a relieved Ricardo met them. And there they live today, with Elián now twenty-one years old, a Cuban in his own country.[3] When the last of the Five returned, Elián took part as an honored guest at their welcoming.

What is most telling about this agonizing story is how the US government thought it was necessary to circumvent their own FBI agents in Miami, not to mention the administration's longtime allies in the Cuban exile community. Like the segregated South in the Kennedy years, federal officials were forced to realize that on the issue of Cuba, South Florida was not part of the United States.

Poor Al Gore. He was the biggest casualty of the Cuban Right's sabotage of the November election. The Miami Cubans' central role in subverting the Florida electoral process that year is mainly forgotten. Incredibly, Gore had supported them on keeping Elián in Florida, but it didn't matter. According to Ann Louise Bardach's detailed account, the exiles were carrying out their payback against the Clinton administration's return of Elián to Cuba.[4]

Gore won the vote in Miami-Dade County that night, though by a close margin of thirty-nine thousand votes. Bush won Florida overall by 537 votes, triggering a recount. Fifteen days later, the Miami-Dade recount still was proceeding, with a green light from the Florida Supreme Court, before the local canvassing board abruptly cancelled its review. One member of the three-member board, judge Myriam Lehr, switched her vote in favor of closing down the recount. Judge Lehr was represented by the same political consultant, Armando Gutiérrez, who was the aggressive public relations spokesman for the Miami relatives of Elián González.[5] Cuban exile US representatives Ileana Ros-Lehtinen and Lincoln Diaz-Balart[6] took to the radio accusing Gore of trying to steal the election.[7] Only hours later, the election board's offices were taken over by a mob whose participants included Republican staffers and furious Cuban exiles.[8] The long struggle to force democracy on Cuba was forcing the end of democracy that day in Florida and, it would turn out, in America.

The story becomes truly venal if one explores the Bush dynasty's knotty Florida connections to Cuban exiles and mobsters from the time of the Bay of Pigs invasion right up to the 1990 election. Of course, the pre-Bush history was long and treacherous; for example, a June 20, 1972, CIA memo noted the need to cover up the Cuban exiles' role in the Watergate burglary:

> Unumb[9] noted a number of inquiries from the press with respect to the Cuban Americans involved in the bugging attempt at the Democratic National Committee headquarters and their alleged involvement in the Bay of Pigs, etc. The Director asked that such inquiries be met with an explanation that we are not prepared to be helpful on this matter.[10]

The first President Bush was the CIA director who covered up the Cuban exiles' murder of Orlando Letelier and Ronni Moffitt in 1976, falsely suggesting to the media that a leftist conspiracy was to blame.[11] When the same Bush became Reagan's vice-presidential running mate in 1980, Jeb Bush moved to Miami where "the cachet of being the vice president's son quickly attracted the support of Miami exiles, who guided him into South Florida's lucrative commercial real estate market."[12] Then Jeb became a leasing agent for, and later partner with, a conservative Cuban American developer, Armando Codina. In 1984 Jeb Bush was Dade County's Republican Party chairman, closely tied to Camilo Padreda, a former intelligence officer under Batista, who became the GOP finance chairman.[13] In 1987, after being appointed Florida secretary of commerce, Jeb managed the congressional campaign of Ileana Ros-Lehtinen, and his father George declared, "I am certain in my heart that I will be the first American president to step on the soil of a free and independent Cuba." Jeb's lobbying was credited with his father George releasing Orlando Bosch from prison in 1990 and subsequently granting him residency.[14] Meanwhile, exile violence in Miami reached its peak levels during the Reagan-Bush years.[15] The publication office of Ricardo's friend Max Lesnik, for example, was bombed eleven times.[16]

When the second Bush president took office, the Republican-exile incest continued. The Cuban who had taken Elián to Disney World, Mel Martínez, was named US housing secretary, while several others who worked on the 2000 Florida recount reaped political rewards. Since the Cuban exiles were directly engaged in the illegal Iran-Contra program, everyone was pleased when Elliott Abrams, convicted of withholding information from Congress, joined Bush's National Security Council. Abrams, a fixture in neoconservative circles, took over the new portfolio of "democracy promotion." John Negroponte, also enmeshed in Iran-Contra, was UN ambassador; Roger Noriega, former aide to Sen. Jesse Helms, became ambassador to the OAS; Emilio González, a Cuban exile military officer, turned up to head the Cuba desk at the White House; José Cardenas of CANF took a State Department post. Bardach does a thorough job of describing how the Bush executive branch was "stockpiled" with Cuban hard-liners.[17] The second Bush refused to extradite Luis Posada Carriles to Venezuela, where he faced charges for the 1976 bombing of the Cubana airliner.

Elections really matter. That was the lesson the Cuban Right took to heart in "winning" the 2000 election for Bush, once again stopping a drift toward rapprochement with every tool at their disposal. One Cuban exile leader told the *Miami Herald* that "if it wasn't for Elián, George Bush would not have won the presidency."[18] As for Al Gore, critics continue to wonder why the Democratic Party leaders exhibited less passion and aggression than the angry Cubans. The *New York Times* and *Miami Herald* both concluded that Gore would have won Florida—by a narrow margin—if every vote intended for Gore had been counted. But Gore's decision not to fight for a state-wide recount was fatal. Perhaps his lifelong adherence to the proper functioning of institutions, assuring their stability and continuity, was a handicap when confronted by Cuban exiles obsessed with their "rights" to shoot, sabotage, bomb, and rig elections. In the end Gore was rejected by the very Cubans to whom he had pandered.

RICARDO: *Would Gore have been better? Yes, on many other issues. But he would have continued all that Torricelli and Helms-Burton stuff. He was more or less moving in the conservative direction he demonstrated in the Elián matter.*

The tragedy of US policy was partly that it sheltered exiles waging war illegally from American soil. That war featured paramilitary groups like Alpha 66, plots to assassinate Fidel, rocket attacks on the United Nations building, the bombing of a civilian Cuban airliner with seventy-three aboard, bombings of hotels and restaurants in Havana, countless acts of violence in Miami, the assassination of a Chilean diplomat in Washington, D.C., assisting the terrorist network known as Condor in Latin America and serving as mercenaries for the CIA in the Angolan and Nicaragua wars. With the CIA's help, they tried to infect Cuba's pig population with swine flu. They blew up offices of Air Canada, Air France, and Japan Airlines. They demanded haven for known terrorists like Orlando Bosch and Luis Posada-Carriles. (Bosch was accused of thirty terrorist operations by the Bush Justice Department, yet the president expedited his release from prison and in 1992 granted him American residency.)[19]

While they were serving as mercenaries in US foreign policy, the Cuban exiles became a cancer on democracy in America. Cuban exiles played a key role in the 1972 Watergate break-in. They turned Miami into a city of crime and corruption; in 1992, Human Rights Watch, a group usually devoted to human rights abroad, chose to list the city of Miami and its police department as responsible for permitting a climate of violence and repression by the Cuban exile community's extremists.[20] They once forced Nelson Mandela to curtail a visit to Miami where he was scheduled to receive an award.[21] So it was consistent with fifty years of past behavior that they would do everything possible to deny the presidency to Al Gore. Unable to defeat Fidel Castro, they could obstruct an election in America which Gore won by 500,000 votes.

CHAPTER 16

Listen, Yankee!

To those who oppose the steps I'm announcing today, let me say that I respect your passion and share your commitment to liberty and democracy. The question is how we uphold that commitment. I do not believe we can keep doing the same thing for over five decades and expect a different result. Moreover, it does not serve America's interests, or the Cuban people, to try to push Cuba toward collapse. Even if that worked—and it hasn't for fifty years—we know from hard-earned experience that countries are more likely to enjoy lasting transformation if their people are not subjected to chaos. We are calling on Cuba to unleash the potential of eleven million Cubans by ending unnecessary restrictions on their political, social, and economic activities. In that spirit, we should not allow US sanctions to add to the burden of Cuban citizens that we seek to help.
—PRESIDENT BARACK OBAMA, DECEMBER 17, 2014

We propose to the government of the United States the adoption of mutual steps to improve the bilateral atmosphere and advance toward normalization of relations between our two countries, based on the principles of International Law and the United Nations Charter. Cuba reiterates its willingness to cooperate in multilateral bodies, such as the United Nations. While acknowledging our profound differences, particularly on issues related to national sovereignty, democracy, human rights, and foreign policy, I reaffirm our willingness to dialogue on all these issues.
—PRESIDENT RAÚL CASTRO, DECEMBER 17, 2014

223

Until the Obama administration, the United States government never heeded the advice of many rational voices over the years who argued for coexistence with Cuba, choosing instead to hear those strident advocates who sought to embargo, isolate, and ultimately overthrow the Cuban Revolution. Republicans have been most explicit in their demands for a rollback, while many liberal Democrats have explored normalization (John Kennedy), turned away from the prospect (Lyndon Johnson), proposed a path to recognition and reversed themselves (Jimmy Carter), or cancelled the prospect after a confrontation (Clinton), failing in the end to achieve that goal for five decades.

One explanation after another fell away with the passage of time. Since the Soviet Union has dissolved, Cuba cannot be its pawn. Since guerrilla wars have subsided in Latin America, Cuba cannot be accused of fomenting them. Since our government has diplomatic relations and trade with one-party states like China, there is no reason why Cuba should be treated differently. If it's about compensation for our casinos, oil and sugar companies, and Cuban families expropriated in 1960, Cuba has negotiated settlements with other countries and says it is willing to negotiate. If it's about political prisoners, Cuba has released many or most of them. If it's about atheism, the Vatican has good relations with Havana. The search for reasons for the impasse could have gone on endlessly, but thankfully ended instead without a new death or catastrophe other than the decades-long embargo itself. Fidel told Robert Pastor and Peter Tarnoff on one of their visits to the island during the Carter era: "Your policy is to wait for me to die, and I don't intend to cooperate." Indeed, Fidel outlasted the embargo, defying all predictions to the contrary.[1]

There is another explanation for how long it has taken which requires returning to C. Wright Mills's early exhortation: *Listen, Yankee.* The title was a complaint that Cubans could not receive a fair hearing as long as the United States officials assumed themselves superior in the relationship, able to bend Cuba to America's will. But wasn't that the basic cry of the Cubans and other small countries from the beginning? When Brzezinski told historians in a 2014 book that "the whole business of Castro seemed to be a piddling affair," he was reflecting a long-standing superiority complex.[2] Brzezinski also referred to Cuba as "an erogenous zone" of foreign policy, according to a colleague, causing a lot of excitement but not mattering very much.[3]

Obama inherits the legacy of the superpower superiority complex that made us blind to the Cuban quest for respect, what the Irish call "parity of esteem."

RICARDO: *Obama has an advantage in being the first president since Carter to take a different approach to the Miami connection, knowing that the Cuban American community is not the same as it once was, that the previous US policy was grounded in the 1960s.*

According to tradition, presidents take bold initiatives at the end of their second term. That's why Max Lesnik's[4] theory is that a solution has to be now, before another president—Hillary, or Jeb Bush, whomever—starts their first term.

The current US policy is biological.[5] Their thinking is that the day we in Cuba don't have a Castro in power, we will be in trouble. But there is also a Helms-Burton problem requiring regime change, so—it may be most comfortable politically for you to keep advancing the same policy of embargo. I do not think the passing of the Castros will create an immediate process toward normalization. The reasons and force behind the current policy are stronger than that. They still have the catastrophic scenario in mind [regime change]. *Even with other Cubans in offer with other last names—Díaz-Canel or whomever—you will still say you oppose the system. Díaz-Canel was a baby or not even born in 1960.[6] So the change from Castro will weaken the US argument a lot, but it doesn't necessarily mean a change from the Right's catastrophe scenario.[7]*

Ricardo was proven wrong when Obama reversed policy in December 2014, but not altogether wrong. Obama could not end the Helms-Burton sanctions and goal of regime change. The Cuban Right and most Republicans will fight him in Congress. Where the Cuban Right and Obama Democrats tend to overlap is in their opposition to the one-party Cuban state with its control over the economy and civic society. The great difference is that Obama sees an evolutionary path to a freer system while the Cuban Right pushes for the Cuban regime's fall.

The common argument is that persistent, principled pressure for human rights and democracy will empower dissidents and Cubans in general to someday flood the streets and bring down the Cuban regime. The models are the fall of former Communist regimes and the Arab Spring. Anything is possible in the future, but this scenario has failed to materialize in the past. Despite brief and occasional street outbursts, there have been virtually no sustained mass protests against the Castro regime for fifty years.[8] If such an uprising were to occur, the Cuban security forces would quell it. If it still spread, a majority of Cubans would be likely to defend their regime against the prospect of either chaos or a Yankee restoration. So too would Latin America and the United Nations. Most analysts, supported by limited public opinion polling, believe that the majority of Cubans prefer gradual and peaceful change over a polarizing bloodbath with a foreseeable outcome.[9]

RICARDO: *Raúl has already said* [in 2013] *he's getting out in five years. When Raúl announced that, nobody here said, well, that's the end of us. The US misperception is that the Cuban system has been the same from the very first day, that the people who attacked Moncada are still around. Yes, there are a few of them, but they are octogenarians.*

And if the [enemies] *didn't succeed in the past, why should we grant them what they couldn't achieve with their plots?*

No doubt internal problems will accompany a transition to a post-Castro future. Simmering rivalries could rise to the surface, based on ideological and personality differences. But the Cuban Communist Party is not simply an aging clique sporting red stars and ready for the morgue of Marxism. It is true that nine of the fifteen-member Politburo are military veterans in their seventies and eighties,[10] but according to a recent analysis by Marc Frank, many young members started filling the ranks of the National Assembly and Council of State in recent years.[11] The 115-member Central Committee is 41.7 percent women, a threefold increase since the previous party congress; 31.3 percent are black or mestizo, a 10 percent growth.[12] A 2008 survey of National Assembly deputies showed 43 percent to be women, 19 percent to be black, 16 percent mestizo, and 6 percent under thirty.[13] These measures of diversity indicate a regime, however authoritarian, that can be flexible and elastic in response to serious grievances. For example, while tightly holding ultimate power, the regime often launches nationwide "consultations"[14] involving millions of Cubans in sometimes-heated discussion of proposed policy changes.

Cuba nevertheless remains a one-party state with significant racial stratification, and a long history of exclusion and persecution of political dissidents and minorities like its LGBT community. In recent years, some of those negative indicators have declined. For example, according to Cuban human rights sources, the number of political prisoners declined from three hundred to 167 between 2006 and 2010.[15] Amnesty International puts the figure at fifty-three prisoners of conscience.[16] In his dying days, my friend Saul Landau, a close friend of Cuba for fifty years, remarked to me that "too many [Americans] think it's supposed to be a paradise. It's not. Cuba just wants to be treated like a regular country." By that he meant that the Cuban revolutionaries, and especially their foreign supporters, were being held to an unrealistic romantic standard. The defensiveness of Cuban society contributes to the tendency to deny admission of flaws deemed to undermine the country's united front and serve the propaganda purposes of the counterrevolution. For example, tolerating or promoting an independent Black Power movement has long been considered divisive, which impedes a full confrontation with the issue. Acceptance of homosexuality in a macho and militarist nation has been seen as weakening national security. A doctrine of "speaking truth to power" would imply that the powerful were lying. Not acknowledging complex contradictions meant not confronting them. Most of these undemocratic features of the Cuban state can be traced to a one-party system with a rigid ideology which insists on the preeminence of class analysis, as if autonomous movements for Afro-Cuban rights, a competitive free press, independent art, or gay liberation would be threatening or diversionary.

The double standards are obvious. The US, for example, exhibits a high tolerance for our own inbred dynasties, the embedded discrimination against women and ethnic minorities, suppression of whistleblowers, and tolerance of torture when practiced by strategic allies like Saudi Arabia. US officials also are frozen in the Cold War belief that reform is possible within our own allied one-party states but apparently never within our one-party opponents. This Cold War formulation, articulated by Reagan's UN representative Jeane Kirkpatrick, fell apart when the Soviet bloc collapsed largely due to Gorbachev's domestic reforms, but the dogma continued to apply toward Cuba. The rigid US view about one-party "totalitarianism" doesn't account, for example, for the evolution of Cuba's policies toward its LGBT community, led by the daughter of Raúl Castro and Vilma Espín, Mariela, born in 1962 not long after her parents emerged from the Sierra Maestra. Mariela, who directs the Cuban National Center for Sex Education (CENESEX), has successfully challenged traditional Cuba thinking on gender orientation, and builds alliances globally with LGBT communities.

It is a serious contradiction to insist on foreign intervention to impose a two-party or multiparty system in Cuba as a pre-condition to democracy. Any such "new" parties would be portrayed as merely the stalking horses for casino-era capitalism or tropical neoliberalism. Scheer and Zeitlin had it right from the beginning: *"Because the United States continues to be publicly committed to the overthrow of the revolution, dissent and criticism in Cuba assume counterrevolutionary implications."*[7]

NORMALIZATION

The signs of gradual normalization were there for all to see.

One sign came in July 2013 when a North Korean vessel was intercepted by Panamanian marines after leaving Cuba with military jet engines, small arms, surface-to-air missiles, and night-vision goggles on board, all in violation of UN sanctions on North Korea. Cuba claimed the parts were antiquated and being sent to Pyongyang for repair and return to Cuba. The contraband was hidden under more than two hundred thousand bags of sugar. Imagine the potential American uproar about Cuba illegally shipping weapons to the nuclear-armed family dictatorship of North Korea! It's not at all clear what the Cubans were up to. But amazingly, the Obama administration made the issue simply go away, without any consequences. The North Korean ship incident was not going to be an impediment to the quiet rapprochement.

A second 2013 example came amidst the controversy over the young American whistleblower, Edward Snowden, who distributed classified documents from the US National Security Agency. On the run, Snowden took refuge in Russia while trying to reach Ecuador. The only flight from Moscow to Quito, however, went through Havana. An unknown party booked Snowden a seat on a June 24, 2013, flight from Moscow to Havana. Snowden didn't show, and instead spent six weeks in the Moscow airport before gaining temporary asylum there. In earlier times, the Cubans might well have expedited Snowden's journey as an act of solidarity. But they didn't. However worthy the whistleblower's cause, it wasn't going to interrupt any below-the-surface plans to patch up the normalization process. Instead of Cuba, Russia gave temporary sancturary to Snowden.

More such incidents lie ahead that could still derail the normalization process, the most dangerous being a crisis over Venezuela. On the positive front, however, besides the many sequential steps that Cuba and the United States have taken, the December 17 annoucements will create irresistible momentum that will be hard to stop.

In 2009, Obama lifted restrictions on US-based Cubans traveling to Cuba to see their families, and allowed unlimited remittances,[18] huge changes from the previous Bush policies. Under Bush, family visits were limited to only fourteen days during a three-year period, and remittances were capped at just $100. Obama's policy shift, promised during the 2008 campaign, did not prevent him from carrying Florida in the presidential election and indeed may have helped him. Politically, the Obama policies divided and diminished the clout of the traditional Cuban exile community, whose right-wing leaders attacked the family remittances as billion-dollar annual subsidies keeping the Castro regime afloat. Obama also re-opened people-to-people licenses for any Americans wishing to visit Cuba, testing the waters for a greater opening.

Meanwhile, the United States and Cuba engaged in practical negotiations on the sorts of issues that nation-states routinely discuss: hemispheric drug enforcement, maritime rescue, reestablishing direct mail service, oil-spill protections, and behind-the-scenes consultation about ending the long war in Colombia. The Associated Press reported from Havana in 2013 that while these were "baby steps toward rapprochement," that "under the radar, diplomats on both sides describe a sea change in the tone of their dealings," leaving many in Washington and Havana "wondering if a breakthrough in relations could be just over the horizon."[19]

Cuba lifted its own travel restrictions significantly too, with a record 184,787 Cubans traveling to the United States on 257,518 separate trips in 2013.[20] Over twenty thousand Cubans will be able to legally visit the United States annually, acquire green cards, and keep their Cuban citizenship, homes, and businesses.[21]

Cuba also gradually opened space for a new generation of private entrepreneurs, according to a 2013 report by Richard Feinberg, former NSC Latin American adviser under Clinton.[22] Raúl Castro is implementing state budget cuts that laid off 137,000 Cubans during his first year in office; his goal is to shift one-third of the state payroll to independent sectors.[23] In *Foreign Affairs*, the journal of the foreign policy elite, Julia Sweig, a protégé of Saul Landau's, published a long essay entitled "Cuba After Communism."[24] (She suggested to me she didn't write the headline.)

In another sign, the European Union moved ahead of Obama toward full normalization of relations. "It is to some extent a vote of confidence in [Cuba's] reforms and [proof] that the new realities in Cuban society are irreversible, and that we want to be on board," EU ambassador to Havana Herman Portocarero told BBC in February 2014.[25] The new EU policy both anticipated the later US path and attempted to position European companies favorably in economic relations with the island.

In terms of global diplomacy, the emergence of a Latin American pope, Francis, was certain to be a helpful factor in swaying American and global opinion toward diplomatic recognition and ending the embargo. The Vatican maintains proper relations with the Cuban government as well as close ties with Cuba's dissidents, seeing itself as mediating the political divide.

RICARDO: *So people will organize a private business here because they got money from Miami. Or they paint their house. Is that bad? Of course you are strengthening the nonsocialist private sector. But should you never have a private barbershop?*[26]

And of course the kind of socialism we are talking about is not what we had in the eighties. This week on Cuban television, for example, they had a story about the neighborhood of La Rampa just around the corner at 23rd between N and O.[27] *On the sidewalk there they have art from the best artists in the sixties, pieces of mosaic, you walk over them because they are encrusted in sidewalk. What happened is that some state enterprise came to do some installation and broke part of the sidewalk, and now a private individual with employees was contracted by the state to solve the problem. A private guy trying to solve a mess caused by the state.*

Concerning the tourists, I don't have a bad view. For decades we've had millions of tourists from Western Europe and Canada. So what!! They haven't changed the country, they mainly come to enjoy life and relax.

These changes, or concessions to the market, are difficult for some Cubans to accept. One with occasional ties to the leadership told me:

Although I am heartened by some of the economic changes that would incentivize people to produce more, I am worried about some of the negative consequences of this newfound Cuban capitalism: older people who can't make ends meet with their paltry earnings and the reduction of items that were previously available through the "libreta" that allowed them to modestly make ends meet.

The skyrocketing prices at the agros are far outstripping the meager salaries that folks are earning. There seems to be a deepening tension between the new "prosperous socialism" that is being preached with the inevitable social inequalities that come with it. If the inequalities come without an adequate safety net for those less fortunate, then many of the gains of the revolution may be lost. Another thing I've noticed is the absence of ideology in the official speech (Raúl's talk on January 1, 2014, being the only exception to that). I was reminded of Quevedo's poem: "Poderoso caballero es Don Dinero."

It is a long history. I was banned on many occasions. The Inter-Parliamentary Union [IPU] organized a number of parliamentary presidents' meetings in New York on the occasion of the

UN anniversary, and I never got a visa. The IPU protested and decided not to meet again in New York and moved their meetings to Geneva, where I attended them.

The Congressional Black Caucus, on the other hand, invited me [regularly] *to participate in their annual conferences but I never got a visa or the authorization to travel from New York to DC. I remember having been invited by* [Rep. Mervyn] *Dymally when he chaired the caucus, and later. The occasion you mention was rather funny; I was not permitted to attend, but a Cuban delegation led by Pedro Saez got their visas and went to Washington invited by US congresswoman Barbara Lee.*

"Democracy-promotion programs" have not been entirely curtailed thus far. The latest to be revealed, a covert program called ZunZuneo, was a Twittter feed directed to Cuban blog-gers in 2012, meant to incite "smart mobs" against the regime.[28] Amazingly, the project was launched *after* the arrest of Gross. Sen. Patrick Leahy denounced the project, which was not dis-closed to congressional leadership, as "dumb, dumb, dumb." State Department spokesperson Marie Harf said it was meant to be "discreet."

Obama not only believes in "democracy programs" and especially Internet expansion in Cuba, but has a penchant for achieving reform goals wherever possible by masking them in conservative arguments. For example, he implemented his Obamacare initiative by repeatedly noting that it was based on RomneyCare, the Massachusetts health policy signed by Republican Mitt Romney. In the case of his Cuba diplomacy, the president often links it to the aspirations for liberty of the Cuban Right, as if he is ushering in a free-market and Internet revolution. He describes his diplomatic success as a victory for democracy, especially for dissidents and bloggers in Cuba, most of whom, by the way, feel betrayed by Obama's initiative.[29]

Obama has glorified, for example, Cuban's most famous dis-sident blogger, Yoani Sánchez, whose *Generation Y* blog depict a drab, paranoid, repressive, frustrating everyday life in Cuba for someone growing up long after the revolution. *Time* magazine proclaimed Sánchez one of the world's one hundred most influential people in 2008. She sometimes seems to receive more Western acclaim than all of Latin America's leading writers put together. According to Wikileaks documents and the Havana-based journalist Marc Frank, Obama even entered into a charade of an interview to promote Sánchez in 2009. The online "answers" that Obama sent in response to several Sánchez questions were actually written by the US Interests Section in Havana, as revealed in a classified US memo disclosed by Wikileaks.[30]

When I was in Havana, Ricardo noticed a Yoani Sánchez book in the pile at my feet. I told him I was reading everything I could about Cuba. When I asked him what he thought of her, he shrugged.

RICARDO: *She's not Pasternak. The Americans are using her.*

The paradox is that Yoani Sánchez and her husband Reinaldo Escobar are critical of the embargo and diplomatic isolation of Cuba by the United States, because they say the US policies are used as a "foreign threat" which Fidel has used to prop up the Cuban regime. Yoani doesn't mention these views in Miami, but seems to have said so in a 2010 interview, according to Salim Lamrani.[31] Her journalist husband has said:

> The United States has made huge mistakes in its policy toward Cuba. The so-called blockade or embargo, the so-called Helms-Burton Act, all have a typically interventionist nature, of a very strong pressure. The main mistake that the United States has committed regarding Cuba is to stubbornly refuse to recognize the legitimacy of the government of Cuba. That's everything.[32]

Obama believes that the Internet will be a liberating instrument for Yoani Sánchez's *Generation Y* to pierce the closed structures of Cuban society. An information war, in this view, is more likely to succeed where invasions, spying and diplomatic isolation have failed. There is no doubt that Cuban officials are concerned about the potential impact of Internet freedom, but more as a crisis to be managed, not as a fatal threat. As Internet access inevitably spreads on the island, the Cubans will have to accommodate a blogosphere more or less independent of the state. The pressure for access to information and greater democracy will grow. That could be benign and very useful for Cuba, if it is distinctly separated from CIA covert operations. Unfortunately, America's National Security Agency policy often blurs any line between democratic exchange and intelligence gathering, perpetuating the widespread Cuban belief that any criticism voiced in the blogosphere should be discounted as serving the interests of Yankee Big Brother.

THE NEW CUBAN DIASPORA

Shifting immigrant tides are fundamental to encouraging normalization. Many excellent studies, including those by Susan Eva Eckstein (2009), Louis Pérez Jr. (1999), and Ruth Behar (1995), point to the same conclusion, that recent generations of Cuban immigrants to America come for economic reasons like most other immigrants, not to join an army led by Batista's ghost.[33] While the first generation was overwhelmingly white, the later groups tend to be brown or black. While the first generation proclaimed, "We shall return," like Gen. Douglas MacArthur in the Pacific, the new generations expect to return often and freely. In 2013 alone, nearly six hundred thousand Americans travelled there, most of them Cuban Americans.[34] In Eckstein's summary, "the New Cubans have done more to change Cuba through their cross-border bonding and income sharing than the rich, powerful exiles who used their clout to make the wall across the Straits as impermeable as possible." She adds that the new ties with the diaspora also have "the unintended effect of undermining the state socialist economy, the socialist system of stratification, socialist precepts, and the socialist normative and socialist order."[35]

RICARDO: *In terms of changing Cuban society, the most effective instruments will be the Cubans coming back. They have been doing this for years. So what? It is a two-way influence. For Cubans here, they get a broader view of Miami and the United States. It changes the mentality of Cuban Americans too, because they see that not everyone here is some kind of terrorist. What freer travel permits is a better understanding of Cuba's realities, and some benefits for the visitors, much cheaper medicines, for example.*

The most effective ambassadors are the Cubans, someone on the corner bringing gadgets back from Miami. When they are in their dining rooms they probably are not pretending to mislead. They will say work is harder in the United States. And they can bring some different elements into the mix here. Maybe some fashion, or music.

Pay attention to this. [Sen. Marco] *Rubio and others strongly oppose normalization for a simple reason that Obama's policy plus our policy of eliminating our travel restrictions may lead to their biggest nightmare. You have a growing segment of Cuban Americans who left Cuba or will want to leave in the future but who want to return to Cuba any time they wish. It's different than the old antagonism of the sixties, when a Cuban was the only person on earth who had to make a decision either to stay in the land of their birth or live forever in another country.*

Cuba was never a minor player in immigration matters. It was second only to Mexico as a source of [legal] *immigrants to the United States. In addition, thousands of Cubans went to the United States, overstayed their visas, and worked. When the revolution happened, the US passed the Cuban Adjustment Act, which was meant to benefit the Batista people, covering all Cubans who left on January 1, 1959, or thereafter. It was the only adjustment act that excluded benefits from those who were there at the time of its passing. They were discriminating against undocumented Cubans who already were there. Now Cuba is eliminating restrictions on our side, and so if the US grants a visa now to any Cuban to go to visit a family member in the United States, if that person remains there, we don't care. This will lead us back to the fifties era with people just going back and forth.*

Ninety-five percent of those who go to the States, come back. No other country is like that. It's not by chance that the Cuban Adjustment Act was adopted in 1966. If a Nicaraguan went to Miami in that time they didn't get a Cuba Adjustment Act.

As a result, the construction of a Cuban anti-Castro community is more and more dissolving. If you were to repeal the law, then Cubans would be more like the other Latinos—hey, they should have a Cuban Adjustment Act! Seriously, now they need alliances. The best position for them will be maybe to advocate for the inclusion of every other Latino living in the United States. It's uncomfortable to see our brothers and sisters facing hostilities from other Latinos in the States now.

What has been the problem is that those elderly Cubans became more American than Cuban. Max Lesnik moved to Miami but retained his Cuban citizenship. Those who were supposed to be fighting to return to Cuba very interestingly became US citizens with a lot of privileges.

The younger Cubans in Florida are Obama voters. He won Florida statewide in 2008 with only 35 percent of the Cuban vote, though taking a majority of young Cuban Americans, and won again in 2012 with 49 percent of the overall Cuban American vote.[36] They were far from isolated. In CNN and Gallup polls, a robust 64 percent of Americans opposed economic sanctions against Cuba as early as 2009, Obama's first year in office.[37] Those majorities prevailed through the December 17 policy changes.

The shift in American public opinion should facilitate the US removal in 2015 of Cuba from the State Department list of states sponsoring terrorism. The desgnation, first made in 1982, is not only false but costs Cuba hundreds of millions of dollars in lost trade annually.[38] Only three other countries are on the terrorism list: Syria and Sudan, where civil wars are killing tens of thousands of people, and Iran, which is engaged in multiple covert operations amidst sectarian conflicts. According to the State Department's own 2012 report, there was "no indication that the Cuban government provided weapons or paramilitary training to terrorist groups."[39] Cuba has opposed the Al Qaeda worldview and politics from the beginning. Where Cuba has supported guerrillas in the past, especially across the Americas, it now enjoys peaceful diplomatic, political, and trade relationships. Cuba provides counsel and diplomatic mediation to Colombia's long-standing guerrilla movement in its efforts at a political settlement. That leaves in Cuba a small number of exiles from the Basque separatist movement, the Black Panthers, and a few others. The most controversial to American authorities is Assata Shakur, a former Panther now residing quietly in Havana. I have known her since the sixties, and visited her at a Havana restaurant in 1999. She does some translating, sees occasional American friends, stays in contact with her daughter in America, and is known to push her aged Volkswagen up the steep Havana streets when her engine sputters out. Since 2005, the FBI has classified her as a "domestic terrorist" and offered a one million dollar reward for her capture. In 2013, the FBI named her a "Most Wanted Terrorist." She lives a guarded life because of the threat of bounty hunters, perhaps from El Salvador or the Cuban exile groups.

Assata's story is not that of a terrorist in any conventional sense, but more a matter of law enforcement rhetoric gone wild. She presumably was involved in criminal acts to gain funds for a black underground network in the early seventies. In 1973, she was pulled over by state troopers on the New Jersey Turnpike, where a violent confrontation broke out. Her comrade and lover, Zayd Malik Shakur, was shot and killed. Assata was grievously wounded. One state trooper was killed, and another badly wounded. Assata was taken to the state's highest security prison where she gradually healed from her wounds. Next, the state authorities indicted her for six other crimes, which resulted in three acquittals and three dismissals of charges. She remained under tight security until 1979 when an underground cell broke her free and arranged her passage to Havana.

Immediately following the December 17 announcement, New Jersey Gov. Chris Christie, Sen. Robert Menendez, and state police called for the Cubans to return Shakur to the United States. Cuba immediately rejected the notion, calling her a political prisoner. Why a shootout with New Jersey state troopers in 1973 qualified her as a "most wanted terrorist" can only be explained by New Jersey's Cuban exile politics. The state troopers understandably want revenge for the killing of one of their own, and for their embarrassment at her escape.

RICARDO: *Regarding Cuba it is unnecessary* [to say the least] *to repeat what has been reiterated—at the highest level—by the Spanish government* [on granting asylum at their request to some Basque militants] *and by the Colombian government* [about the guerrillas that have been meeting with them in Havana seeking a peaceful resolution of their conflict]. *Giving refuge to some Americans—such as Assata—has also been used by Washington in a preposterous manner. Assata is not a terrorist but an intellectual and a symbol of Afro-American resistance.*

On the other hand, since January 1, 1959, the United States has been home to the worst criminals of the Batista era and after. All of them protected and employed by the US as active terrorists whose actions have also involved killing people in US territory. Posada Carriles and Orlando Bosch are just two examples of such a systematic policy of terrorism promotion.[40]

For several decades, until 2008, Nelson Mandela and the ANC, were on that terrorist list and were kept there by Democratic and Republican administrations alike. Mandela was classified as a ter-

rorist when he was incarcerated—after having been captured by
the apartheid regime with the direct participation of the CIA—and
was still considered a terrorist after having been freed and remained
on that list when he was president and after having received the
Nobel Peace Prize and was kept in that list when he was well into
retirement from public life. Do you want a better joke?

DEMANDING DEMOCRACY?

The reader will have noticed by now that this is not another of
countless books on Cuba that begin with a denunciation of dictatorship and a long listing of political prisoners. To be taken seriously in mainstream publishing, an American writer must make
clear that he or she harbors no sentimentalism toward Fidel
Castro and his revolution. Such concerns have merit, but the
premise clouds any deeper or more expansive portrait of Cuba.
It is like reducing all of American society and politics to the fact
that a young black man is killed by police every twenty-four hours
and our prisons hold one-fourth of all the world's inmates. There
is no question that Cuba suffers what can be politely called a def-
icit of democracy. C. Wright Mills worried about this prospect in
Listen, Yankee over forty years ago. Numerous books have been
written on the subject over the years by many persuasive authors
including Jacobo Timerman and Alma Guillermoprieto.[41]

My own views were stated by Pete Seeger as long ago as 1971:

At present Cuba may be headed for the same trouble
that has hobbled the USSR and China, by limiting
criticism to certain prescribed channels." He went on
to make a trenchant observation: socialism "rarely pro-
duces people ambitious for money or prestige, but it
almost never seems to produce the brilliant noncon-
formist.[42]

But the criticisms miss the central point. After more than fifty years of pressure that would have caused virtually any other one-party state to fall, Cuba still stands. After fifty-years of failed "democracy promotion," another perspective is needed.

Where does Ricardo Alarcón fit in the debate over democracy in Cuba? As a leading Cuban official for many decades, he shares some responsibility for many policies for which Cuba is legitimately criticized. The Cuban archives in time may reveal his dissents on given policies; for his institutional loyalty he absorbs a drumbeat of criticism. In 2008 in Havana, he was put on the defensive by student questioners with complaints about Internet access and everyday economic frustrations; the videoed exchange went viral, cementing an impression among critics that Alarcón was something between an apologist and a dinosaur. Yet Alarcón has survived many shakeups and purges to the consternation of critics like Ann Louise Bardach, who can't explain his survival, especially since she considers him to have "a dicey personal relationship with the Castros."[43]

Ricardo is hardly going to denounce the revolution or the party to which he has devoted his life. But it would be a terrible mistake to fail to see that he has been a powerful, pragmatic reformer working from within the Cuban Revolution to reform and modernize the structures he fought to build. He could not very well represent the Cuban government in its long quarrel with the United States and at the same time be a domestic critic.

In 1993, according to Gott, he was chosen to "bring back life to the National Assembly ... as its new president ... [h]is task was to preside over what were, in effect, Cuba's fledgling attempts to install a new kind of 'participatory democracy' ... [and he] soon articulated an intelligent defense."[44]

Having said that, *poder popular* rested on a different vision than the American version of participatory democracy. But we in the States never faced the full wrath of the Pentagon, the CIA, and a blockade. Even in a more open and democratic atmosphere, the FBI's COINTELPRO programs were crucial in splintering, disrupting, and damaging our American social movements. The repression by our own government contributed directly to many of us becoming sectarian, factional, pushed toward violence. The style of the mainstream mass media gave rise to cults of personality with all the corollary damage to grassroots democracy. Given the greater pressure it was under, it's hard to imagine how the Cuban Revolution survived in any form, much less how it earned respect in most of the world.

Cuba took the path of Marxism-Leninism when it appeared to the leadership that the Soviet Union was their only protection against the United States. The original revolutionaries were hunted men and women who learned to live and struggle in shadowy spaces far from an open society. They brought those habits of clandestinity from the days of the 26th of July movement to the consolidation of the Cuban Communist Party in 1965, four years after the Bay of Pigs. In another decade, they evolved further, establishing the National Assembly, a parliamentary structure representing domestic constituencies, and brought back Ricardo from his foreign service to head the new institution. (For a rough comparison, the United States Senate didn't become a directly elected body until 1913.)

It was after the Soviet collapse that Ricardo assumed leadership of the National Assembly. In 1992, the 1976 Constitution was amended, providing for the direct election of deputies. The transfer of state-owned property to new joint ventures was permitted, with the number rising from two in 1990 to 112 by 1993. The US dollar was legalized as the principal currency for traded goods and services for the first time since being introduced in the US occupation. Also in 1993, self-employment opportunities were restored in principle for private businesses after being banned since 1968. Agricultural cooperatives and farmers' markets began to replace state-owned farms. These were evolutionary reforms, although the monopoly of political power in the hands of the Communist Party remained intact.

A forgotten reason for the Cuban government's lingering

resilience is that Cuba actually progressed in many areas over the course of the last fifty years in its overall quality of life and economic achievements, despite the embargo. It is no paradise. But how many countries would have stabilized and improved at all after a revolution, an invasion, constant covert attacks, an economic embargo, and the fall of its most powerful ally? As a November 2012 Congressional Research Service report noted, Cuba's real GDP went from 5.8 percent (2004) to 11.2 percent (2005), 12.1 percent (2006), 7.3 percent (2007), and then cratered to 1.4 percent in 2009 partly due to the Wall Street economic crisis before crawling back toward 3 percent in 2013.[45] More important, for decades Cuba has ranked among the countries in the High Human Development category defined by the United Nations, for its achievements in health care, literacy, and education.[46] At over seventy-nine years, Cuba's life expectancy is competitive with or slightly above that of the United States.[47] It has one of the highest per capita numbers of doctors of any country in the world. Its classical ballet is known everywhere. Cuba was fifty-ninth out of 186 countries in the UN development index in 2012, higher than nearly every Latin American and Caribbean nation. Though lying in a deadly hurricane corridor, Cuba's disaster preparedness is unmatched. Cuban athletes have collected 196 gold, silver, and bronze medals at the Olympics since the revolution, as opposed to only twelve before 1959.[48]

These achievements occurred while Ricardo presided over the National Assembly under the domination of the Communist Party, and go far toward explaining why the Cuban system, for all its flaws, retains a core legitimacy in the eyes of most Cubans.

How many Cubans? To estimate a percentage, the Cuban-based journalist Marc Frank borrows terminology from Eastern Europe during the Cold War, using the category of "grey zone" to describe citizens who are dissatisfied but unwilling to rebel against the system. By this standard, he estimated in 2013 that a majority of Cubans fell in the grey zone—"increasingly restless for change"—and wrote that Raúl Castro was trying to win them back.[49] A 1995 *Nuevo Herald*/Gallup underground poll showed 31 percent significantly dissatisfied, while 76 percent were "somewhat" or "very" satisfied with their lives, and 58 percent felt the revolution had more successes than failures.[50] That's a popular base for regime *reform*, not regime change.

RICARDO: *What is going on now in Latin America, among the ALBA countries, is a pattern composed of a "diversity which is multi-colored but not yet rainbow"* [quoting his 2006 article]. *And with the help of the neoliberal trend backfiring, for the first time in Latin America, we are having a real social movement that would have been condemned by the old guard. It was very difficult for them to understand it was not "the end of history" but we were entering a new period of history. Ironically, it gave more opportunity to the revolutionary movement. Why? Because the concept of a centralized* [revolutionary] *leadership across boundaries disappeared, and because of the new way in which information goes around in the present world.*

The future of Latin America is far from settled. But obviously, if Cuba intends to bond and integrate with Latin America there is no possibility of their exporting the current single-party model of the Cuban Communist Party. The Cuban Revolution will have to accept the fruits of its long advocacy of an independent region of the Americas, which for now includes a democratic electoral path enabling the advancement of social equality, regulated economies including corporations, cooperatives and worker-run enterprises, and regional integration in defense, diplomacy, and development. That's not communism, nor does it mean capitulation to Wall Street and the unregulated market. It means a permanent process in which to struggle toward an economy and politics under popular control. It's a future that Ricardo Alarcón has helped to shape.

EPILOGUE

Old friends are passing quickly. One of them, Saul Landau, who died of cancer in late 2013, was a regular link between Ricardo and myself. Saul was inspired by the Cuban Revolution in 1960 and spent his lifetime traveling there, writing books and articles, documentary films, serving as a hopeful go-between in the long process of normalization. Saul was there as a founding member of Fair Play for Cuba. Saul was there as a translator for C. Wright Mills. Decades later, Saul was passing messages between Kissinger and Fidel. Saul sometimes lamented that the Cuban dream was fading. His daughter Carmen attended medical school in Cuba, married a Cuban, gave Saul a grandson. Saul mentored and opened doors for Julia Sweig, who became the Cuba expert at the prestigious Council of Foreign Relations. In recent years, Saul undertook the grueling journey to interview Gerardo in a California desert prison. In one of his final projects, Saul filmed a documentary interview with Mariela Castro, Raúl's daughter, Cuba's leading advocate of LGBT rights—Saul had met her in San Francisco and thought her to be a "great lady." Saul also sent me a flurry of emails proposing that Cuba should agree to take the US detainees from Guantanamo in exchange for the United States giving back the prison site. His brain never ceased.

In the final days when Saul's health problems became terminal, Ricardo issued a lengthy tribute on behalf of the Cuban people and government.

Days before he died, I visited Saul at his home near the sea, in Alameda, California. He was suffering, barely able to move, busy holding last conversations with old friends like California senator and former congressman John Burton, who came along with me to say goodbye.

Looking at Saul's tired frame, I thought of Cuban history. We were all so young when the revolution was born, vibrant, new, experimental, radical. Whatever troubles, even nightmares, lay ahead, we would overcome them. In a surprisingly short time, great things were achieved. At midlife, power consolidates, with all its contradictions. We experienced unexpected setbacks and divisions. Power becomes middle-aged, then simply old. The process is not a choice, neither for a movement nor for a single human being, not for Cuba's revolution and not for Fidel and Raúl Castro. Revolutions have similar phases to the human: the bloody eruption of birth, innocence and idealism, the forceful assertion of autonomous identity, the struggle with inner and outer foes, the responsibilities of power, then decline and atrophy, with renewal and revision coming on the terms of the next generations for whom the past is ancient history.

Having already shaken the world and altered politics in favor of the dispossessed, the Cuban people are entering a new chapter in what Martí called the vast and beautiful space of "our America."

ACKNOWLEDGMENTS

I want to thank my wife Barbara, and sons Troy and Liam, who have accompanied me to Cuba where they wandered in wonder while I spent hours and sometimes days in interviews with Cuban contacts, most importantly Ricardo Alarcón, usually on the empty sixth floor of the Hotel Nacional. I must especially thank Ricardo himself, a leader of the Cuban Revolution and state for over five decades, for his patience with my hundreds of questions since we first began our interviews in 2006. His many years of listening to often-insufferable US diplomats perhaps prepared him well for our fifty hours of back and forth over seven years. His daughter Margarita has gone out of her way to support and sometimes interpret the conversation over time. Many other Cubans, including some who were there from the early revolutionary years right up to the diplomatic achievement of December 17, 2014, have been incredibly open with their observations.

I remained in close touch for years with my late good friends Saul Landau and Len Weinglass. Saul, a San Francisco Bay area graduate student and young journalist, took the sociologist C. Wright Mills on a 1960 trip to Cuba where he interviewed Fidel at length and then wrote the best-selling *Listen, Yankee* in homage to which I have titled this book. Saul wrote hundreds of articles and filmed numerous documentaries about the Cuban Revolution through all its twists and turns. Even though Saul felt at times that the Cuban revolutionary dream had "faded," he remained a passionate historian, occasional citizen-diplomat, and defender of Cuba until he succumbed to cancer in 2013. In his final days, Saul was finishing a documentary about a new heroine of his, Mariela Castro, daughter of Raúl Castro and niece of Fidel, who became an elected member of the Cuban parliament and is a passionate advocate of LGBT equality.

Len Weinglass became one of my best friends after we met in Newark in 1965, where I was a young community organizer and he had opened a law practice after Yale Law School and the Air Force. Our lives were changed by the massive urban rebellion of July 1967, which occurred in an atmosphere charged with revolutionary aspirations—fueled in part by the Cubans in Havana and the triumph of their successful revolution. Len was a brilliant member of the team of lawyers defending the Chicago Eight, including myself, when we faced federal charges of conspiring to disrupt the Chicago Democratic convention in 1968. He went on to conduct methodical defenses of many of the most controversial radicals of our time, far from his roots at Yale. But his most challenging case of all was that of the Cuban Five, a group of Cubans who illegally infiltrated the United States to monitor the Cuban exiles attempting to subvert the Castro regime from protected sanctuaries in Florida. The Five were charged variously with conspiracy to murder, illegal entry, and false documentation when they were rounded up in Miami in September 1998. Since impossible cases were Len's specialty, I suggested that he take the Cuban Five case on federal appeal, which Len did with steady success. He was reading an appellate brief for one of the Cuban Five on his deathbed, alongside Tolstoy's *War and Peace*, when he died of cancer in 2011.

Indeed there are only a few survivors left among those who were present in 1959 when the US-supported Batista regime fled Havana before the approaching insurgents, whose leader, Fidel Castro, spoke in Havana while a white dove descended to his shoulder. When I began researching this book, Alfredo Guevara, a lifetime friend of Fidel and Raúl Castro, described the moment as the "pre-post-Castro era." He too passed away in 2013, at eighty-seven. Another early revolutionary, Enrique Oltuski, passed away shortly after I interviewed him in the nineties. Another old friend of Fidel's, who left Cuba over communism but promoted détente, was Max Lesnik, who is still around, having survived multiple bombing assaults in Miami for promoting dialogue. I also was pleased to interview Manuel Yepe, an early Prensa Latina editor who brought Mills to meet Fidel in the Sierra in 1960, and his sociologist-feminist partner Marta Núñez.

On the American side I want to thank Ethel Kennedy and her son Bobby Jr., for reminiscing about those perilous times when the Kennedys and Fidel were on the brink of global war, and sharing with me their recollections of how President Kennedy and his brother, US attorney general Robert Kennedy, saw the unfolding drama. The Kennedy family's subsequent reconciliation and friendship with the Cubans is an important model of reconciliation for the future.

I must thank also the many US officials, diplomats, and American historians who were willing to be interviewed for the chapters on the foiled history of past attempts at reconciliation: Greg Craig, Morton Halperin, Wayne Smith, William LeoGrande, Peter Kornbluh, Richard Feinberg, and Robert Pastor all gave willingly of their time and personal knowledge. Tim Rieser in the office of Sen. Patrick Leahy was invaluable. US Congress members including Karen Bass, Jim McGovern, and Barbara Lee kept me aware of their continuous advocacy for a new policy. The State Department's Jack McGrath shared the official US perspective with me. Julia Sweig, a protégé of Saul Landau's now at the Council on Foreign Relations, provided expert insights. William Orme at the United Nations Development Program helped me sift through data about Cuba's place on their Human Development Index. The *Nation*'s editor, Katrina vanden Heuvel, was a constant source of encouragement. Authors including Harvard's Jonathan Hansen, Salim Lamrani, Piero Gleijeses, and Gerald Horne were generous with their work, and I wish to thank Harvard's Institute of Politics for holding a seminar in 2014 where I shared my findings.

I must thank profusely Andrés Pertierra, a Cuban American philosophy student at the University of Havana, now in Washington,

250 ▪ *Listen, Yankee!*

who fact-checked and researched numerous substantive footnotes meant to enrich the history and background of many events described in this book. Andres's father, the Cuban-born human rights attorney José Pertierra, always has offered wise advice and friendship, as has his wife, the Cuban journalist Rose Miriam Elizalde.

Jill Hamberg, a lifelong follower of Cuba, sent me blogs and articles about the island virtually every day for the past year. Sue Horton of the *Los Angeles Times* and Gary Reed of the *Sacramento Bee* were willing to test the waters by publishing my op-ed pieces when people were scoffing at the notion that there would be normalization of relations between Cuba and the United States.

Among the many numerous Cuban solidarity and reconciliation activists who shared their memories were Antonio Gonzales, John McAuliff, Sandra Levinson, Phil Hutchings, and former California Sen. John Burton. My longtime friend Andy Spahn never tired of lobbying President Obama to do the right thing. Michael Thelwell and Courtland Cox were helpful with insights into Stokeley Carmichael's stance toward the Cuban Revolution, Pan-Africanism and the US black liberation struggle. Alycia Jrapko of the Committee in Defense of the Cuban Five has been tireless in including me in her forums from Los Angeles to Washington, D.C. Joe Perez of Cuba Travel has never failed in arranging flights and introductions.

My research assistant Emma Taylor did a great job of steering the manuscript through the shoals of creation. She never made a mistake.

Finally, I want to thank the crew at Seven Stories Press in New York. My publisher, Dan Simon, took a risk on me even when I couldn't exactly explain what this book would be about. He believed me when I said I would only know the purpose if he let me write it. Great thanks to Ruth Weiner for promotion, Liz DeLong for her managerial stability, Jon Gilbert for production, Stewart Cauley for the jacket design, and Lauren Hooker for her assiduous proofreading at the last minute. Thank you for Dan's leadership and everyone's collective passion for a story that, until now, hasn't been told.

Any infelicities or flaws in *Listen, Yankee!* are my own. On December 17, 2014, came the wonderful news—just as the last parts of the book were being finalized—that our country and Cuba had decided to normalize relations, requiring a rapid revision for the best of reasons.

—TH, Los Angeles, January 20, 2015

NOTES

Preface: The Day They Said Would Never Come

1. On January 8, 2015, serious rumors of Fidel's death were circulating among close observers of Cuba. It turned out that the deceased was a Kenyan named Fidel Castro. The Cuban leader is eighty-eight years old.
2. Pilgrimage to Rincón for the feast day of San Lázaro, http://www.cubaabsolutely.com/aboutcuba/article_religion.php.
3. *Wall Street Journal,* December 20–21, 2014.
4. Andrew Roth, "Hawkish Russian Emissary to Visit Cuba's Leaders," *The New York Times*, December 20, 2014.
5. It will be interesting to watch the conflict play out over major league baseball, where Cuban teams and stars are competitive with the best in North America. As of 2014, twenty-two Cuban ballplayers were in the major leagues, with several excelling in their positions. But because of the embargo, Cuban players have had to migrate illegally and renounce their citizenship, and they are not allowed to send remittances home. The major league offers big salaries and insists that Cubans not play winter ball in their home country for fear of injuries. The Cubans will want to see their players star in the major league and make good money, while remaining Cuban nationals, paying taxes to Cuba, and representing Cuba internationally. It is conceivable that an MLB team will locate in Havana. See *The New York Times*, December 18, 2014, one day after the official announcement.
6. Sen. Robert Torricelli (D-NJ) authored 1992 legislation signed by Bill Clinton, that tightened the embargo and, in Title II, provided a funding stream for pro-dissident projects in Cuba. Pertierra is referring to an apparent denial of access to Viagra in Cuba.
7. The convicted informants are Miguel Alvarez and his wife, Mercedes Arce, serving sentences of thirty and fifteen years, respectively. Alvarez, known as "Miguelito," was friendly with every American who visited Ricardo, and was present at every diplomatic or government meeting involving Ricardo as well. The chatter among many in Havana was that Ricardo was at fault for not detecting the informant at his side. He was forced to become a virtual recluse for nearly two years before the case was resolved.
8. From "The Great Surprise," Ricardo's commentary in *Punto Final,* December 26, 2014.
9. Jimmy Carter froze his original promise of normalization when the Cubans fought in Angola and were accused of being Soviet pawns. Bill Clinton resumed the thaw, then froze it after the 1996 incident when Cuba shot down exile planes flying out of Miami. The Helms-Burton Act, which Clinton signed, was a gesture of support toward the wealthy Cuban American lobby based in Miami.
10. The Cuban Five were René González and Fernando González, released in 2013 and 2014, respectively, and Gerardo Hernández, Antonio Guerrero, and Ramón Labañino,

flown home on December 17. The latter three all have families in Cuba and returned as national heroes on the same day that Alan Gross flew to Washington, D.C.

11. Head of Cuba's agency for North American Affairs.
12. Cardinal Jaime Ortega.
13. $20 million has been regularly budgeted by the administration for "democracy programs" in Cuba—of the sort that Gross carried out.

Introduction: Two Old Guys Talking

1. C. Wright Mills, *Letters and Autobiographical Writings* (University of California Press, 2000), 311.
2. Ricardo Alarcón, "Waiting for C. Wright Mills," *The Nation*, April 9, 2007.
3. Editorial Board, "Cuba's Impressive Role on Ebola," *The New York Times*, October 19, 2014.

Chapter 1: "A Heroic Creation"

1. Notable Quesadas include Gonzalo de Quesada y Aróstegui (1868–1915) who would go on to compile José Martí's seminal writings and extract permission from then American governor Leonard Wood to build the National Library. Another prominent figure is president Carlos Manuel de Céspedes y Quesada (1871–1939), who in turn was the son of the nation's first president.
2. Hugh Thomas, *Cuba: The Pursuit of Freedom* (Da Capo, 1998), 838.
3. After decades of internal instability, the young Cuban republic found a period of relative stability after the revolution of 1933 and the creation of the extremely progressive constitution of 1940. Although the next decade was characterized by systemic corruption and increased inequality, the major impulse of political movements was toward reform from within instead of attempts at revolution. As time went on, radical reformist movements like the Orthodox Party, of which Fidel was a congressional candidate, gained tremendous political momentum and seemed poised to be swept into power in the coming 1952 elections. Preempting the vote, Batista took power and suspended the 1940 constitution, silencing grievances and leaving no legal avenues for change. In response to this, Fidel organized an attack on several targets, in particular the Moncada military barracks in the heart of Santiago de Cuba, the nation's second largest city. Although his 1953 attack failed militarily, Fidel was able to turn the incident into a public relations success through the *sub rosa* publication of his historic speech during his trial. Convicted and sentenced to fifteen years in prison, he spent only two behind bars before being the subject of a political amnesty along with his co-conspirators in 1955, after which he swiftly fled to Mexico in self-imposed exile. There he built up an expeditionary force that returned to the island with Fidel at its head in 1956, beginning the guerrilla war that would culminate in Batista fleeing the country with the rebels hot on his heels, on New Year's Eve 1958.
4. Chibás had made a very public and specific accusation of corruption against a public official. The official demanded proof of the accusation, which Chibás had promised to provide, citing the same sources that had informed him of the story in the first place. Finding out that there was no evidence and, perhaps, that the whole story had been an excuse to discredit those criticizing corruption, Chibás committed suicide so as to clean himself and his party of the shame.
5. The Directorio was a student organization largely composed of the most radical and politically minded members of the FEU, including student president at the time, José Antonio Echeverría.

6. Scheer and Zeitlin, along with Saul Landau, were early New Left intellectuals attracted to the revolution, spending weeks there interviewing workers and intellectuals, including Che Guevara, beginning as early as 1959. Their 1963 book, *Cuba: Tragedy in our Hemisphere* (Grove Press), later republished as *Cuba: An American Tragedy* (Penguin, 1964), remains an important work.

7. To be precise, on August 30, 1953, the PSP described the Moncada assault as "a rabble-rousing, undisciplined, desperate initiative, typical of a petty bourgeoisie without principles and compromised by gangsterism." Néstor Kohan and Nahuel Scherma, *Fidel* (Seven Stories Press, 2010), 41.

8. The Moncada numbers are from Thomas, *Cuba*, 838.

9. Andy Gravette, *Globetrotter: Cuba* (New Holland Publishers, 2007), 103.

10. The Moscow-mandated Popular Front strategy prohibited the more radical strategies of the CP's early years, breeding discontent in its ranks and causing the more radical individuals to seek other outlets when Batista took power in 1952. Worsening its reputation during this period and since is the fact that it used its relative safety from Batista's secret police to publicly criticize and attempt to divide those who did rise up against the dictatorship. It would only compound the wounds of that time that many of these same figures in the CP would find leadership roles in the post-Batista regime.

11. Fidel speech on September 4, 1995, in Kohan and Scherma, *Fidel*, 31.

12. Thomas, *Cuba*, 605–606, 618.

13. Scheer and Zeitlin, *Cuba: An American Tragedy*, 121.

14. Richard Gott, *Cuba: A New History* (Yale, 2004), 147.

15. Mariátegui was a more complex thinker than I can do justice to. He was branded a follower of Leon Trotsky, even though he had not read such works as *Permanent Revolution*. The Cuban Communists would have supported Stalin's banishment of Trotsky to Mexico and subsequent assassination. One of Mariátegui's formulations bore a resemblance to both Trotsky and the Cuban Revolution's model. Mariátegui rejected in his era the "class collaboration" model adopted by the Cuban Communists with Batista in the 1950s in favor of a complete revolution bypassing the "stage" of a "national democratic revolution" in which revolutionaries collaborate with the "bourgeois" and "patriotic" sectors of the business class. The Castro revolution, in bypassing that stage, echoed Mariátegui's belief that the business sector was too compromised by international capitalism (or Yankee imperialism) to stand for genuine independence and substantial improvements for the Cuban working class. For a general treatment that contextualizes Mariátegui, consult "The Left in Latin America since c. 1920" by Alan Angell, in Vol. VI of Leslie Bethell's monumental collaborative work *The Cambridge History of Latin America* (Cambridge University Press, 1994).

16. Ricardo refers to the February 1924 article by Mella, "Lenin Coronado," in *Juventud* magazine.

17. The "power struggle" quote is attributed to Manuel Piñeiro in Julia E. Sweig, *Inside the Cuban Revolution: Fidel Castro and the Urban Underground* (Harvard University Press, 2004), 10. As a young revolutionary, Piñeiro helped smuggle arms left behind in the failed palace insurrection to the Sierra guerrilla front (Thomas, *Cuba*, 930). He became the Cuban revolutionary government's chief of intelligence for many decades. Piñeiro, genially known as "Barbarroja" (for his red beard) died in a car accident in 1998.

18. Thomas, *Cuba*, 928.

19. Ibid., 930.

20. "Cuban Rebel is Visited in Hideout," *The New York Times*, February 24, 1957.

21. The Mexico Pact was negotiated between Echeverría of the Directorio and Fidel's M-26-7 in August 1956, uniting their forces in a revolutionary commitment to Batis-

ta's overthrow, a broad reform program and a post-Batista coalition including dissident Cuban military leaders.

22. Thomas, *Cuba*, 930.
23. Ibid.
24. Marquitos was a drama student at the University of Havana Theater. He was in the youth branch of the Communist Party. He had been assigned to inform the party of the activities of the Directorio. He personally visited the hideout on the afternoon of April 19. On April 20, he contacted police colonel Esteban Ventura Novo, who promptly surrounded the location and proceeded to massacre Directorio members using automatic machine guns. Ramón L. Bonachea and Marta San Martín, *The Cuban Insurrection, 1952–1959* (Transaction Publishers, 1974), 127–130.
25. Personal interview with Andrés Pertierra at University of Havana, 2013.
26. Thomas, *Cuba*, 931, 1319.
27. Ibid., 1319.
28. Ibid.
29. Bonachea and San Martín, *The Cuban Insurrection*, 127–130.
30. Personal interview with Andrés Pertierra.
31. Nancy Stout, *One Day in December: Celia Sánchez and the Cuban Revolution* (Monthly Review Press, 2013), 329.
32. Hugh Thomas writes that the "general attitude of the Directorio was anti-communist, democratic, middle class and basically Catholic despite what has sometimes been suggested since," 927. The Directorio also carried out urban sabotage and later attempted to establish a guerrilla base of its own in the Sierra. Its slain leader, Echeverría, would have been one of the revolution's foremost figures. After the revolution, the Directorio was integrated into the ORI (Organizaciones Revolucionarias Integradas), an initial attempt to merge the revolutionary factions before the transition to the PSP, or new Communist Party.
33. The Ten Years' War (1868–1878) was the first sustained war of independence in Cuba. An irregular army of property owners, peasants, and freed slaves prosecuted a relatively successful guerrilla war for a decade against all the efforts of the Spanish military. Eventually, the war stagnated, morale ebbed, resources ran low, and the extremely capable Spanish general, Arsenio Martínez Campos, took the field. The cumulative result of these changes led to the Pact of Zanjón (1878) where most of the Cuban forces agreed to surrender.

Chapter 2: The Revolutionary War, 1956–59

1. The vessel, which barely survived the trip, stands in a place of honor in old Havana today.
2. Nancy Stout, *One Day in December*, 126.
3. Frank País (1934–1957) headed the urban guerrilla branch of the M-26-7 in the eastern part of the island. He led the diversionary uprising in Santiago that was to coincide with the landing of the *Granma* in late 1956, as well as a series of other urban operations. The Batista regime was able to track him down and murder him in cold blood on July 30, 1957.
4. Gott, *Cuba: A New History*, 163.
5. Sweig, *Inside the Cuban Revolution*, 231.
6. Oltuski interview with Tom Hayden, Havana.
7. The tallest skyscraper in Havana, finished in 1956.
8. Rolando Masferrer's infamous private army, Los Tigres (The Tigers), quickly became known for their brutal methods against rebel forces and civilian sympathizers.

9. The reference to Masferrer is from an unpublished Alarcón interview with Salim Lamrani in Havana in 2006. Masferrer (1918–1975) was both a Communist Party senator and staunch supporter of Batista. His paramilitary groups provided Batista with protection and executed alleged subversives. In the United States he was apparently acquainted with Mafia bosses like "Santo" Trafficante and Teamsters leader Jimmy Hoffa. Masferrer even met on one occasion with president John Kennedy to discuss an invasion of Cuba. According to an FBI agent interviewed by Ann Louise Bardach for her *Cuba Confidential* (2002), "to some extent the *gangsterismo* of Havana was transported to Miami by a handful of early *batistiano* arrivals, guys like Rolando Masferrer. . . . They set up shop here just like they did in Havana—running protection rackets and illegal gambling, primarily *bolita*, which flourished until the lottery became legal." Masferrer, who had earned enemies in all directions, was blown to pieces by a bomb in Miami, in 1975.

10. Jane Franklin, *Cuba and the United States: A Chronological History* (Ocean, 1997), 34. See also *Cuban Revolution Reader*, ed. Julio Garcia Luis (Ocean, 2008), 120–123.

Chapter 3: The Cuban Revolution and the American New Left

1. Now the American Society of News Editors.
2. Julia S. Chen, "Castro Comes to Cambridge," *The Harvard Crimson*, June 1, 2009.
3. Van Gosse, *Where the Boys Are: Cuba, Cold War America, and the Making of the New Left* (Verso, 1993).
4. Ibid., 90.
5. Matt Schudel, "Activist and filmmaker Saul Landau dies at 77," *The Washington Post*, September 10, 2013.
6. Thomas, *Cuba*, 1277.
7. Van Gosse, *Where the Boys Are*, 140.
8. Ibid.
9. Ibid., 144, 146.
10. The Cubans claimed that the hotel's management had demanded a $2,000 cash advance for their continued stay, either out of suspicion that they lacked the funds, or in an attempt to insult the delegation and ensure that they would leave of their own volition. Since the Cubans had already been the target of assassination attempts and negative attention, the latter intention can at least be understood.
11. Salim Lamrani, unpublished manuscript. Another very serious academic, Felix Roberto Masud-Piloto, also stands by this 100,000 figure in his book, *From Welcomed Exiles to Illegal Immigrants: Cuban Migration to the US, 1959–1995* (Rowman & Littlefield, 1996), 7.
12. An apocryphal tale about his death states that when given a final chance to convert, and to thus escape eternal damnation, he asked the officiating Catholic priest if Spaniards also went to the heaven the cleric spoke of. Upon hearing the affirmative, Hatuey is said to have responded by saying that he would prefer to go to hell.
13. Richard Price, ed., *Maroon Societies: Rebel Slave Communities in the Americas* (Doubleday/Anchor, 1973), 1, 3, 49–55.
14. *The North Star*, April 27, 1849.
15. C.L.R. James, Appendix, "From Toussaint l'Ouverture to Fidel Castro," *The Black Jacobins* (Vintage, 1963), 392–418.
16. Ibid., 391.
17. In his 1961 "Prose Contribution to the Cuban Revolution," Ginsberg wrote: "Now the Cuban revolutionary government, as far as I can tell, is basically occupied by immediate practical problems & proud of that, heroic resistances, drama, uplift, reading & teaching language, and *totally unoccupied as yet with psychic exploration* . . ." Ginsberg

wrote that Carlos Fraqui, a Cuban writer, "parroted the US imperialist line against marijuana" and told Ginsberg that "it should be easier for a poet to understand a revolution than for a revolution to understand poetry." Ginsberg would continue to insist, and would eventually be joined by many in the counterculture, that the Cuban Revolution should have prioritized his values. Cuba prevented the emergence of a drug culture, but forty years after Ginsberg's protest, began lifting restrictions on gay rights and producing films such as *Strawberry and Chocolate* (1993).

18. Van Gosse, *Where the Boys Are*, 147.
19. Scheer and Zeitlin, *Cuba: An American Tragedy.*

Chapter 4: C. Wright Mills, Cuba, and the New Left

1. C. Wright Mills, "Letter to the New Left," in *New Left Review*, No. 5, September–October 1960.
2. Mike Forrest Keen: *Stalking Sociologists: J. Edgar Hoover's FBI Surveillance of American Sociology* (Transaction Publishers, 2004), 174–176.
3. Régis Debray, *Revolution in the Revolution?* (Grove, 1967).
4. C. Wright Mills, *Letters and Autobiographical Writings*, 12.
5. Ibid., 319.
6. Ibid., 324.
7. "Oriente," meaning "east," refers to the then-province of Oriente, which is now made up by the provinces of Granma, Bayamo, Holguín, Las Tunas, and Guantanamo.
8. C. Wright Mills, *Letters and Autobiographical Writings*, 324.
9. "Mills's Return," Alarcón lecture, Workshop at XXVII International Conference of Latin American Studies Association (LASA), Montreal, September 7, 2007.
10. C. Wright Mills, *Listen, Yankee* (Ballantine Books paperback, 1961), 43.
11. Ibid., 39.
12. Ibid., 44.
13. Ibid., 113.
14. Ibid., 46.
15. Ibid., 98–99.
16. Ibid., 107.
17. Ibid., 100.
18. Ibid., 104.
19. Tom Hayden, "Port Huron Statement," *Inspiring Participatory Democracy: Student Movements from Port Huron to Today* (Paradigm, 2012), 152.
20. Ibid..
21. Ibid., 153.
22. Ibid., 154.
23. Ibid., 166.
24. Mills, *Listen, Yankee*, 179.
25. Ibid., 182.
26. Ibid., 179.
27. Ibid., 106.
28. Ibid., 100.
29. Ibid.
30. Ibid., 179.
31. Ibid., 166.

Chapter 5: From the Missile Crisis to Counterinsurgency

1. Gott, *Cuba: A New History*, 58.

2. Letter from José Martí to Manuel Mercado, May 18, 1895, Encampment of Dos Ríos. At the time, Martí was embedded with independence forces as they marched through Oriente. He was still in the process of composing the letter when the unit he was moving with was caught in a Spanish ambush. Martí died in the battle.

3. The Platt amendment refers to an imposed addendum to the Cuban constitution (1901) that had been proposed by congressman Orville Platt. It allowed the United States to intervene in Cuban affairs whenever Washington saw fit. This effectively nullified Cuban national sovereignty. Cuban representatives who had met in Havana to decide on the details of the new constitution were coerced into including the insulting amendment with the threat of continued US occupation if they refused.

4. Carlos Manuel de Cespedes (1819–1874) was elected president of Cuba during the first independence war. He had been a freemason, along with many of the key conspirators prior to the outbreak of the war. Knowing that large, closed-door meetings of important local figures would draw attention, Cubans used the seemingly innocuous practice of visiting local masonic lodges to plan their uprising.

5. When the Ten Years' War broke out, sugar plantations were already common throughout the island, although the largest were mostly exclusive to the western half of the island. For this reason, the west is also where most of the enslaved black population lived. Wary of supporting independence, slave owners and those economically dependent on them became the bulwark of the Spanish regime. It was not without reason that they feared the road to independence would lead to slave uprisings and eventually outright abolition. Many of these same plantation owners had purchased or inherited Spanish aristocratic titles, hence Ricardo's reference to "aristocracy."

6. The policy of burning down sugar plantations had originated when Cubans burned down their own properties in the east to keep the Spanish from receiving any revenue from their seizure. After seeing the worst slavery had to offer in the west, the policy quickly became a moral imperative as well.

7. Raúl Roa (1907–1982) was a prominent Cuban intellectual from before the revolution who brought his years of experience and intellectual capacity to foreign affairs on behalf of the post-Batista government. His experience in the struggle against Machado and the resulting revolution of 1933 bridged the generational divide between both revolutions.

8. Van Gosse, *Where the Boys Are*, 149.

9. In Ted Sorenson's *Counselor: A Life at the Edge of History*, 705; cited in Thomas, *Cuba*, 1417.

10. Joint Soviet-Cuban statement, September 2, 1960, in Franklin, *Cuba and the United States*, 58.

11. Gott, *Cuba: A New History*, 198.

12. Ibid., 203.

13. Ibid., 206.

14. *Verde Olivo*, October 6, 1968; cited in Thomas, *Cuba*, 1416.

15. When the Ten Years' War drew to a close with Pact of Zanjón, between Spain and the Cuban rebels, a small group of radicals, under the leadership of Antonio Maceo, broke away and continued the war for a short period. Because of this, in Cuban history, Baraguá is a symbol of quixotic defiance, with signs in Havana reading "Cuba will be an eternal Baraguá."

16. Gott, *Cuba: A New History*, 205

17. Thomas, *Cuba*, 1415, citing an interview with Che by Ricardo Rojo, in *Che Guevara*, 130.

18. Thomas, *Cuba*, 1409.

19. Franklin, *Cuba and the United States,* 58. Franklin's sources are a 1984 speech by Fidel, a Soviet general at an 1989 conference on the crisis, and another Russian official at a 1992 conference.
20. Thomas, *Cuba,* 1413.
21. Ibid., 1417.
22. Ibid., 1407–1408.
23. Sorenson, *Counselor,* 706; cited in Thomas, *Cuba,* 1413.
24. Gott, *Cuba: A New History,* 196.
25. Bertrand Russell, *Unarmed Victory* (Simon & Schuster 1963), 29; cited in Thomas, *Cuba,* 1407.
26. It was during this speech that President Kennedy revealed to the public evidence of offensive mid-range Soviet nuclear missiles in Cuba that were capable of striking key locations throughout the hemisphere. This was particularly significant because it disproved Soviet claims that all missiles were simply defensive and non-nuclear. Kennedy went on to call for their removal and announced a naval quarantine around the island until the situation was resolved.
27. *Common Sense,* Vol. 4, No. 2, New York, December 1962.
28. Robert Dallek, "JFK vs. the Military," *The Atlantic,* September 10, 2013.
29. Thomas, *Cuba,* 1417.
30. For a full exposition of his ideas, read Edward Geary Lansdale, *In the Midst of Wars: An American's Mission to Southeast Asia* (Fordham University Press, 1991).
31. Evan Thomas, *Robert Kennedy: His Life* (Simon and Schuster, 2013), 148.
32. Lansdale on Mongoose in Fabian Escalante's *The Secret War,* 13–14.
33. *US Army/Marine Corps Counterinsurgency Field Manual* (University of Chicago Press, 2008), 73–75.

Chapter 6: JFK's Assassination

1. Thurston Clarke, *JFK's Last Hundred Days* (Penguin, 2013), 250.
2. The National Archive likes to emphasize the fact that less than half a million documents are still "postponed in full," or completely withheld from the public. Millions of other pages still contain at least partial redactions due to supposed security concerns.
3. To date, the CIA continues to contend that they cannot release at least 295 documents from his file because they would cause "extremely grave danger" to national security. The documents may be released in 2017, but the CIA may attempt to keep them classified. See Scott Shane, "C.I.A. Is Still Cagey About Oswald Mystery," *The New York Times,* October 16, 2009.
4. Ibid.
5. The reader might recall that the revolutionary Directorio is the name of the armed radical offshoot of the student federation (FEU) that led the failed assault on the Presidential Palace in 1956. They later added *13 de Marzo* (13 of March) to their name in memory of the date of the attack.
6. Interview with Jefferson Morley, November 12, 2013.
7. Scott Shane, "C.I.A. Is Still Cagey About Oswald Mystery," *The New York Times,* October 16, 2009.
8. Jefferson Morley, "Celebrated Authors Demand that the CIA Come Clean on JFK Assassination," *Salon,* December 17, 2003.
9. Joannides exercised an "important degree of control" over the Directorio, according to one CIA report. *The New York Times,* October 17, 2009.
10. Gus Russo, *Live by the Sword* (Bancroft Press, 1998), 44; Jefferson Morley, *Our Man in Mexico* (Kansas, 2008), 130, 163. For the size of his team, see Franklin, *Cuba and the United States,* 46.

11. "US Select Committee to Student Government Operations," US Senate, November 20, 1975, 71.

12. This refers to the downing of the U-2 spy plane near Banes, Cuba, during the height of the Cuban missile crisis. The plane's pilot, Major Rudolf Anderson Jr. (1927–1962), perished in the crash.

13. In Arthur Schlesinger's history, *Robert Kennedy and His Times* (Houghton Mifflin, 1978), 541. Donovan also reported to the White House that Fidel was "a most intelligent, shrewd, and relatively stable political leader," 541, footnote.

14. Thomas Mann was the State Department's premier expert on the region, gaining the unofficial title "Mr. Latin America." He had opposed the Bay of Pigs vociferously in the preceding months.

15. Edward C. Keeper et al., *Foreign Relations of the United States, 1961–1963, Vol. XI: Cuban Missile Crisis and Aftermath* (United States Government Printing Office, 1996), Document 320.

16. Fabian Escalante, *JFK: The Cuba Files*, 42; Arthur Meier Schlesinger, *Robert Kennedy and His Times* (Houghton Mifflin Harcourt, 1978), Vol. 1, 543.

17. Thurston Clarke, *JFK's Last Hundred Days* (Penguin Press, 2013); Robert Dallek, *Camelot's Court: Inside the Kennedy White House* (Harper, 2013); David Talbot, *Brothers: The Hidden History of the Kennedy Years* (Free Press, 2007); James Douglass, *JFK and the Unspeakable: Why he Died and Why it Matters* (Touchstone, 2010).

18. Dallek, *Camelot's Court*, 384.

19. Gleijeses, *Conflicting Missions*, 15.

20. Talbot, *Brothers*, 222–223.

21. Ibid., 224.

22. Ibid.

23. Dallek, *Camelot's Court*, 384, 387; James Douglass, *JFK and the Unspeakable*, 177, 248–249.

24. Ibid., 390.

25. Ibid., 387.

26. Ibid.

27. Ibid., 391.

28. Ibid.

29. Talbot, *Brothers*, 229.

30. Ibid.

Chapter 7: Latin American Revolution

1. McCone, in *Foreign Relations of the United States, 1961–63* (Government Printing Office, 1964), Vol. 10, 955.

2. Nancy Stout, *One Day in December*, 211.

3. Dr. Osvaldo Dorticós (1919–1983) was hand-picked for the presidency by Fidel to replace a troublesome interim predecessor. While never achieving the power usually associated with the title of president, Dorticós contributed ideas to the new government and was not an entirely inert figurehead.

4. Present were former president Lázaro Cárdenas of Mexico, then-Chilean senator Salvador Allende, and peasant leaders and socialists from Brazil, Uruguay, and beyond. Franklin, *Cuba and the United States*, 48.

5. Gott, *Cuba: A New History*, 184.

6. Ibid., 197.

7. Despite the restoration of the constitution of 1940 being a rallying point of the struggle against Batista, Fidel ruled by decree until 1976, when a new explicitly socialist constitution as drafted.

8. According to Gleijeses, *Conflicting Missions*, 12.

9. In the First Declaration of Havana, Fidel identified himself with the "Our America" that Bolívar, Hidalgo (Mexico), San Martín (Argentina), O'Higgins (Chile), Tiradentes (Brazil), Sucre (Venezuela), and Martí (Cuba) "wished to see free." In Gott, *Cuba: A New History*, 184.

10. Ibid., 191.

11. Ibid., 217.

12. Debray, *Strategy for Revolution: Essays on Latin America* (Jonathan Cape, 1970), 108.

13. It is important to note that although his death in captivity was officially ruled a suicide by the government, this explanation has long been contested by supporters who point to a lack of suicidal tendencies in his past and to suspicious circumstances surrounding his death.

14. Betancourt 49.18 percent, URD/PCV 34.61 percent, COPEI 16.21 percent.

15. Roque Dalton, *Small Hours of the Night: Selected Poems of Roque Dalton*, ed. Hardie St. Martin (Curbstone Press, 1996), 189.

16. Ibid., 111.

17. Dermot Keogh, "El Salvador 1932. Peasant Revolt and Massacre," *The Crane Bag Magazine*, 1982, Vol. 6, No. 2, 7.

18. Theresa Whitefield, *Paying the Price: Ignacio Ellacuria and the Murdered Jesuits of El Salvador* (Temple, 1995).

19. Hardie St. Martin, "Love Falls Like a Generous Rain," preface to *Small Hours of the Night: Selected Poems of Roque Dalton* (Curbstone Press, 1996).

20. It is difficult to overstate the importance of Casa de las Americas to Latin American artists and writers during this period. Despite Cuba's own questionable cultural policies and the obvious leftist agenda of the institution, it gave recognition, support, and sometimes even asylum along with a paying job to progressive and radical figures in Latin American culture whose work was often banned and whose personal safety was in danger in their home countries.

21. Dalton, *Small Hours of the Night*, 169, 172–173.

22. As a great poet, he was seen as having a higher calling than soldiering, which is something almost anyone could do. See Margaret Randall, *More than things* (University of Nebraska Press, 2013), 29.

23. Whitefield, *Paying the Price*, 61.

24. Though publicly denied at first, the FMLN eventually admitted the truth.

Chapter 8: Enter and Exit Régis Debray

1. In both cases, this refers specifically to the party officially recognized by Moscow, the *Parti communiste français* (PFC). For attitudes to Algerian independence, see Allison Drew, *We are no longer in France: Communists In Colonial Algeria* (Manchester University Press, 2014). And regarding Vietnam, see Alain Ruscio, *Les communistes français et la guerre d'Indochine, 1944–1954* (L'Harmattan, 1985).

2. Régis Debray, "Latin America: The Long March," *New Left Review*, No. 33, September–October 1965.

3. Debray, *Praised Be Our Lords: The Autobiography* (Verso, 2007), 16.

4. Ibid., 24.

5. Ibid., 29.

6. Régis Debray, "Le Castrisme: La Longue Marche de l'Amérique Latine," *Les Temps Moderne*, No. 224, January 1965.

7. George Ciccariello-Maher, *We Created Chávez: A People's History of the Venezuelan Revolution* (Duke University Press, 2013), 19.

8. Debray, *Praised Be*, 39.

9. "Initiated" is Debray's term for it. See *Praised Be*, 22.

10. For the details on this period of training in Cuba, read Debray, *Praised Be*, 22, 39, 42.

11. For a comprehensive and sympathetic history of Che's guerrilla front in Africa, see Piero Gleijeses's masterful *Conflicting Missions* (2003). In 2013, I interviewed the author, who lives in Washington, D.C., and teaches at Johns Hopkins' School of Advanced International Studies.

12. Gleijeses, *Conflicting Missions*, 216. Gleijeses cites Gianni Mina's interview with Fidel in *An Encounter with Fidel* (Ocean, 1991), 225.

13. Debray, *Praised Be*, 46.

14. Ibid., 69.

15. Ibid.

16. Debray, *Revolution in the Revolution?*

17. Ibid., cover blurb.

18. Ibid., 29.

19. Jon Lee Anderson, *Che*, (Grove, 1997), 694–695.

20. Ricardo and Debray both agreed that the Soviet pursuit of "peaceful coexistence" with the United States was at the expense of third world countries where rebels were seeking Soviet support for wars against Western colonial powers.

21. The Bolivian Communist Party opposed the armed struggle and may have included informants who led the CIA to Che. At one point, however, the party's chairman, Mario Monje Molina, demanded leadership over the foco, which Che resisted. One of Monje's objections was that Che's column included only a minority of Bolivians. Another was Che only saw Bolivia as a springboard to Argentina and the Andes.

22. Debray, *Praised Be*, 65.

23. Debray, *Revolution in the Revolution?*, 21.

24. Gabriel García Márquez and Roberto Pombo: "Subcomandante Marcos: The Punch Card and the Hourglass," *New Left Review*, May–June 2001.

25. Anderson, *Che*, 703.

26. According to Che's notebooks, Debray was described as "white bread" (*pan blanco*), and he "stated too vehemently how useful he could be on the outside." Quoted in Anderson, *Che*, 713.

27. Debray, *Praised Be*, 130.

28. Ibid., 131.

29. Ibid., 130.

30. Anderson, *Che*, 713.

31. Ibid., 718.

32. Led by Reies Lopez Tijerina, a Chicano land grant movement staged occupations in 1966–1967, and engaged in a shootout at the courthouse in Tierra Amarilla, New Mexico, on June 5, 1967. When federal troops were sent, the raiders took to the mountains in northern New Mexico until they were eventually tracked down.

33. The Chicago Seven refers to eight radical activists, including myself, who were indicted by the Nixon administration, and tried and convicted in February 1970 for conspiracy to disrupt the 1968 Democratic convention in Chicago. The case was won in the 7th US circuit court of appeals.

34. *Scanlan's Monthly*, January 1971. The numbers were based on reported incidents and categorized according to acts against police (423), high schools (392), and the military (101).

35. Kirkpatrick Sale, *SDS: The Rise and Development of the Students for a Democratic Society* (Random House, 1973), 445.

36. *Foreign Relations of the United States, 1964–1968, Vol. V, Vietnam, 1967*, Document 386: "Memorandum From the President's Assistant (Jones) to President Johnson," Washington, November 4, 1967.

37. Sale, *SDS*, 444.

38. According to a 1969 survey published by *Fortune* magazine, "Che Guevara was a more popular figure than Johnson, Nixon, Humphrey, or Wallace"—Sale, *SDS*, 480.

39. *Verde Olivo*, Havana, December 21, 1969.

40. Special Forces members James Jackson Jr., Dan Pitzer, and Edward Johnson.

41. The black and white photograph of Che that is now world-famous is named the "Guerrillero Heróico" (Heroic Guerrilla Fighter). It was taken by Korda while Che was marching in Havana along with thousands of others in protest of the explosion that destroyed the French freighter *La Courbre* on March 4, 1960. The exact cause of the explosion is unknown to this day, but Cuban authorities at the time claimed it was an act of CIA sabotage. The vessel had been carrying tons of Belgian arms recently purchased by the Cuban government, despite numerous attempts by US authorities first to dissuade and later to impede the sale. Many Cubans presumed that the CIA was behind the action, which further inflamed already deteriorated relations with Washington.

42. The Tet Offensive, which began on January 31, 1968, was a surprise military operation by North Vietnamese and Viet Cong forces, around the Vietnamese holiday of Tet. The scope of the assault and the unexpected nature of the onslaught caught US and South Vietnamese forces off guard. It is often considered a turning point in the war, in favor of North Vietnam.

43. Tom Hayden, "Two, Three, Many Columbias," *Ramparts Magazine, June* 15, 1968.

44. Conversation with Richard Goodwin, 1988. According to historian Joshua Freeman, "Richard Goodwin later said that one of his influences in writing the Great Society speech had been the SDS's Port Huron Statement, whose principal author, Tom Hayden, had adopted some of the cadences and tone that John Kennedy had used in his inaugural address, a measure of how much mainstream liberalism and movements to its left had penetrated one another by the mid-sixties"—Freeman, *American Empire, 1945–2000* (Viking, 2012), 204–205.

45. The Catholic worker movement is a tendency founded during the Great Depression that pushed left-leaning American Catholics to take action to promote social justice and other progressive causes. Although a broad movement, each unit operates autonomously and without organizational structure. The far better-known Peace Corps was founded by President Kennedy in 1961 to channel American volunteers to foreign countries—in order to bring assistance while members of the corps would also serve as unofficial ambassadors for the United States abroad, improving the nation's international image.

46. Before Kennedy's murder in 1963, SDS decided to branch out to build community-based movements in ghettos, barrios, and the hollows of Appalachia. We wanted to create an "interracial movement of the poor" in tandem with the SNCC Mississippi Project. I moved to Newark with a team of twelve in June 1964, and remained nearly four years. We succeeded in building a base among the voiceless poor, but the effort crumbled as national resources were devoted to Vietnam.

47. Sargent Shriver (1915–2011) was a friend in the Kennedy and Johnson administrations. After serving as the first director of the Peace Corps, he went on to head President Johnson's "War on Poverty."

48. The Alliance for Progress was an international initiative under the Kennedy administration created to promote economic cooperation between the United States and Latin America. The publicly espoused goals were benign, but Che, as well as others

among the region's Left, saw behind it an attempt to reform the system of exploitation without changing its essential nature.

49. Debray, *Praised Be*, 130.
50. Carlo Feltrinelli, "Comrade Millionaire, Part Two," *The Guardian*, November 2, 2001.
51. Debray, *Praised Be*, 119.
52. Régis Debray and Salvador Allende Gossens, *The Chilean Revolution: Conversations with Allende* (Pantheon Books, 1972), 119.
53. Debray, *Praised Be*, 110.
54. Jean Paul Sartre, "Preface" to Frantz Fanon's *The Wretched of the Earth* (François Maspero, 1961).
55. The Cultural Revolution, sometimes known by the above-mentioned full title, was a process that took place in China between 1966 and 1976 at the behest and encouragement of Mao to battle "bourgeois" tendencies that had supposedly usurped the Chinese revolution. Spurred on by his so-called *Little Red Book*, numerous Maoist fanatics proceeded to perform a purge of heterodoxy in both high governmental offices and in local government.
56. Debray, *Praised Be*, 130.
57. Ibid., 128.

Chapter 9: The Revolutionary Flame

1. From Mark Rudd's thoughtful autobiography, *My Life with SDS and the Weathermen* (Norton, 2009), 41.
2. In his televised appearance on August 24, 1968, Fidel publicly supported the USSR's action against the "liberal" reforms that were leading to "counterrevolution" in Czechoslovakia.
3. The Tlatelolco massacre, which occurred on October 2, 1968, was the shooting of hundreds of unarmed students by the Mexican armed forces as a response to the growing strength and momentum of the student movement. The bullets were quickly followed by bulldozers, chasing away survivors and maiming the fresh corpses of the students that had been killed. Thousands more were beaten and jailed, and a notable number simply disappeared. The ensuing chaos of the incident made it difficult to reach an objective estimate of the death toll, but witnesses claim to have seen hundreds of corpses. It is considered by Latin Americans to be one of the most infamous massacres in the region's long and bloody history.
4. Rudd, *My Life*, 143.
5. Ibid., 42.
6. Carlos Rafael Rodríguez (1913–1997) was a Cuban, Marxist, economist, intellectual, and one of the key political figures of twentieth-century Cuba. Serving as the head of the Cuban institution that directed and regulated agricultural reform (INRA), he was dubbed the "economic czar" by international media. In the following decades, he would serve as the Cuban representative to numerous countries in the Soviet bloc and would represent the island nation at important international events. He would also be the one to represent the Cuban Communist Party in Fulgencio Batista's democratically elected 1942 government, as a part of the freshly forged alliance between the two old enemies.
7. Oglesby, *Ravens In the Wind* (Scribner, 2008), 233. Oglesby attributes this quotation to Bernadine Dohrn.
8. Sale, *SDS*, 500, 571.
9. Carlos Marighella was a Brazilian author of a handbook on urban guerrilla warfare, *Minimanual of the Urban Guerrilla* (1969).
10. Karen Wald, handwritten notes in my files.

11. Ayers, *Fugitive Days*, 228.

12. Ibid., 247.

13. Rudd, *My Life*, 261–262.

14. See the Weathermen Manifesto, "You Don't Need a Weatherman to Know Which Way the Wind Blows," June 18, 1969.

15. Rudd, *My Life*, 110. Rudd, who helped set the blaze too, quotes J.J. as saying, "These motherfuckers have got to fall."

16. Jeremy Varon, *Bringing the War Home: The Weather Underground, the Red Army Faction, and Revolutionary Violence in the Sixties and Seventies* (University of California Press, 2004), 172–173.

17. Kevin Gillies, "The Last Radical," *Vancouver Magazine*, November 1998, 82.

18. Kate Phillip, "Palin: Obama is 'Palling Around With Terrorists,'" *The New York Times*, October 4, 2008.

19. David Corn, "Clinton Bashes Obama's Weathermen Connection, But What About Her Own?," *Mother Jones Magazine*, April 17, 2008.

20. The term was made famous by the 1965 book of the same name by Robert Taber, which opens with: "The guerrilla fights the war of the flea, and his military enemy suffers the dog's disadvantages: too much to defend; too small, ubiquitous, and agile an enemy to come to grips with."

21. Carlos Fraenkel, "A Guerrillero-Gentleman," *The Nation*, January 20, 2014.

22. Henry Kissinger: *Years of Upheaval* (Boston, 1982), 785.

Chapter 10: The Cuban Revolution Goes Global

1. Piero Gleijeses, *The Cuban Drumbeat* (Seagull Books, 2009), 19.

2. Piero Gleijeses, "The View From Havana: Lessons from Cuba's African Journey, 1959–1976"—in Gilbert M. Joseph and Daniela Spenser, *In from the Cold: Latin America's New Encounter with the Cold War* (Duke University Press, 2008), 112–113.

3. Ibid.

4. Gleijeses, *The Cuban Drumbeat*, 23.

5. Gleijeses, *Conflicting Missions*, 97.

6. Wilfred Burchett, *Southern Africa Stands Up* (Urizen Books, 1978), 89.

7. Speech and interview, Claybourn Carson, SNCC fifty-year anniversary, Shaw University, North Carolina, April 15, 2010.

8. Taylor Branch, *At Canaan's Edge* (Simon and Schuster, 2006), 486–487.

9. Chaney, Goodman, and Schwerner were activists participating in a voter registration drive in June, 1964, when they were arrested by the local authorities. They were held incommunicado and concerned friends who called the facility where they were being held were lied to by officers who stated flatly that the three activists were not in their custody. Upon their release late at night, they were captured by a group of locals, including KKK members, who had been lying in wait, in collusion with local authorities. The KKK murdered all three and disposed of their bodies in the hinterland. The incident caused national outrage, spurring a federal investigation and resulting in relatively light sentences for some of those involved.

10. *Newark News*, August 19, 1966; cited in Kevin Mumford: *Newark, A History of Race, Rights, and Riots in America* (New York University Press, 2007), 109.

11. Peniel Joseph, *Stokely: A Life* (Basic Books, 2014), 29.

12. Peniel Joseph, *Stokely: A Life* (Basic Books, uncorrected proofs, 2013), 198. This refers to the classic work, C.L.R. James, *The Black Jacobins: Toussaint L'Ouverture and the San Domingo Rebellion* (1938).

13. Stokely Carmichael with Ekueme Michael Thelwell, *Ready for Revolution: The Life and Struggles of Stokely Carmichael (Kwame Ture)* (Scribner, 2003), 580.

14. Joseph, *Stokely* (2014), 203.
15. Stokely with Thelwell, *Ready for Revolution*, 582.
16. Joseph, *Stokely* (2014), 202.
17. Ibid., 204.
18. Ibid., 208.
19. Ibid., 205.
20. Ibid., 207; Stokely with Thelwell, *Ready for Revolution*, 589.
21. Joseph, *Stokely* (2014), 205–206.
22. From my 2013 interview with Courtland Cox.
23. Joseph, *Stokely* (2014), 202; Stokely with Thelwell, *Ready for Revolution*, 591.
24. Gleijeses, *Conflicting Missions*, 193.
25. Interview on December 17, 2013.
26. In a later interview, Thelwell argued that he and Stokely detected a racial stratification running through the Cuban Revolution, despite the presence of a few Afro-Cubans in its leadership. This racism, according to Thelwell, was rooted in the structure of the previous century's plantation economy and could not be alleviated without a black consciousness movement in Cuba. Such a prospect seemed divisive to the Cubans, leading to sharp disagreement which took years to heal over. The same charges were leveled by another Black Panther leader who took temporary exile in Cuba, Eldridge Cleaver.
27. Stokely with Thelwell, *Ready for Revolution*, 633. In his autobiography, Stokely Carmichael and Charles V. Hamilton, *Black Power: The Politics of Liberation in America* (Vintage, 1967), Stokely says that "the CIA was now propagating the smear that I was a CIA agent," and "the Cubans began to withdraw from us," 696. Fidel had just promoted Stokely as an international hero and provided Cuba's material support.
28. Gleijeses, *Conflicting Missions*, 193–194
29. Thelwell, *Ready for Revolution*, 692.
30. Carmichael and Hamilton, *Black Power*, 632. More on Stokely's effort, from his autobiography: "I'd written to every legitimate liberation organization to check out the possibility of serving with them. I really wanted to participate as a front-line fighter." His description appears immediately after he mentions that Makeba was at a New York concert and he was meeting with liberation groups in Tanzania.
31. Carmichael and Hamilton, *Black Power*, 626.
32. Ibid.
33. Carl Stokes, Cleveland, 1967; Richard Hatcher, Gary, 1967; Matthew Carter, Montclair, 1968; Luska Twyman, Glasgow, Ky. 1968; Howard Nathaniel Lee, Chapel Hill, 1968; Charles Evers, Lafayette, Mississippi, 1969; Kenneth Gibson, Newark, 1970; James McGee, Dayton, 1970; James Ford, Tallahassee, 1972; Ted Berry, Cincinnati, 1972; Coleman Young, Detroit, 1973; Clarence Lightner, Raleigh, 1973; Maynard Jackson, Atlanta, 1973; Tom Bradley, Los Angeles, 1973; Lyman Parks, Grand Rapids, 1973; Walter Washington, Washington, D.C., 1975; Henry Marsh, Richmond, 1977; Lionel Wilson, Oakland, 1978; Ernest Morial, New Orleans, 1978; Richard Arrington, Birmingham, 1979. Much of the national leadership behind these electoral victories came from the 1967 Black Power conference organized by the late Amiri Baraka.
34. Gleijeses notes US intelligence files from 1963 through 1973, and specifically one on Cuban foreign policy, dated September 15, 1967—in *The Cuban Drumbeat*, 82.
35. Matthews cited by Richard Gott in *Cuba: A New History*, 255; originally in *The New York Times*, March 4, 1976; also cited in Piero Gleijeses, *Conflicting Missions*, 391.
36. Gleijeses, *Conflicting Missions*, 187–189.
37. Gott, *Cuba: A New History*, 251.

268 ▪ *Listen, Yankee!*

38. David H. Shinn and Joshua Eisenman: *China and Africa: A Century of Engagement* (University of Pennsylvania Press, 2012), 339.

39. Godfrey Mwakikagile, *Congo in the Sixties* (New Africa Press, 2014), 86.

40. Piero Gleijeses, *Visions of Freedom: Havana, Washington, Pretoria, and the Struggle for Southern Africa* (UNC Press Books, 2013), 302; Tom Wicker, "In The Nation: Savimbi and Marcos," *The New York Times*, February 21, 1986.

41. Gott, *Cuba: A New History*, 252.

42. Letelier and his American assistant Ronni Moffitt were killed on September 21, 1976, by a car bomb planted by Cuban exiles operating on the orders of the Chilean dictator Augusto Pinochet. George H.W. Bush, then the CIA director, initially blamed the bombing on leftists, apparently as an intentional diversion. The Cuban exiles were part of a multi-country assassinations and terror network named Operation Condor, operating with at least tacit support from US authorities. For a more detailed look at the assassination, Cuban exile participation, and tacit US support for Operation Condor, see John Dinges, *The Condor Years: How Pinochet and his Allies Brought Terrorism to Three Continents* (The New Press, 2005).

43. On October 6, 1976, seventy-three people, mainly young Cuban athletes, perished when their Cubana Airlines plane exploded on its way from Barbados to Havana because of bombs planted by Venezuelan operatives at the behest of Cuban exiles with CIA ties and training. The alleged mastermind was a US intelligence asset, Luis Posada Carrilles, a longtime leader of Miami's Cuban exile groups. Posada is currently at liberty in Miami despite an outstanding Interpol warrant for his arrest.

44. The authoritarian and quasi-fascist Estado Novo was, in 1974, one of the last remaining right-wing, colonialist holdouts left in Europe. Extremely conservative and unabashedly proud of its colonial possessions, the regime was in bad repute with many of its neighbors, as well as large sectors of its own population, when a group of progressive-minded generals overthrew it in the so-called Carnation Revolution, on April 25, 1974. The new regime systematically recognized the independence of its foreign colonies in the following years, many of which had ongoing armed struggles against Lisbon's control dating from the days of the Estado Novo.

45. In July, 1975, president Gerald Ford authorized the CIA to send funds, arms, and assistance to both the FNLA and UNITA as a part of a covert operation known as AI-FEATURE. The operation became public and the public backlash resulted in the Clark Amendment, which severely limited the US government's ability to intervene directly in the conflict without congressional approval.

46. Gleijeses, *The Cuban Drumbeat*, 27

47. Gleijeses, *Visions of Freedom*, 29.

48. Gleijeses, *The Cuban Drumbeat*, 42.

49. Ibid., 62.

50. Gott, *Cuba: A New History*, 255.

51. When Mandela visited Havana in 1991, he was greeted by hundreds of thousands and asked approvingly, "What other country can point to a record of greater selflessness than Cuba has displayed in its relations to Africa?"—in Gleijeses, *The Cuban Drumbeat*, 73.

52. Burchett, *Southern Africa Stands Up*, 94.

53. Gleijeses, *The Cuban Drumbeat*, 34.

54. The *Isla de la Juventúd* (Isle of Youth) was originally the *Isla de Pinos* (Isle of Pines), where Fidel and countless other political prisoners had languished at the infamous *Presidio Modelo* (Model Prison). After the revolution triumphed the new government closed the prison, renamed the island, and several years later opened several schools for Cuban and foreign students there.

Chapter 11: The Liberal Democrats' Default: The Carter Era

1. Wayne Smith, *The Closest of Enemies* (Norton, 1987), 86.
2. William M. LeoGrande and Peter Kornbluh, *Back Channel to Cuba: The Hidden History of Negotiations Between Washington* (UNC Press Books, 2014), 94.
3. Ibid., 97.
4. Ibid., 99.
5. Smith, *The Closest of Enemies*, 85–90. Smith complained that having read over the interviews with Fidel, he has come to "the painful suspicion that they were right and I was wrong."
6. Smith's account references a statement by Rusk made on February 25, 1964; in Smith, *The Closest of Enemies*, 89.
7. The Dominican Republic had only just returned to democracy after three decades under one of the bloodiest dictators in the history of the Americas, General Rafael Leonidas Trujillo, who had enjoyed support from Washington almost until the time of his assassination by Dominican conspirators in 1961.
8. LeoGrande and Kornbluh, *Back Channel to Cuba*, 104.
9. Ibid., 115.
10. Anderson, *Che*, 726.
11. LeoGrande and Kornbluh, *Back Channel to Cuba*, 112.
12. Ibid.
13. Smith, 122–123. Brzezinski gave a not-for-attribution statement to the press on November 16, 1977, in which he said that Cuba's operations in Angola made normalization "impossible."
14. Robert Kaplan, "Supremacy by Stealth," *The Atlantic*, July 1, 2003.
15. "Discovering the Caribbean" is a sarcastic Cuban way of describing the continuous flow of US envoys and experts who wander like Columbus until discovering the tropics without quite knowing where they are.
16. Refers to the Ten Years' War (1868–1878).
17. http://www.granma.cubaweb.cu/2013/12/13/interna/artico2.html
18. Kennedy is reported to have said that he wanted "to splinter the CIA into a thousand pieces and scatter it to the winds."
19. Stephen Schlesinger, "Ghosts of Guatemala's Past," *The New York Times*, June 3, 2011.
20. Jack Anderson, "Castro Stalker Worked for the CIA," *Washington Post*, February 23, 1971; "6 Attempts to Kill Castro Laid to CIA," *Washington Post*, January 18, 1971.
21. Gott, *Cuba: A New History*, 261.
22. Smith, *The Closest of Enemies*, 97.
23. LeoGrande and Kornbluh, *Back Channel to Cuba*, 130–131. And personal interviews with Saul Landau.
24. Personal interview with Saul Landau, 2011.
25. Franklin, *Cuban and the United States*, 131.
26. Ibid., 132.
27. Smith, *The Closest of Enemies*, 107.
28. Tom Hayden, "Young a Symbol of 'New Politics,'" *St. Petersburg Times*, April 11, 1977; originally published in *Los Angeles Times*.
29. Ibid.
30. Smith, *The Closest of Enemies*, 15.
31. Ibid., 122–123.
32. Refers to the so-called Downing Street Memo, named after the residence of the Prime Minister of the UK, in which the minutes of a meeting of senior British ministers are recorded and intelligence figures explain that they believed the information

building up to a possible war in Iraq was being fixed. The memo's leak to the public caused public outrage.

33. Smith, *The Closest of Enemies*, 123–124. The "study" in question is described by Smith as follows: "It consisted of two pages, the first a list of countries, with the CIA's estimate of how many Cuban civilian and military personnel were in each, and the second a map showing where the countries were. Some study!" It had apparently been requested by Brzezinski merely as a reference of the Agency's current estimates. Several of these estimates were dead wrong, but Smith doesn't attribute any malicious intent to the report.

34. Ibid., 123.

35. Gott, *Cuba: A New History*, 260.

36. Ibid., 260.

37. Ibid., 265.

38. In conversation and in his writings, Pastor repeatedly refers to the "Soviet general" in a way suggesting that Cuban troops were servile mercenaries to Moscow in Ethiopia. The Soviet officer was General Vasily Petrof, who was charged with coordinating "the *counteroffensive* against Somalia," which underscores that the military action was deterrent in nature ("The Soviet-Cuba Liaison," by Captain Gary Payton, *Air University Review*, November–December 1979). The roots of the Soviet role went back to czarist times, according to Payton. The original aspiration was to unite those of Orthodox faith by cultivating ties with the feudal aristocracy of then-Abyssinia. There was an exchange of ambassadors in the 1880s and a brief establishment of a New Moscow Colony in 1889, when Western colonial powers were dividing Africa into their spheres of interests.

39. Lars Schoultz, *That Infernal Little Cuban Republic: The United States and the Cuban Revolution* (University of North Carolina Press, 2011), 292. Sol Linowitz was the former US Representative to the Organization of American States, 1966–1969. His commission's report was based on findings that previous policies had failed and that a new approach of phased, reciprocal steps toward normalization be taken.

40. Robert A. Pastor, "The Carter-Castro Years," in *Fifty Years of Revolution, Perspectives on Cuba, the United States, and the World*, ed. Soraya Castro Marino and Ronald Pruessen (University Press of Florida, 2012), 248.

41. The second Strategic Arms Limitation Treaty, which would have put more stringent caps on US and Soviet missile production, was signed in 1979 by both parties but was never formally ratified in Congress, which was too divided on the merits of the treaty.

42. LeoGrande and Korhbluh, *Back Channel to Cuba*, 224.

43. Pastor, "The Carter-Castro Years," 257.

44. Ibid., 258.

45. Patrick Jude Haney, *The Cuban Embargo: The Domestic Politics of an American Foreign Policy* (University of Pittsburgh Press, 2005), 28.

46. Pastor, "The Carter-Castro Years," 246.

47. Gleijeses, *Conflicting Missions*, 363. It is known as the Clark Amendment after the congressman who proposed it, Sen. Richard Clark.

48. David Binder, "House Vote Ends Aid to Angolans in Rebuff to Ford," *The New York Times*, January 28, 1976.

49. William G. Howell and Jon C. Pevehouse, "When Congress Stops Wars," *Foreign Affairs*, September–October 2007.

50. Gleijeses, *Conflicting Missions*, 332.

51. Godfrey Mwakikagile, *Congo in the Sixties* (New Africa Press, 2014), 86.

52. Shinn and Eisenman, *China and Africa*, 339.

53. Gleijeses: *Visions of Freedom*, 302.

54. Tom Wicker, "In The Nation; Savimbi and Marcos," *The New York Times*, February 21, 1986.
55. Samuel P. Huntington et al., *The Crisis of Democracy* (New York University Press,1975), 113.
56. Commonly referred to as the Powell Memorandum.
57. Robert E. Quirk, *Fidel Castro* (W. W. Norton & Company, 1995), 819.
58. The document they produced, "A New Inter-American Policy for the Eighties," is popularly known as "The Santa Fe Report."

Chapter 12: The Clinton Years: Yielding to the Cuban Right

1. Clinton never dodged the draft outright, but he does seem to have done everything in his power, short of breaking the law, to avoid going. See the editorial piece, "Bill Clinton's Vietnam Test," *The New York Times*, February 14, 1992.
2. James V. Grimaldi, "Clinton Quiet About Own Radical Ties," *Washington Post*, May 19, 2008.
3. Ann Louise Bardach, *Cuba Confidential: Love and Vengeance in Miami and Havana* (Vintage, 2002), 145.
4. Although the president of CANF stated to the press that "Jorge was never a man who believed in terrorism," the undeniable fact is that there exists a June 1965 CIA report which states that Canosa had presented his handler with a proposal "to blow up a Cuban or Soviet vessel in Veracruz, Mexico," along with numerous other documents detailing additional operations. See http://www2.gwu.edu/~nsarchiv/NSAEBB/NSAEBB288/index.htm.
5. LeoGrande and Kornbluh, *Back Channel to Cuba*, 271.
6. US Secretary of State Madeleine Albright said, "As I understand it, it was a chance encounter that Mr. Castro initiated." See "Clinton shook Castro's hand," *BBC*, September 8, 2000.
7. Bardach, *Cuba Confidential*, 128.
8. Salim Lamrani, 31.
9. Ibid., 31–32.
10. The *Período Especial en Época de Paz* is the name Fidel gave to the new day that was dawning with the imminent collapse of the USSR, in a speech on October 10, 1991, the anniversary of the first independence war. This epoch-defining speech attempted to explain the hardships that were to come—equivalent, he argued, to wartime shortages, but in a time of peace.
11. State Security is the intelligence branch of the Cuban government charged with investigating potential threats to the standing order and, if possible, to prevent them. As opposed to emblematic G-men in the United States, Cuban agents of State Security often walk around in plainclothes, although those working in the Interior Ministry are usually dressed in military fatigues.
12. These Committees, abbreviated as CDRs, were originally convened with grassroots participation in order to watch for terrorist activity and attempts to subvert the revolution. In addition, they would organize activities that would help maintain the neighborhood, or that would be the organs through which a locality would request resources from the government for special projects. As time went on, however, they grew to be an extension of the government security apparatus.
13. Parapolice units made up of pro-government civilians who watch and respond to dissidents.
14. Gott, *Cuba: A New History*, 330–331. The language in quotation marks is from the law itself.

15. Octavio Paz (1914–1998) was a Mexican intellectual, poet, diplomat, and essayist of the Left. He was well respected, even by his opponents, as a man of principle after having resigned as Mexican ambassador to India in protest over the massacre of students in Tlatelolco Plaza, in 1968, mentioned above. See Enrique Krauze, "The Wars of Octavio Paz," *The New York Times*, March 30, 2014.

16. Louis A. Pérez, *Cuba in the American Imagination: Metaphor and the Imperial Ethos* (University of North Carolina Press, 2008), 25.

17. In 1994, thousands of Cubans and Haitians (refugees from the overthrow of the elected Haitian president Jean-Bertrand Aristide three years earlier), protested their deprivation and fled on rafts on the sea, earning their name *los balseros*, or "the Rafters." Under US law, the Cubans could become legalized once they touched ground in the United States, and therefore many were turned back and held in Guantanamo. That September, "the numbers were so large that the United States was obliged to make a major and permanent change in its policy toward Cuban migration, as Castro had hoped. The two countries made a deal in September, negotiated on the Cuban side by Ricardo Alarcón, to bring the crisis to an end." In Gott, *Cuba: A New History*, 300.

18. This refers to the February 1996 shoot-down of two planes belonging to the Cuban exile group Hermanos al Rescate (Brothers to the Rescue), after they tried to repeat their illegal violation of the airspace around Havana. This is incident is explored in greater detail later in this book.

19. Anthony Lake and Samuel "Sandy" Berger were national security advisers to Bill Clinton.

20. Refers here to the second war of independence (1895–1898), which achieved what the Ten Years' War (1868–1878) was unable to do.

21. The *malecón* is a sea wall, parts of which date back to the colonial era, which follows the lip of Havana Harbor. Walking along the *malecón* or meeting there with friends is a favorite pastime of Cubans.

22. Stephen Kimber, *What Lies Across the Water* (Fernwood, 2013), 107. Published in Canada, Kimber's is the best researched book released so far.

23. Former New Mexico governor and US cabinet official often deployed by the Clinton administration on Latin America-related issues. "They put me in charge of the bad guys they can't talk to," Richardson told me in 2011.

24. In *Back Channel to Cuba*, LeoGrande and Kornbluh write that, in 2011, Richardson said that "he could not remember to whom he had spoken" at the White House.

25. White House aide Richard Nuccio said the Brothers "got exactly what they were hoping to produce"—LeoGrande and Kornbluh, *Back Channel to Cuba*, 314.

26. As explained earlier, of the three planes that Brothers to the Rescue sent, only one got away. Basulto was on that plane, which quickly turned back toward Miami once the other planes were shot down.

27. Frank, *Cuban Revelations*, 182.

28. Bardach, *Cuba Confidential*, 132.

29. E-mail correspondence, August 12, 2013

Chapter 13: Rethinking Marxism, Rethinking the Americas

1. Gott, *Cuba: A New History*, 244.

2. I had a similar experience when I spent several weeks in the Soviet Union in late 1975. I brought a close personal friend, a committed scientific socialist, to a clinic to treat his advanced cancer. In the cancer ward, all the patients were a jaundiced yellow or green, yet it was forbidden to tell them they had cancer. When my friend died an agonizing death in an advanced treatment ward a few months later in Houston, he

cursed his belief in science as a faith that had shaken him in the Soviet hospital as well.

3. Raúl Castro's daughter, Mariela, is internationally known for supporting marriage equality and LGBT rights, fifty years after Allen Ginsberg was expelled from Cuba and homosexuality was officially a counterrevolutionary crime.

4. Fidel Castro and Frei Betto, *Fidel and Religion: Castro Talks on Revolution and Religion with Frei Betto*, Introduction by Harvey Cox (Simon and Schuster, 1987).

5. Richard Gott, *In the Shadow of the Liberator, Hugo Chávez and the Transformation of Venezuela* (Verso, 2000), 18.

6. In February 1992, the young mestizo officer, Hugo Chávez, attempted a progressive coup in response to the neoliberal policies of the existing government, since he felt there was no solution within the electoral system. When the coup fell apart and he realized that further fighting would be a waste of lives, he surrendered himself to the government. He was allowed to appear on Venezuelan television to convince other rebels to put down their arms. He also took the opportunity to emphasize that they were only surrendering "*por ahora*" (for now).

7. Javier Corrales, "Hugo Boss," *Foreign Policy*, January 4, 2006.

8. In Istán Mészáros's interview with Chávez, cited by John Bellamy Foster in foreword to Marta Harnecker's "Latin America and Twenty-First Century Socialism," *Monthly Review*, July–August 2010.

9. The 1988 elections were so blatantly rigged that years later ex-president Miguel de la Madrid admitted that he had rigged the election of his successor, Carlos Salinas de Gortari, and that the ballots had been burned to remove all traces. See Ginger Thompson, "Ex-President in Mexico Casts New Light on Rigged 1988 Election," *New York Times*, March 9, 2004. While the 2006 election has not been irrefutably proven to have been rigged, many generally consider it to be at least undermined by dishonest practices.

10. Harnecker, "Latin America and Twenty-First Century Socialism," 7.

11. Rodriguez quoted by Gott, *In the Shadow of the Liberator*, 109–117; cited by Bellamy, xvii.

Chapter 14: A New Model in Our Americas

1. Czech-born Hans Kelsen (1881–1973) was a formidable legal and political scholar who spent nearly three decades at the University of California, Berkeley. He was also deeply involved in the war crimes tribunals that followed World War II. His writings provided a strong defense of democracy and judicial independence against the executive branch.

2. A common point of discussion in Cuban historiography is the strain placed on democratic political mechanisms used by *mambises* during the struggle for independence. The earliest political systems used by Cubans in the Ten Years' War were quickly found to be impractical, presupposing ideal peacetime conditions in terms of legislative quorums and limiting the powers of the executive. Local *caudillos* (warlords) were also capable of manipulating the system and subverting it, without sufficient centralized power. Martí and others struggled to find a balance between guaranteeing the basic elements for democracy, the cause for which they were risking their lives in the first place, and the practical concessions the war imposed upon them.

3. Most of the indigenous peoples living in the Spanish-dominated Antilles were wiped out by a combination of disease and an extremely intense forced-labor system known as the *encomienda*. Natives were "commended" to the care of Spaniards who would exploit them to an extent possibly worse than that of slaves later, because slaves had to be purchased while Indians merely had to be caught. Although indigenous peoples

are mentioned throughout the rest of the colonial period, even playing important roles in fighting off piratical attacks in the seventeenth century, they became increasingly rare as time went on. It seems that the last remains of indigenous populations have been fully absorbed into the melting pot of the general populace.

4. Mills warned of the merging interests of two bureaucratic collectivisms, the Soviet state and American corporate capitalism. Among Western liberals, this "détente" was seen as a good thing because it lessened the risk of superpower warfare. For Ricardo and the third world, détente resulted in proxy wars like Vietnam, while reinforcing the shared interests of the superpowers in the global status quo. In retrospect, the Cold War was a struggle for dominance to the end, with the "socialist bloc" set back or dissolved.

5. Not to inflate the issue, but citing Rosa Luxemburg's critique is quite the opposite of the view taken by Che Guevara in his September 14, 1961, interview with Maurice Zeitlin. When Zeitlin extolled Luxemburg's criticism of Leninism, Che replied: "She was a great revolutionary, and she died a revolutionary as a consequence of her political mistakes"—in Scheer and Zeitlin, *Cuba: An American Tragedy*, 343.

6. The 1999 anti-WTO demonstrations in Seattle were led by the AFL-CIO and a rainbow.

7. Nicholas Watt, "'Blue-Eyed Bankers' to Blame for Crash, Lula Tells Brown," *The Guardian*, March 26, 2009.

8. Alexei Barrionuevo, "In Obama Visit, Brazil's Leader Aims to Mend Fences," *The New York Times*, March 17, 2011.

9. Mariel Bay is an excellent, deep natural port to the west of Havana. The lack of extensive urbanization and its natural characteristics make it the ideal port of entry for extremely large international vessels. In 1980, it became infamous for being the center of the Mariel boatlift, in which 125,000 Cubans traveled to the United States, including mentally ill and violent inmates who were placed on boats headed for Florida in an act of spite on the part of the Cuban government. Since then, the bay has largely laid dormant. With the advent of the new port, it is set to be the beating heart of economic revitalization and renewed international trade, as well as the flagship project of reformism.

10. The reader may be surprised by this, but it is technically true. Cuban law allows for 100 percent foreign ownership. However, in practice, such a concession is rarely, if ever, made.

11. In addition to limiting our own trade with Cuba, after Helms-Burton, the US government now prosecutes even non-American companies that trade with the island nation. The penalty can be a fine to the tune of millions of dollars.

Chapter 15: Rescuing Elián González, Losing Al Gore

1. During the Clinton administration, she was legal counsel to the State Department. She currently heads diplomatic negotiations with Iran.

2. Ethel Kennedy interview, February 6, 2014.

3. Elián was born on December 6, 1993.

4. Bardach, *Cuba Confidential*, 309–325.

5. See *Deadlock, The Inside Story of America's Closest Election* (Public Affairs, 2001), 125.

6. Diaz-Balart's grandfather, Rafael, was the lead lawyer for United Fruit and a former Batista cabinet member. In Bardach, *Cuba Confidential*, 320.

7. Tim Padgett, "Mob Scene in Miami," *Time Magazine*, November 26, 2000.

8. Ibid.

9. This is likely a reference to John Unumb, a CIA agent.

10. CIA document in "Family Jewels" (1973), FOIA electronic reading room, CIA-retrieved, December 18, 2013, 297.
11. Bush's CIA passed the word to *Newsweek* and other US media that the Chilean junta was not involved. The CIA told *Newsweek*, for example, that "the bomb was too crude to be the work of experts and because the murder, coming while Chile's rulers were wooing US support, could only damage the Santiago regime"—*Newsweek*, October 11, 1976. The CIA had more than ample reasons to doubt their own explanation, however. As deputy assistant secretary Hewson Ryan noted, "we knew fairly early on that the governments of the Southern Cone countries were planning . . . some assassinations abroad in the summer of 1976. Whether if we had gone in [to proactive diplomatic meetings on the subject], we might have prevented this, I don't know. But we didn't"—Peter Kornbluh, *The Pinochet File: A Declassified Dossier on Atrocity and Accountability* (The New Press, 2004), 362–363.
12. Bardach, *Cuba Confidential*, 314.
13. Ibid., 315.
14. Duncan Campbell, "The Bush Dynasty and the Cuban Criminals," *The Guardian*, December 1, 2002.
15. Bardach, *Cuba Confidential*, 116.
16. Vivian Lesnik Weisman's documentary film, *The Man of Two Havanas* (Latinovision, 2008).
17. Bardach, *Cuba Confidential*, 322.
18. Ibid., 319.
19. Ibid., 201.
20. Ibid., 106.
21. Ibid., 105–106.

Chapter 16: Listen, Yankee!

1. Pastor, "The Carter-Castro Years," 237–260.
2. LeoGrande and Kornbluh, *Back Channel to Cuba*, 214.
3. Ibid., 192.
4. Max Lesnik is one of Ricardo's oldest friends. Max, eighty-four years old, has lived in Miami since 1961, when he left Cuba in a quarrel over communism. He grew up with Fidel and takes frequent trips to the island. He is an advocate of reconciliation and has been involved in dialogues and papal visits at the highest level.
5. This refers to the strategy known in US circles as the "biological solution," which refers to letting biology "solve" the "Fidel problem" through his inevitable death.
6. Miguel Díaz-Canel, Cuba's first vice president since 2013, was born in 1960.
7. The so-called catastrophe scenario would mean the chaotic fall of the Cuban government, similar to the fall of Communist regimes in Eastern Europe.
8. The biggest exception to a general lack of mass protests is the so-called *maleconazo* twenty years ago, in 1994, when hundreds of Cubans took to the streets protesting the dire conditions of the "special period," looting government stores and shutting down important parts of the city after spreading out from poorer neighborhoods. The protest was successfully defused by a countermarch personally led by Fidel.
9. The Cuban-born journalist Mark Frank makes the same assessment: "Discontent runs deep in Cuba, where no one has made a living wage for two decades, but most Cubans are seeking change through reform and evolution of the system, not in open alliance with Washington and Miami's political establishment which seeks regime change"—in *Cuban Revelations: Behind the Scenes in Havana* (University Press of Florida, 2013), 207.

10. "Cuba's Military Power Elite," *Cuba Facts*, Issue 61, January 14, 2014. By another count, according to Cuban-born Nelson Valdés, there are six military men and eight civilians on the present Politburo—correspondence with Nelson Valdés, University of New Mexico, January 27, 2014.
11. Frank, *Cuban Revelations*, 248.
12. Ibid., 250.
13. Arnold August, *Cuba and Its Neighbors* (Palgrave MacMillan, 2013).
14. These can be thought of as a sort of non-legally binding plebiscite.
15. Frank, *Cuban Revelations*, 205.
16. Ibid.
17. Scheer and Zeitlin, *Cuba: An American Tragedy*, 250.
18. Lamrani, 43–44.
19. Paul Haven, "Cuba, US Try Talking, But Face Many Obstacles," *Associated Press*, June 21, 2013.
20. Patricia Rey Mallén, "Cuba's First Year of Immigration Reform: 180,000 People Leave the Country . . . And Come Back," January 14, 2014.
21. Julia E. Sweig and Michael J. Bustamante, "Cuba After Communism: The Economic Reforms that are Transforming the Island," *Foreign Affairs*, July–August 2013.
22. Richard E. Feinberg, "Soft Landing in Cuba? Emerging Entrepreneurs and Middle Classes," Brookings Institution, Latin America Initiative, November 2013.
23. Sweig and Bustamante, "Cuba After Communism," *Foreign Affairs*, July–August 2013.
24. Ibid.
25. "EU agrees to launch negotiations with Cuba," *BBC*, February 10, 2014.
26. According to Mark Frank, there were 1,669 barber shops and beauty parlors in Cuba in 2011 before control was returned to private owners. In *Cuban Revelations*, 176.
27. *La Rampa*—"The Ramp"—is a tourist-oriented neighborhood of a few city blocks that contains both the Hotel Nacional and the Habana Libre, along with numerous clubs and bars. The hill that starts at the Habana Libre, at 23 and M streets, then slopes downward toward the *malecón*. Although there are residences along these short blocks, the entire economy of the street life is centered on tourism.
28. Desmond Butler, Jack Gillum, and Alberto Arce, "US secretly created 'Cuban Twitter' to stir unrest," *Associated Press*, April 4, 2014.
29. "Sudden US Thaw Worries Cuban Dissidents," *The New York Times*, December 27, 2014.
30. "Questions from Yoani Sánchez to POTUS," *Wikileaks*, US Interests Section, August 26, 2009. In Frank, *Cuban Revelations*, 180.
31. Salim Lamrani, "Forty Questions for Yoani Sanchez," *Palgrave* blog; without citing his source, Lamrani quotes her as saying: "The blockade has provided the regime with a perfect excuse to maintain its intolerance, its control, and its repression of internal dissent. If economic sanctions were to end tomorrow, I doubt very much that the effects would be felt." The reason her statement seems credible is because of its consistency with the filmed interview of her husband.
32. Reinaldo Escobar interview in the Tracey Eaton documentary, *Diplomacy Derailed* (2013).
33. Susan Eckstein, *The Immigrant Divide: How Cuban Americans Changed the US and Their Homeland* (Routledge, 2009); Louis A. Pérez Jr., *On Becoming Cuban: Identity, Nationality, and Culture* (University of North Carolina Press Books, 1999); *Bridges to Cuba*, ed. Ruth Behar (University of Michigan Press, 1995).
34. Christine Armario, "Cuba Suspends Consular Services in US," *Associated Press*, April 14, 2014. Cuban Americans traveling to Cuba spend an average of $3,238 USD per person while visiting.

35. Susan Eva Eckstein, *The Immigrant Divide: How Cuban Americans Changed the US and Their Homeland* (Routledge, 2009), 8. Over one million Cubans emigrated to the United States between the 1959 revolution and the decade of the 2000s—"Washington most warmly welcomed Cubans when they served its Cold War geopolitical agenda." About 225,000 came between 1959–1962, after Castro took power. Between 1965–1973, another 260,000 came on so-called Freedom Flights. In the eighties and nineties, the United States clamped down on immigration in hopes of inspiring an Eastern-European-style uprising. From 1985–1994, the United States issued only 11,222 visas. On three occasions, 1965, 1980, and 1994, Fidel unilaterally let Cubans leave "to defuse and deflect domestic discontent." See Eckstein, 12–13.

36. Sweig, *Inside the Cuban Revolution*, 268.

37. Lamrani, 71.

38. Between April 2013 and June 2014, Cuba estimates a loss of $205.8 million in rum and cigar sales alone. *Russia Today*, September 10, 2014: "Cuba calculates loss of 54 yr US embargo at $1.1 tn."

39. "Cuba still on the US list of state sponsors of terrorism"—Paul Richter, *Los Angeles Times*, May 30, 2013.

40. Orlando Bosch is one of the more rabid of the anti-Castro terrorists. In 1968, he fired a homemade bazooka at a Polish freighter that was entering Miami's Biscayne Bay, the freighter's only crime being that Communists ruled in Warsaw. In the late eighties and early nineties, even the US Justice Department wanted him deported as an undesirable and, more specifically, a terrorist. It took a presidential action on the part of Bush *pére* for him to go free, but only after making Bosch promise to no longer support the use of force for regime change in Cuba. Bosch would later call this vow a "farce." He died, free and unrepentant, in Miami, in early 2011.

41. Jacobo Timerman, *Cuba: A Journey* (Knopf, 1990); Alma Guillermoprieto, *Dancing with Cuba: A Memoir of the Revolution* (Vintage, 2005).

42. Pete Seeger, *Pete Seeger in his own Words*, ed. Rom and Sam Rosenthal, (Paradigm, 2012), 186.

43. Bardach, *Without Fidel: A Death Foretold in Miami, Havana and Washington* (Scribner, 2009) 205.

44. Gott: *Cuba: A New History*, 294.

45. Congressional Research Service, November 6, 2012, 21.

46. Interview with William Orme, director, UN Development Program, 2013. Orme stresses that the three factors that constitute the rankings are difficult to compute. Cuba ranks low on income measured by purchasing power, but near the top in health and education. The reason, he says, is that the Cuban state has subsidized basic necessities, causing per capita purchasing power to appear lower than it is in reality.

47. These are not based on official Cuban statistics, which could be accused of bias and manipulation, but instead on the figures used by the World Bank, available on their own website. Average life expectancy has remained steady at seventy-nine years since 2009.

48. The total number of medals won by Cuban athletes in the Olympics, without counting winter events, is 208, of which twelve were won during the first half of the twentieth century. This is based on a table supplied to the author by the Olympic Committee's Press Office, also available on the organization's website.

49. Frank, *Cuban Revelations*, 66.

50. Ibid., 66–67.

INDEX

Abrams, Elliott, 220
activist generation, 36
ADA. *See* Americans for Democratic Action
Adams, John Quincy, 45, 170
Africa. *See also specific countries*
  Cuba and, 125–26, 136–44, 148–49, 158–59
  Guevara in, 87, 137
  post-colonial, 137
  US-Cuban relations and, 159–60
African Americans, 33–34, 128–30
African wars, xxv, 126
Afrocubanismo, 126
Afro-Cuban rights, 228
Alarcón, Margarita, xxii–xxiii, 1, 8–9
Alarcón de Quesada, Ricardo, xii, xxi–xxii, 1–3
  the Bay of Pigs and, 47–48
  Brothers to the Rescue shoot down and,
    176
  Crocker and, 144
  Cuba and, 241
  December 17 agreement and, xxviii–xxix
  diplomatic career, 28, 48–49
  González, E., and, 213–14, 216
  Guevara and, 24–25
  Levinson and, 113
  "Marx After Marxism, The Global Fight
    for Immigrant Rights in a Neo-Lib-
    eral Economy," 203–4
  Mills and, 38–39
  National Assembly of People's Power
    and, 4–5
  Perea and, 26–29
  Rodriguez, F., and, 17
  Tarnoff and, 171–72
  US-Cuban relations and, 150–51
Algeria, 125
Allende, Salvador, 74–75, 107, 122, 195
Alliance for Progress, 57
Almeida, Juan, 23
Alpha 66, 221
Althusser, Louis, 85–86
American Peace Corps, 6
Americans for Democratic Action (ADA), 54
ANC, 141–43

Anderson, Jack, 154
Angola, 6, 137–39, 155
Annexationist Project, 170
anti-communism, 40–41
anti-globalization, 200, 204–6
anti-nuclear movement, 52–56
Arbenz, Jacobo, 66, 76, 154
Armed Forces of National Resistance
  (FARN), 83
Assassinations Records Review Board
  (ARRB), 61
Attwood, William, 69
Ayers, Bill, 118

Bachelet, Michelle, 123
balseros (rafters), 214
Baraka, Amiri, 34
Bardach, Ann Louise, xxi–xxii, 179
  Cuba Confidential, 166, 178
Basulto, José, 173, 175
Batista, Fulgencio, xi, 11–12, 25–26
  Cuban Communist Party and, 14
  Directorio attack on, 17–18
  September 1933 coup, 13
the Bay of Pigs, 47–48, 154
  prisoner release, 52, 66
  US-Cuban relations and, 52
Beals, Carleton, 32
Beat Generation, 34
Behar, Ruth, 9, 235
Berger, Sandy, 173
Berle, A. A., 38
Berlin Wall, 190–91
Betancourt, Rómulo, 74, 77–78
Bissell, Richard, 76
Black Jacobins (James), 129
Black Panther Party for Self-Defense, 97–98,
  238
Black Power, 127, 134, 228
Blanqui, Auguste, 93
Bolivar, Simon, 76, 93, 197
Bolivia, 122–23
  Guevara in, 88–89, 93–94
  US and, 94–95

bolsa familia (family allowance), 208
Bosch, Orlando, 222, 239
BRAC (Bureau for the Repression of Communist Activities), 27
Brás, Juan Mari, 75
Brazil, 8, 122, 207–9
 Cuba and, 210
Brazzaville Protocol, 141–44
Brecht, Bertolt, 119–21
Bremer, Paul, 199
brigadistas, 111
Brothers to the Rescue, 177–78
 Cuban shoot down of, 173–76, 179, 182–83
Brown, Sam, 153
Brzezinski, Zbigniew, 147, 157–58, 225
Buchaca, Edith García, 19
Buckley, William F., Jr., 48
Bundy, McGeorge, 67
Bureau for the Repression of Communist Activities. *See* BRAC
Burgos, Elisabeth, 87, 101
Burton, John, 246
Bush, George Herbert Walker, 147–48, 168
 Cuban Right and, 219–20
Bush, George Walker, 148, 193, 218–19
 Chávez and, 194
 Cuban Right and, 220–21
 Cuba policy, 230
Bush, Jeb, 220

Cabral, Amílcar, 132–33, 137
CANF. *See* Cuban American National Foundation
Canosa, Mas, 166
capitalism, 191, 200
 Cuban, 232–33
 Latin American, 212
Caracazo, 191
Carbó Serviá, Juan Pedro, 19–20
Caribbean, 128–29, 196
Carmichael, Stokely, 95–96, 103, 127–28
 Black Power and, 134
 in Cuba, 129–30
 Cuban Revolution and, 130–33
 global tour, 131–35
 SNCC and, 131, 134
Carriles, Posada, 239
Carson, Clay, 127, 133
Carter, Jimmy, xxiii, 137, 153–64
 Castro, F., and, 162–63
 Cold War and, 153
 Cuban policy, 140, 155, 159–61
 Puerto Rican nationalists and, xxviii–xxix
 Young and, 160–61
Casa de las Americas, 81
Castro, Fidel, xi, 3, 22, 23
 ABC interview of, 68–69

assassination attempts, 64, 70
 Brothers to the Rescue shoot down and, 177–78
 Carter and, 162–63
 Chávez and, 191–92
 CIA and, 70, 146–47
 Clinton and, 166
 Cuban missile crisis and, 50–51
 Cuba's House of Representatives and, 11–12
 Debray and, 88–90, 107–8
 First Declaration of Havana, 74
 "History Will Absolve Me" speech, 14
 imprisonment of, 11
 Johnson and, 145–46
 Kennedy, J., and, 51–52, 64, 66–70
 Khrushchev and, 51
 Kissinger and, 155
 Matthews's interview of, 13–14
 Mills and, 36–38
 proclamation of 1959, 40
 religion and, 190
 revolutionary mission of, 136–37
 Second Declaration of Havana, 74
 in Sierra Maestra, 47
 US and, 31–34, 61–62
 visit to UN, xi–xii
Castro, Mariela, 228, 245
Castro, Raúl, xi, 23, 155, 243
 December 17 agreement and, xiii–xvi, xxviii
 imprisonment of, 11
 Obama and, xii, 210–11
Castro's Final Hour (Oppenheimer), 168
The Causes of World War Three (Mills), 35, 42–43
Cayetano Carpio, Salvador, 80–81
CENSEX. *See* Cuban National Center for Sex Education
Central America, xvii, 123
Central American Wars, 8
Cespedes y Quesada, Carlos Manuel de, 13, 46
Chávez, Hugo, 79, 122
 Bush, G. W., and, 194
 Castro, F., and, 191–92
 US and, 193–94
Chibás, Eduardo, 11
Chicano movement, 4
Childs, Lawton, 180
Chile, 74–75, 107
 socialism in, 195
China
 Cuba and, 8
 Nixon and, 162
 Soviet Union and, 92
 US and, 149
Christie, Chris, 239
CIA, xxvii

Castro, F., and, 70, 146–47
Congress and, 154
congressional oversight committees and, 163
covert operations, 163
Guevara and, 146–47
Kennedy, J., and, 63–64, 68
National Student Association and, 47
Operation Mongoose, 49, 63
US-Soviet relations and, 162
Cienfuegos, Camilo, 3, 23, 25
cimarones, 33
Civil Rights movement, 4, 48, 127, 135–36
Clark, Ramsey, 130
Clinton, Bill, xv, xxiii, 147, 165–83
   Brothers to the Rescue shoot down and, 178
   Castro, F., and, 166
   Cuban-Americans and, 181
   Cuban refugees and, 179–80
   Cuba policy, 165–67
   trade embargo and, 168
   wedge politics, 166
Clinton, Hilary Rodham, 165
Closest of Enemies (Smith), 159
Codina, Armando, 220
COINTELPRO programs, 241
"cold peace," 56
Cold War, xxiii, 4, 40, 228
   Carter and, 153
   US-Cuban relations and, 161–62
Colombia, xiv, 196
colonialism, xxv, 6
Columbia University student strike, 104
"Committee of 75," 159
communism, 40–41, 60–61, 156, 244. *See also* BRAC; Cuban Communist Party
Communist Party, xix
   Cuban Revolution and, 40–42
   in Latin America, 92
Congress, US
   CIA operations and, 154
   Cuban Americans in, xvi
   December 17 agreement and, xviii
   foreign policy and, 163
   US-Cuban relations and, 163–64
congressional oversight committees, 163
Cosa Nostra, 2, 14. *See also* Mafia
counterinsurgency, 56–58
Cox, Courtland, 128, 131–32
Craig, Gregory, 214–17
Crocker, Chester A., 143, 144
Cuba. *See also* US-Cuban relations
   Africa and, 125–26, 136–44, 148–49, 158–59
   African Americans and, 33–34
   African wars and, xxv
   Alarcón, R., and, 241

American Embassy in, xv, xxxi
Angola and, 138–39, 155
Brazil and, 210
Brothers to the Rescue shot down by, 173–74, 179
Bush, G. W., and, 230
capitalism in, 232–33
Carter and, 140, 155, 159–61
Castro regime in, 226–27
China and, 8
Clinton, B., and, 165–67
Colombia and, xiv
democracy in, 201, 228, 240–41
dissidents in, xviii–xix
economy, 242
elections, 242
EU and, 231
foreign policy, 125–26
government, xv, xvii, xix
health care, xiii, 5–6, 187
humanitarianism, 5–6, 125–26
human rights, 227–28
imperialism, 126
independence, 33, 45–46
internationalism, 125, 136, 140–41
Internet in, 233–34
Johnson and, 145
Kennedy, J., and, 54, 64–67
Latin America and, 8, 212, 244
LGBT community in, 228
Mafia in, 2, 13
Marxism-Leninism in, 11
Miami-based attacks on, 173
Mills in, 36–37
North Korea and, 229
Obama and, 234–35
one-party system in, 228–29
Oswald and, 62
Pope Francis and, 231
post-Castro, 227
progress in, 242–43
regime change in, 225
religion in, 190
SDS in, 110–11
South African apartheid and, 6, 138–39
stature in world, 210–11
travel restrictions, 230
on United Nations Human Development Index, xvi
US annexation of, 45, 152
US counterinsurgency efforts in, 57–58
US public opinion of, 237–38
US students traveling to, 110–12
US terrorist campaign against, 138
Venezuela and, 194–95
Vietnam and, 100–101
Cuba Confidential (Bardach), 166, 178

Cuba Lobby, 147–49, 165
Cuban Adjustment Act, 236–37
Cuban airspace
　Brothers to the Rescue shoot down by,
　　173–75
　Cuban exiles shot down in, xxiv
Cuban American National Foundation
　(CANF), 166, 214
Cuban-Americans, xv, xxviii, 52–53
　Clinton, B., and, 181
　in Congress, xvi
　in Cuban airspace, xxiv, 173
　Cubans' spying on, xxviii
　in Miami, 7, 222
　Obama and, 225, 237
　waging of war by, 221–22
　Watergate and, 219
Cuban Communist Party (Popular Socialist
　Party, PSP), 11, 13–14, 20–21
Cuban Democracy Act (Torricelli law), 147,
　167–68
Cuban diaspora, 235–40
Cuban Five, xx, xxii–xxiii
　December 17, 2014 and, xxiii–xxxi
　Gross exchange, xxiv, xxx–xxxi
　release of, xxv
　trial and conviction of, 174
Cuban immigrants, 9–10, 172
　December 17 agreement and, 206–7
Cuban mafia, 172
Cuban missile crisis, 45–58
　Castro, F., and, 50–51
　Guevara and, 50
　Kennedy, J., and, 49
　SDS and, 53–54
　Soviet Union and, 49–51
　trade embargo and, 51–52
　US-Cuban relations and, 52
Cuban National Center for Sex Education
　(CENESEX), 228
Cuban refugees, 166
　Brothers to the Rescue and, 173
　Clinton, B., and, 179–80
　in Guantanamo, 180
　return of, 177, 181–82
Cuban Revolution, xii, xiii, xvii–xviii, xxiii,
　4, 16
　African Americans and, 128–30
　Carmichael and, 130–33
　Communist Party and, 40–42
　Debray and, 87–88, 94
　history of, 45–47
　Latin America and, 73–74, 76–77
　Mafia and, 154
　Martí and, 45
　Mills and, 35–44
　New Left and, 31–34, 55

power struggles within, 16
US and, 7, 96–98
Vietnam and, 95
women in, 26
Cuban revolutionaries, 11–12
Cuban Revolutionary Party, 33
Cuban Revolutionary War, 23–29
Cuban Right, American, xv, xvi
　Bush, G. H. W., and, 219–20
　Bush, G. W., and, 220–21
　Bush, J., and, 220
　González, E., and, 215–16
　Gore and, 218–19, 221
　Obama and, 226
　Venezuela and, 194
Cuban-Soviet relations, 41–42, 159–60, 162,
　187, 189, 242
　alliance, 49, 66
　dissolution of USSR and, 202
　economy and, 185–86
Cuban War of Independence, 46, 151–52
Cubela, Rolando, 70

Dalton, Roque, 80–82
Daniel, Jean, 66, 69–70
Davidson, Carl, 102
Days of Rage, 116
Debray, Regis, 5, 85–108
　in Bolivia, 88–89
　Castro, F., and, 88–90, 107–8
　Cuban Revolution and, 87–88, 94
　Guevara and, 89–90
　Latin American revolution and, 87
　release of, 103, 106–7
　Revolution in the Revolution?, 88, 91–100
December 17 agreement, xxiii–xxxi
　Alarcón, R., and, xxviii–xxix
　Castro, R., and, xiii–xvi
　Congress and, xxviii
　Cuban Five and, xxiii–xxxi
　Cuban immigrants and, 206–7
　Gross and, xxix–xxx
　Obama and, xiii–xvii
　talks leading to, xxv–xxvi
　US-Cuban relations and, xiii–xiv
de Gaulle, Charles, 89
Dellinger, David, 102
democracy
　in Central America, 123
　in Cuba, 201, 240–41
　electoral, 200
　in Latin America, 7, 122–23, 200
　participatory, 200
　programs, xxiv, xxxi, 233
Diaz-Balart, Lincoln, 219
Directorio. See Revolutionary Directorate

Directorio Revolucionario Estudiantil (DRE), 61–62
di Suvero, Henry, 32
Dobrynin, Anatoly, 71
Dohrn, Bernardine, 110, 113–14, 118
Donovan, James, 66
Dorticós, Osvaldo, 74
Douglass, Frederick, 34
DRE. *See Directorio Revolucionario Estudiantil*
Dreke, Víctor, 132
Dubois, W. E. B., 45
Dulles, Allen, 76, 154

Ebola epidemic, 5–6
Echeverría, José Antonio, 17, 21
Eckstein, Susan Eva, 235–36
Eder, Richard, 145
Eisenhower, Dwight D., 31, 41, 154
electoral democracy, 200
Elrod, Richard, 116
El Salvador, 123
    guerillas in, 79–84
    the *Matanza*, 80
    US and, 84
ERP. *See* People's Revolutionary Army
Escobar, Reinaldo, 234
Estrada, Oscar, 132
Ethiopia, 140, 158–59
European Union (EU), 231
Evans, Rowland, 130

FAA. *See* Federal Aviation Administration
Fair Play for Cuba Committee (FPCC), xii, 32, 59, 245
Falla, Laureano Batista, 21
family allowance. *See bolsa familia*
Fanon, Frantz, 125
Farabundo Martí, Agustín, 80
Farabundo Martí Front for National Liberation (FMLN), 83
FARN. *See* Armed Forces of National Resistance
FBI, 37–38, 241
Federación Estudiantil Universitaria (FEU), 3
Federal Aviation Administration (FAA), 176–77
Feinberg, Richard, 177, 231
Feltrinelli, Giangiacomo, 107
Ferlinghetti, Lawrence, 34
FEU. *See Federación Estudiantil Universitaria*
Fidelistas, 2
Fitzgerald, Desmond, 70
Flacks, Dick, 56
FMLN. *See* Farabundo Martí Front for National Liberation
foco, 24, 88–89, 115
Ford, Gerald, 163

FPCC. *See* Fair Play for Cuba Committee
FPL. *See* Popular Liberation Forces-Farabundo Martí
Francis (Pope)
    Cuba and, 231
    December 17, 2014 agreement and, xxix
    Latin America and, 190
Frank, Marc, 178, 227, 234, 243
Frank, Waldo, 32
Frappier, John, 112
Freedom Summer, 7
Funes, Mauricio, 83, 123

Garcerán, José, 17
Genovese, Vito, 2
Ginsberg, Allen, 34
Gleijeses, Piero, 76, 126, 132–33
globalization, xvi, 200, 204
Gold, Terry, 115
Goldwater, Barry, 48
González, Elián, 7, 172, 213–22
    Alarcón, R., and, 213–14, 216
    Cuban Right and, 215–16
González, Fernando, 174
González, Juan Miguel, 214–15, 217–18
González, René, xxv, xxvii, 141, 151, 174
Good Neighbor policies, xvii, 10
Goodwin, Richard, 68, 73
Gore, Al, 167, 213
    Cuban Right and, 218–19, 221
Gott, Richard, 24, 50, 158, 241
Graham, Bob, 180
Grant, Frances, 74
Green Berets, 57, 154
Gross, Alan, xxiii–xxiv, xxvii–xxviii
    Cuban Five exchange, xxiv, xxx–xxxi
    December 17, 2014 agreement and, xxix–xxx
Guantanamo, 51, 170, 180
Guatemala, 76, 154
Guererro, Antonio, xxiii, 174
guerillas, 238
    in El Salvador, 79–84
    in Venezuela, 77–79
guerrilla war
    foco theory of, 24
    in Latin America, 76–77
Guevara, Ernesto "Che," 3, 13, 23
    in Africa, 87, 137
    Alarcón, R., and, 24–25
    in Bolivia, 88–89, 93–94
    capture of, 94–95
    CIA and, 146–47
    Cuban missile crisis and, 50
    death of, 95
    Debray and, 89–90
    Goodwin and, 73

284 ▪ *Listen, Yankee!*

idea of armed struggle and, 90–91
Kennedy, J., and, 68
as revolutionary icon, 101–2
Guillén, Nicolás, 126
Guillermoprieto, Alma, 240
Gutiérrez, Armando, 219

Haitian Revolution, 33–34
Halperin, Morton, xxiv–xxv, 174, 177
Cuban refugees and, 179–82
Harf, Marie, 233
Harnecker, Marta, 200
Hays, Dennis, 171
Helms, Richard, 70
Helms-Burton legislation, xv, xix, xxiii, xxiv,
147, 168–69, 173–74
trade embargo and, 177
Hernandez, Gerardo, xxiii, xxvi–xxvii, 174
Hernández Martínez, Maximiliano, 80
"heroic creation," 16, 23
High Human Development, 243
Holder, Eric, 215, 216
Hoover, J. Edgar, 131
Horne, Gerald, 34
Hotel Nacional, 2–3
"How a Cuban Spy and His Wife Came to
Be Expectant Parents," xxvi
Howard, Lisa, 68–69, 145
"the Humboldt Seven massacre," 18–20
Huntington, Samuel, 164
Hutchings, Phil, 110–11

ICBMs, 151
immigration, xvii, 9
normalization and, 235–40
Ingenieros, José, 13
INRA (National Institute of Agrarian
Reform), 38
Inter-American Association for Democracy
and Freedom, 74
Interest Sections, xv, xxiii, xxx, 155
internationalism, 189
Cuban, 125, 140–41
International Monetary Fund, xv
Internet, xvi, 233–34
Iran-Contra program, 220

Jacobs, John, 116–17
James, C.L.R., 34
Black Jacobins, 129
Jefferson, Thomas, 45
Jennings, Peter, 112
Jiménez, Martha, 19
Joannides, George E., 61–63
Joannides files, 61, 64
John Paul II (Pope), 190
Johnson, Lyndon, 100

Castro, F., and, 145–46
Cuba policy, 145
"Great Society" speech, 105
Jones, LeRoi, 34
Juventud Socialista (JS), 27

Kaplan, Robert, 149
Kelsen, Hans, 200
Kennedy, John F., 6, 78
assassination of, 59–72
the Bay of Pigs and, 154
Castro, F., and, 51–52, 64, 66–70
CIA and, 63–64, 68
counterinsurgency and, 56–57
Cuban missile crisis and, 49
Cuba policy, 54, 64–67
Guevara and, 68
Peace Corps and, 47
trade embargo and, 74
Kennedy, Robert, Jr., 65
Kennedy, Robert F., xiii, 55, 65–67, 104–5
Kerry, John, xxix, 150
Khrushchev, Nikita, 49–51
King, Coretta Scott, 156–57
King, Martin Luther, Jr., 104, 127
Kirkpatrick, Jeane, 228
Kissinger, Henry, 123, 154–55, 245

Labañino, Ramón, xxiii, 174
Lake, Anthony, 173, 176
Lamrani, Salim, 233
Landau, Saul, xix–xxi, 32, 155, 231, 245–46
Mills and, 36–37
Lansdale, Edward, 57
Lansdale proposal, 57–58
Lansky, Meyer, 2
Latin America
capitalism in, 212
Communist Party in, 92
Cuba and, 8, 212, 244
Cuban Revolution and, 73–74, 76–77
democracy in, 7, 122–23, 200
Francis (Pope) and, 190
governance, 65
guerrilla war in, 76–77
leaders in, 195–96
Marxism in, 15, 197
nationalism, 122
neo-liberalism in, xviii, 5
New Left in, 190
political revolution in, 196–97
presidents in, 123
revolution in, 73–84, 87
US and, xvii, 10, 40, 211
Leahy, Patrick, xxv–xxviii, 233
Leary, Timothy, 114
Lebrón, Lolita, xxix

Lechuga, Carlos, 69, 71
Lehr, Myriam, 219
LeMay, Curtis, 49
Leninism, 11, 242
Lesnik, Max, 225, 237
Letelier, Orlando, 219
"Letter to the New Left" (Mills), 36
Levinson, Sandra, 112–13
LGBT community, Cuban, 228
Lifton, Robert Jay, 149
Linowitz Commission, 160
Listen, Yankee! (Mills), xxiii, 4, 35, 39, 224–25
Llano, 24–25
Locker, Michael, 112
Luciano, Charles "Lucky," 2
Lula da Silva, Ignacio, 122, 207–9
Luxemburg, Rosa, 204
Lynd, Staughton, 96, 105

M-26-7 movement. See 26th of July Movement
MacArthur, Douglas, 235
Maceo, Antonio, 25, 46, 51
Machado, Gerardo, 13–15
Machado, José, 20
Maduro, Nicolás, 194
Mafia
    American, in Cuba, 2, 13
    Cuban, 172
    Cuban Revolution and, 154
    Kennedy assassination and, 61
Makeba, Miriam, 133
Mandela, Nelson, 140, 149, 222, 239
Manifest Destiny, 10, 11
Mankiewicz, Frank, 155
Mariátegui, José Carlos, 15–16, 197
Marighella, Carlos, 122
Maroon resistance communities, 33–34
Martí, José, 10, 16, 33, 45–46, 129
Martin, Lionel, 112
Martínez, Mel, 220
Marx, Karl, 202–3
"Marx After Marxism, The Global Fight for Immigrant Rights in a Neo-Liberal Economy" (Alarcón, R.), 203–4
Marxism, 186, 189–90, 202, 242
    in Latin America, 197
    "Latin Americanization" of, 15
    re-examination of, 196
Marxism-Leninism, 11, 242
"Marxism without Marx," 5
Marxist revolutionary ideology, 36, 92
Masferrer, Rolando, 26
Massip, Anotonio, 20–21
the Matanza (El Salvador), 80
Matthews, Herbert, 13–14, 17, 23–24, 32, 96, 137
McCarthy, Eugene, 106

McCone, John, 68–69
McGovern, George, 64
McGovern, Jim, xxviii
Meissner, Doris, 215, 216
Mella, Julio Antonio, 15–16, 46
Menendez, Robert, 239
Meredith, James, 127
Mexico, 196
"Mexico Pact," 17
Miami, Florida, 7, 173, 222
Miliband, Ralph, 38
military-industrial complex, 41
Mills, C. Wright, xxiii, 4, 240, 245
    Alarcón, R., and, 38–39
    Castro, F., and, 36–38
    The Causes of World War Three, 35, 42–43
    in Cuba, 36–37
    Cuban Revolution and, 35–44
    Landau and, 36–37
    "Letter to the New Left," 36
    Listen, Yankee!, xxiii, 4, 35, 38, 39, 224–25
    New Left and, 34–44
    The Power Elite, 35
    White Collar, 35
Mitterrand, François, 108
Mobutu, Joseph, 137, 138
"modus vivendi," 74, 87
Moffitt, Ronni, 219–20
Moncada attack, 14, 17
Monje Molina, Mario, 88
Montes, Melida Anaya, 83
Morales, Evo, 90, 121–22, 122–23
Morley, Jefferson, 61–63
MPLA, 137–38
Mujica, José, 123
My Lai massacre, 115

Nader, Ralph, 156, 164
Namibia, 144
National Assembly, 242
National Assembly of People's Power, 4–5
National Institute of Agrarian Reform. See INRA
National Security Agency, US, 229
National Student Association, 47–48
Nation of Islam, 127
Negroponte, John, 220
neo-liberalism, xviii, 5, 202, 206
Neto, Agostinho, 137–38
Newfield, Jack, 54–55
New Left, 4
    anti-nuclear movement and, 52–56
    Cuban Revolution and, 31–34, 55
    in Latin America, 190
    Mills and, 35–44
New Left Notes (SDS), 98
Newton, Huey, 133

Nicaragua, 76, 123
Nichaman, Julie, 100
Nixon, Richard, 31, 66, 100, 119, 147, 154, 158
    China and, 162
Non-Aligned Movement, 6
non-recognition policies, 6
Noonan, Peggy, xvi
Noriega, Roger, 220
normalization, 9–10, 229–35
    Brothers to the Rescue shoot down and,
        177–78
    immigration and, 235–40
    Venezuela and, 230
North Korea, 114, 229
Novak, Robert, 130
nuclear war, 49–50, 53–54. *See also* Cuban
    missile crisis
Nuñez, Marta, 37
Nyerere, Julius, 132

Oanh, Xuan, 188
OAS. *See* Organization of American States
Obama, Barack, xi, 118
    anti-Venezuela sanctions bill, 194
    Castro, R., and, xii, 210–11
    Cuban-Americans and, 225, 237
    Cuban Right and, 226
    Cuba policy, 234–35
    December 17 agreement and, xiii–xvii
    Gross's release and, xxviii
    Lula and, 209
    US-Cuban relations and, 151–52
    Venezuela and, 194
Oglesby, Carl, 111
Ojeda, Fabricio, 77–79
OLAS. *See* Organization of Latin American
    Solidarity
Oltuski, Enrique, 25
Operation Mongoose, 49, 63
Operation Phoenix, 58
Oppenheimer, Andrés, 168
Ordoqui, Joaquín, 19
Organization of American States (OAS), 73,
    146, 154–55
Organization of Latin American Solidarity
    (OLAS), 129
Organization of Solidarity with the People
    of Asia, Africa and Latin America. *See*
    OSPAAAL
Ortega, Daniel, 123
the Orthodox Party, 11
OSPAAAL (Organization of Solidarity with
    the People of Asia, Africa and Latin
    America), 126–27
Oswald, Lee Harvey, 59–61
    Cuba and, 62
Oughton, Diana, 115

Padreda, Camilo, 220
Paine, Tom, 149
País, Frank, 23–24, 27
Panetta, Leon, 181
participatory democracy, 200
Pastor, Robert, 148, 159–62
"Patria o Muerte", 16
Paz, Octavio, 169
Peace Corps, 47, 57, 105–6
Peña, Frederico, 181
People's Revolutionary Army (ERP), 80–81,
    82
Perea, Margarita, 26–29
Perez, Adriana, xxvi–xxvii, xxx
Pérez, Louis, Jr., 235
Pérez Jiménez, Marcos, 77–78
Pertierra, Andrés, 19–20
Pertierra, José, xix
Peru, 15
"Peter Pan" exodus of 1960-1962, 214
Petraeus, David, 58
Piñeiro, Manuel, 75–76, 103
Pinochet, Augusto, 195
Platt Amendment, 46, 170
political prisoners, 239
Popular Front policy, 13
Popular Liberation Forces-Farabundo Martí
    (FPL), 80–81, 82
Popular Socialist Party. *See* Cuban Commu-
    nist Party
Port Huron Statement, 4–5, 36, 40–41
Portocarero, Herman, 231
Portugal, 138
Portuguese colonialism, xxv
Posada-Carriles, Luis, 222
Powell, Lewis F., 164
The Power Elite (Mills), 35
PSP. *See* Cuban Communist Party
Puerto Rican nationalists, xxviii–xxix
Punto Cero military training complex, 87

radical theory, 36
rafters. *See balseros*
Rand, Ayn, 191
Ray, Michele, 101
Reagan, Ronald, xxiii, 147
reform, 207
religion, 189–90
Reno, Janet, 215
Reston, James, 130
Revolutionary Directorate (*Directorio*), 12,
    17–18, 20–22
Revolution in the Revolution? (Debray), 88,
    91–100
Reyes, Rodolfo, xxi–xxii, 140–41
Richardson, Bill, 176
Ricks, Willie, 127

Rieser, Tim, xxv–xxvii
Roa, Raúl, 48, 89
Robbins, Terry, 115, 117
Roche, John, 54
Rodríguez, Carlos Rafael, 111
Rodríguez, Enrique Nuñez, 172
Rodríguez, Félix, 95, 146
Rodriguez, Fructuoso, 12, 16–19
Rodríguez, José Machado, 19
Rodriguez, Marcos Armando "Marquitos,"
    19–21
Rodríguez, Simón, 197
Roosevelt, Franklin, xvii, 10
Rosales, Joe Westbrook, 19
Roselli, Johnny, 154
Ros-Lehtinen, Ileana, 219–20
Rousseff, Dilma, 122, 210
Rudd, Mark, 104, 110
Rusk, Dean, 52
Russell, Bertrand, 53
Russia, 15. *See also* Soviet Union

Sale, Kirkpatrick, 111
Sánchez, Celia, 25
Sánchez, Yoani, 233–34
Sánchez Cerén, Salvador, 83–84
Sanchez-Parodi Montoto, Ramon, 152
Sandinistas, 76, 164
Santamaría, Haydée, 14
Sarraf, Rolando, xxvii
Savimbi, Jonas, 137
Sawyer, Diane, 216
Scheer, Robert, 14–15, 34
Schlesinger, Arthur, Jr., 54
Schumpeter, Joseph, 201
SDS. *See* Students for a Democratic Society
Seeger, Pete, 240
September 1933 coup, 13
Shackley, Theodore, 63
Shakur, Assata, 238–39
Shakur, Zayd Malik, 238
Sherman, Wendy, 171
Shultz, George, 143, 144
Sierra Maestra, 25, 47
Sinatra, Frank, 2
SLATE, 32
slavery, 125–26
Smith, Wayne, 145–46, 157
    Closest of Enemies, 159
SNCC. *See* Student Nonviolent Coordinating
    Committee
Snowden, Edward, 229–30
socialism, 92, 186, 190, 202
    in Chile, 195
    21st Century Socialism, 193, 195
"solidarity movements," 8
Somalia, 140

Sorensen, Ted, 51
South Africa, 139
South African apartheid, xxv, 5, 141–44
    Cuba and, 6, 138–39
Soviet Union. *See also* Cuban-Soviet relations;
    US-Soviet relations
    China and, 92
    Cuban missile crisis and, 49–51
    dissolution of, 185, 188–89, 202
Spain, 33
Spanish-American War, 46
Standard Oil, 66
States Sponsors of Terrorism, 237–38
Stein, Jean, 1
Stevenson, Adlai, 69, 145
Stone, I. F., 55
Student Nonviolent Coordinating Commit-
    tee (SNCC), 52, 104, 127
    Carmichael and, 131, 134
Students for a Democratic Society (SDS),
    xii, 4, 116
    in Cuba, 110–11
    Cuban missile crisis and, 53–54
    New Left Notes, 98
    protests, 53–54
Summit of the Americas, xvii
"Superpower Syndrome," 149–50, 225
SWAPO, 141–43
Sweig, Julia, 17, 231, 245

Tarnoff, Peter, 170–72, 177
"terrorist state" designation, xiv–xv, xxxi
Tet Offensive, 103
Thelwell, Michael, 128, 133
Third World, xvii, 41, 125–27
    immigrants, 205
Thomas, Hugh, 19
Los Tigres, 26
Timerman, Jacobo, 240
Tito, Josef Broz, 69
Torricelli, Robert, 167
Torricelli law. *See* Cuban Democracy Act
tourism, xiv, xvii–xviii, 3, 8
trade, xiv, xvii
trade embargo, xv, 149
    Clinton, B., and, 168
    Cuban missile crisis and, 51–52
    Helms-Burton and, 177
    Kennedy administration and, 74
Trafficante, Santo, 2
travel, xiv
travel restrictions
    to Cuba, xx–xxi, 230
    to US, 231
Treaty of Paris, 46
Tutu, Desmond, 5
21st Century Socialism, 193, 195

26th of July Movement (M-26-7), 12, 17, 21–22, 27, 42

United Fruit, 65–66, 76
United Nations (UN), xvi
  Castro, F., and, xi–xii
  Human Development Index, xvi
  US-Cuban relations and, xvii
United States (US)
  annexation of Cuba by, 45, 152
  anti-Cuba terrorist campaign, 138
  Bolivia and, 94–95
  Castro, F., and, 31–34, 61–62
  Central America and, xvii
  Chávez and, 193–94
  China and, 149
  Cuban immigrants to, 9–10
  Cuban Revolution and, 7, 96–98
  El Salvador and, 84
  foco in, 115
  foreign policy, 163
  Latin America and, xvii, 10, 40, 211
  plots to overthrow Castro, F., and, 61–62
  public opinion of Cuba in, 237–38
  revolution in, 97–100
  Soviet Union and, 49–50
  students traveling to Cuba from, 110–12
  "Superpower Syndrome" and, 149–50
  travel restrictions, 230
University Reform movement, 12–13
urban underground revolutionary movement, 24
Uruguay, 123
US. *See* United States
US Agency for International Development (USAID), xxiv
US-Cuban relations, xii, xvi–xvii, 5–6
  Africa and, 159–60
  Alarcón, R., and, 150–51
  Bay of Pigs and, 52
  Brothers to the Rescue shoot down and, 177–78
  Cold War and, 161–62
  Congress and, 163–64
  Cuban missile crisis and, 52
  December 17, 2014, xiii–xiv
  diplomatic channels, 71, 183
  González, E., and, 213–14
  normalization and, 229–35
  Obama and, 151–52
  policy and, 147–48
  public opinion and, xvi
  "Superpower Syndrome" and, 149–50, 225
US-Soviet relations, 49–50, 71, 148–49, 162, 186

Valdés, Ramiro, 23
Valdés Vivo, Raúl, 100
Vallejo, René, 37, 38, 102

Vance, Cyrus, 155
Van Reigersberg, Stephanie, 170
Venceremos Brigade, 7–8, 103, 110
Venezuela, 8, 122, 191–92
  Caracazo, 191
  Cuba and, 194–95
  Cuban Right and, 194
  electoral process, 193
  guerillas in, 77–79
  normalization process and, 230
  Obama's policy towards, 194
Vidal, Josefina, xxviii
Vietnam, 90–91, 95–96, 188
  Cuba and, 100–101
  Cuban Revolution and, 95
  Operation Phoenix, 58
  Tet Offensive, 103
Vietnam War, 115
Villoldo, Gustavo, 146

Wagner, Robert F., Jr., 31
Wald, Karen, 112
Warren Commission, 61
Watergate, 115, 219
Weather Underground, 109
  bombings, 114–15
  today, 117–18
Weinglass, Leonard, xix–xxi, 175
White Collar (Mills), 35
Wood, Leonard, 46
Workers Party, Brazil's, 208–9
World Economic Forum, 208
World Social Forum, 207–8
World Trade Organization, 5
Worthy, William, 95

X, Malcolm, 33, 99, 127

YAF. *See* Young Americans for Freedom
Yepe, Manuel, 37
Young, Andrew, 153, 156–57
Young Americans for Freedom (YAF), 48

Zapatistas, 123
Zeitlin, Maurice, 14–15
ZunZuneo, 233